KU-592-647

History in the early years
Second edition

Hilary Cooper

NEWMAN COLLEGE
BARTLEY GREEN
BIRMINGHAM B32 3NT
CLASS 372.89
BARCODE 01118064
AUTHOR COO

London and New York

First published 1995
by Routledge

Second edition published 2002
by RoutledgeFalmer
11 New Fetter Lane, London EC4P 4EE

Simultaneously published in the USA and Canada
by RoutledgeFalmer
29 West 35th Street, New York, NY 10001

RoutledgeFalmer is an imprint of the Taylor & Francis Group

© 2002 Hilary Cooper

Typeset in Palatino by
Keystroke, Jacaranda Lodge, Wolverhampton
Printed and bound in Great Britain by
The Cromwell Press, Trowbridge, Wiltshire

All rights reserved. No part of this book may be reprinted or
reproduced or utilised in any form or by any electronic,
mechanical, or other means, now known or hereafter
invented, including photocopying and recording, or in any
information storage or retrieval system, without permission in
writing from the publishers.

British Library Cataloguing in Publication Data
A catalogue record for this book is available from the British Library

Library of Congress Cataloging in Publication Data
A catalog record for this book has been requested

ISBN 0–415–27145–2

Contents

PART IV
Three case studies   **175**

PART V
In-service workshops   **201**

Illustrations

FIGURES

BOXES

Editor's preface

Each book in this series focuses on a specific curriculum area. The series relates relevant learning theory or a rationale for early years learning to the practical development and implementation of subject-based topics and classroom activities at the infant level (i.e. Reception, YI, Y2). It seems that the majority of existing books on primary education and the primary curriculum focus on pupils aged 7–11 years. It is hoped that this series presents a refreshing and much needed change in that it specifically addresses the first three years in school.

Each volume is intended to be an up-to-date, judicious mix of theory and practical classroom application, offering a wealth of background information, ideas and advice to all concerned with planning, implementing, monitoring and evaluating teaching and learning in the first three years in school. Theoretical perspectives are presented in a lively and interesting way, drawing upon recent classroom research findings wherever possible. Case studies and activities from a range of classrooms and schools illuminate many of the substantial issues related to the subject area in question.

Readers will find a similar pattern of contents in all the books in the series. Each discusses the early learning environment and the transition from home- to school-based learning, and addresses the key questions of what this means for the early years teacher and the curriculum. Such discussion inevitably incorporates ideas on the knowledge which young children may have of subjects and an overview of the subject matter itself which is under scrutiny. As the thrust of the series is towards young children learning subjects, albeit in a holistic way, no doubt readers will wish to consider what is an appropriate content or rationale for the subject in the early years. Having considered young children as learners, what they are bringing into school in terms of prior knowledge, the teacher's task and the subject matter itself, each book then turns its attention to appropriate methods of planning, organising, implementing and evaluating teaching and learning activities. Crucial matters such as assessment, evaluation and record-keeping are dealt with in their own right, and are also referred to and discussed in ongoing examples of good practice. Each book concludes with useful suggestions for further staff room discussion/INSET activities and advice on resources.

As a whole, the series aims to be inspirational and forward looking. As all readers know so well, the National Curriculum is not 'written in concrete'. Education is a dynamic process. While taking due account of the essential National Curriculum framework, authors go far beyond the level of description of rigid content guidelines to highlight *principles* for teaching and learning. Furthermore, they incorporate two key messages which surely underpin successful, reflective education, namely 'vision' and 'enthusiasm'. It is hoped that students and teachers will be inspired and assisted in their task of implementing successful and progressive plans which help young learners to make sense of their world and the key areas of knowledge within it.

Joy A. Palmer

Acknowledgements

There has been increasing emphasis over the past five years on developing partnerships between teacher training institutions and schools, on reflection on practice and on practitioner research. There has also been increased emphasis on centralised control of the curriculum, and on mechanistic and piecemeal approaches to teaching and learning. I am therefore grateful to the students and teachers who worked with children to investigate questions, illustrate points and exemplify ideas suggested in the first edition of this book. I remain grateful to the PGCE students whose dissertation studies examined children's responses to stories, artefacts and pictures and, in particular, to Lyn Clarke, Hilary Croft, Joanne Edwards, Virginia Hunt and Shelley Moore. I am grateful to the class teachers who undertook case studies to illustrate a variety of approaches to planning and assessment (Angela Kinsett, Julie Giles and Rosie Alston); to Teresa Clark, Humanities Inspector in Lewisham; and to Joan Blyth, who has done so much to initiate and support the teaching of history to young children. I would like to thank teachers who have shared their ideas through projects, especially Ann Dingdale, co-ordinator of the Women in History Key Stage 1 Biography Project, and Jonathan Barnes, for the infectious enthusiasm and expertise in teaching medieval history to 5- and 6-year-olds that he shared at Historical Association workshops.

Many teachers and student teachers responded to the first edition by further exploring some of the unanswered questions it raised. Janet Liddle investigated children's concepts of time when they first entered her Nursery class (p. 20); Debra Vickers discovered some amazing insights when she listened to children in her playgroup talking about 'old things' (p. 20); Catherine Garside describes how she promoted and assessed children's learning through role-play in a castle (p. 28); Julie Woodward shows how she intervened to help children participate in developing play in 'an old shop' and 'an old kitchen' (p. 30). When Joanne Reeves took her Reception class on a local walk they discovered evidence of an old water-mill (p. 36) while Alison Coleman helped her Nursery class to differentiate between role-play and reality at a living history site (p. 36). Renewed thanks are due to Pat Etches who worked with trainee teachers and her year 1/2 class at Stramongate School, Kendal, investigating links between history and the Literacy Hour (p. 92) and the spiritual, cultural and moral dimensions of a history topic (p. 112). Thanks are also due to Elizabeth Hart and Sarah Spink who allowed me to visit their Teddy Museum made by Nursery and Reception class children (p. 175). I am also grateful to Liz Elliott for advice on current computer software.

My thanks are due to the many colleagues in schools and other early years settings and in teacher training institutions whose case studies published since 1995 have been woven into and included in this second edition.

Finally, I am grateful to Donald Johnson and Thora Cartwright for their patience and good humour in preparing the manuscript for this second edition with such meticulous care.

Introduction

The 1995 edition of *History in the early years* celebrated the statutory inclusion in 1991 of history as an integral component of a broad and balanced curriculum for all 5- to 8-year-olds. It drew on the resources which had been developed to support history education for young children, ranging from books and replica artefacts to education services in museums, art galleries and living history reconstructions and through organisations such as the National Trust and English Heritage. It honoured the professionalism, energy and enthusiasm with which many teachers, who had not previously seen history as appropriate for very young children, explored its potential, using local and oral sources, music and art, story and rhyme to develop children's curiosity about the past and to reconstruct their own accounts of the past through retelling stories and in imaginative play. *History in the early years* aimed to show teachers how, by using these resources and activities, they are developing, in embryonic ways, the strands of historical thinking which lie at the heart of the processes of historical enquiry: tracing causes and effects of change over time; asking questions about historical sources – incomplete traces of the past which remain; understanding the reasons why there is often more than one valid interpretation of the past. It gave an overview of research into the development of children's historical thinking within each of these three strands and showed how, by analysing their own practice, teachers can modify, extend and contribute to this research.

Since 1995 there have been four major, centrally initiated, changes of emphasis in early years education. The 2002 edition of *History in the early years* explores the implications of the changes and ways in which they can make a positive impact in developing the history dimensions of children's early education.

First, *Curriculum Guidance for the Foundation Stage* (DfEE/QCA 2000a) offers all early years practitioners working in playgroups, nurseries and Nursery and Reception classes in schools, shared understanding of how they may plan for, teach and assess children's understanding of the past, through meaningful experience, across six broad areas of learning:

personal, social and emotional education; communication, language and literacy; mathematics development; physical development; creative development; and knowledge and understanding of the world. Within the area of Knowledge and Understanding of the World, children are expected to 'find out about past and present events in their own lives and those of their families and other people they know'.

However, this learning goal also has potentially rich links with goals in each of the other areas. The second edition of *History in the early years* considers how a variety of history focuses can be developed in holistic ways based on the Foundation Stage Guidance in DfEE/QCA 2000a. Part I, An Introduction to History in the Foundation Stage, has been expanded to show how each of the three strands of historical thinking referred to above (understanding changes over time, interpretations of the past, and deductions and inferences from sources) can be developed in pre-school settings. There is an emphasis on assessment through play. Part II, which considers how teachers can build on this embryonic capacity for historical thinking during the first three years of school, is enriched by many case studies undertaken since the first edition. Part III considers approaches to planning; in particular, it analyses ways of planning for continuity and coherence across the Foundation Stage and Key Stage 1, despite potential tensions created by different approaches to curriculum structure. At both stages the emphasis is on a holistic approach. In Part IV, a new case study describes a four-week sequence of work with a history focus on toys and games, now and then, within an integrated curriculum, taught to a Nursery and Reception class in an Early Years Unit, using the Foundation Stage Guidance.

An enhanced profile recently given to education in pre-school settings has raised our awareness of what young children know about the past before they begin formal schooling. There are powerful ways in which this knowledge shapes their sense of identity and so we need to take this into account in the experiences we provide for them. In a recent study (Cooper 2000a), when pre-school children in five European countries were asked what they knew about 'the past' they showed that they knew a great deal about dinosaurs, 'The Flintstones' and creation stories. But in England, Greece and the Netherlands they also mentioned the World Wars. In Romania they spoke of 'the revolution' ('my dad did not take part but there are bullet holes in the walls'), and in Greece they spoke of 'the Greek war of Independence'. They said their families were a main source of information. Between the distant and recent past they described vivid but partially understood images: 'stone elephants, old and broken', 'a collapsed church'. Even the youngest children need the opportunity to discuss their 'unofficial images of the past' and to make sense of them (Phillips 1998), for the time and circumstances in which we are born and the things that happen around us provide all sorts of messages we need to discuss and decode within an open and inclusive society (Gallagher 1998).

It has also been officially rediscovered that 'play' is a necessary adjunct to learning and the pioneers of early years education, whose work was light years away from target-driven prescriptive education, are back in fashion.

Second, the revised *National Curriculum for England and Wales* (DfEE/QCA 1999a: 3–24) placed considerable emphasis on both the values and skills which are expected to underpin the whole curriculum. Values and principles include: the importance of working in partnership with parents and the local community; providing opportunities for all children to achieve their potential in rich and varied contexts; promoting pupils' spiritual, moral, social and cultural education; education for citizenship. Key skills which should be developed across the curriculum include: literacy and numeracy and information technology skills; personal and social skills; thinking skills – information processing, reasoning, enquiry, creative and evaluation skills. Ways in which both values and skills may be planned for in history are specifically discussed in Part III, Chapters 7 and 8, and are integrated throughout the book. However, an attempt to approach the curriculum from a 'value-centred' perspective re-emphasises the need to make links between areas of learning and between subjects, and for teachers to collaboratively define their own principles for teaching and learning rather than identify piecemeal opportunities for developing discrete values or skills. This approach is discussed further in Chapter 8.

Another attempt to develop a holistic approach has been a renewed emphasis on the central importance of creativity (DfEE/QCA 1999b), drawing on recent research on multiple intelligences. This is discussed in Chapter 8. Implications of research on different learning styles, for planning activities and for providing equal opportunities, are considered in Chapter 8.

Third, since 1995, Schemes of Work for teaching history from Reception to year 2 have been produced (DfEE/QCA 1998a) as guidance for schools where planning lacked clear objectives. It was intended that schools should 'use as little or as much of the schemes as they find helpful, including their use to develop or refine their own schemes of work' (Harrison 2000). However, some schools seem to adapt them very little to suit the needs of their pupils and exploit their local resources; many schools seem to have abandoned the initiative in developing their own schemes. 'The schemes give us confidence that we are doing the right thing. We are all open to so much criticism now', said one primary headteacher who had been a brilliantly innovative teacher of history. This seems very sad. It is hoped that *History in the early years* will fly a few flags for confident and creative teaching.

Fourth, the place of history in the Key Stage 1 curriculum was, to some extent, marginalised by the introduction of *The National Literacy Strategy* (DfEE/QCA 1998b) and *The National Numeracy Framework* (DfEE 1999). However, the appropriateness of developing literacy and numeracy across the curriculum is recognised as teachers become familiar with the strategies and as potential links with history are clearer. Sometimes history and literacy or numeracy objectives can be achieved simultaneously; at other times, literacy- and numeracy-focused sessions can be linked by content to history activities taking place at other times. Appropriate linkages and references to relevant case studies are discussed in Chapter 5.

Finally, since 1995, as more and more early years teachers have explored the rich variety of ways in which history can be taught to young children, a plethora of small-scale classroom-based case studies has emerged, which are woven into this edition.

We have indeed come a long way since my grandmother, aged 5, received a prize book from Cosgreaves School in 1869 called *A Day at the Seaside by Mrs Barnard*. It begins with Emma Somerton mending her stocking. This inspires her mother to spend the next 140 pages instructing her in the whole of European and Asian history, all commendably linked to the history of stockings. 'The Ancient Britons painted themselves red and blue before stockings were invented. . . . However, in the reign of Edward VI, knitting was a common employment. Cotton had not yet been brought to England and things were made of wool.' By page 10 Emma learns that silk was taken to Spain by the Arabs, 'during the reign of Adderhaman III who ruled Cordova from AD 912 to AD 961'. On page 11, she is reminded that 'the Emperor Tacitus made it unlawful for men to wear silk unmixed with ordinary substances', and that 'silk comes from the caterpillar *Phaloena Mori* which was domesticated in China . . .'. Fortunately for 5-year-olds today, the emphasis is on *doing* things to investigate their own questions: talking to older people, finding out how things work, making drawings or models of places they have visited, listening to stories and exploring them through imaginative play.

An awareness of the past is as important for an individual as it is for a society. Through history we can find out about, share and become part of the record of the human race. It is an awareness which, nurtured when young, grows throughout life.

> In childhood it may have the same appeal as a fairy story or a tale of adventure; in later life it may come to have a philosophical meaning . . . a subject that is capable of interesting you as a child and does not fail to reward you, has ever deeper interest for a grown man.
>
> (Rowse 1946: 49)

Part I reviews research which suggests the embryonic but genuine historical thinking of which 3- to 5-year-old children are capable and shows how this can be developed in interesting, holistic and meaningful contexts during the Foundation Stage of their education. Part II considers how the processes of historical enquiry can be extended during Key Stage 1. In Part

III, issues concerning planning across the Foundation Stage and Key Stage 1 are considered. Case studies in Part IV describe how history-focused topics were planned and taught in Nursery and Reception classes, and at Key Stage 1. Part V gives suggestions for workshops for teachers which could help them to plan and implement a school policy document which meets the needs of their school. The workshops are intended to be fun, for exciting teaching is the product of confident, informed reflection on practice by teachers who are constantly developing their own interests and expertise and, above all, enjoying themselves.

Prologue

We are going by car from Balaq Dakhrur to Heliopolis. I am in the back. The leather of the seat sticks to my bare legs. We travel along a road lined at either side with oleander and jacaranda trees, alternate splashes of white and blue. I chant quietly: 'Jacaranda, oleander . . . jacaranda, oleander . . .' And as I do so there comes to me the revelation that in a few hours times we shall return by the same route and that I shall pass the same trees in reverse order – and that, by the same token, I can look back upon myself now . . .

Here is a child thinking about time, experiencing a sudden illumination about chronology and a person's capacity for recollection . . .

'Jacaranda, oleander' . . . This is an incident infused with a sense of language quite as much as with the perception of the nature of time, the possession and control of the decorative words, the satisfaction of being able to say them, display them . . .

Penelope Lively 1994: 1–2*

This is how Penelope Lively begins *Oleander, Jacaranda*, in which she remembers and examines her emerging perceptions of time, as a child in Egypt, over fifty years ago. She captures what educational psychologists might clinically describe as significant moments in child development but when Penelope Lively describes them they are brilliant glimpses of 'the rainbow experience we have all lost'. As teachers we are sometimes in danger of too much 'scientific observation'. To begin with this quotation from the work of an author I so much admire is a plea to readers not to lose sight of their own childhood selves or the 'rainbow experiences' of children.

* The author and publisher are grateful to Penelope Lively and Penguin Books for permission to reproduce an extract from *Oleander, Jacaranda: A Childhood Perceived.*

Part I

An introduction to history: the Foundation Stage

There are three interdependent strands to historical thinking. First, historians are concerned with tracing changes over time; changes may be rapid or gradual. They analyse the various causes of change and the effects of change on people's lives. Changes may be political, economic, social, technological or cultural; changes in one area affect other aspects of life. Some changes are more significant than others.

Second, historians construct accounts of past times. Their accounts depend on the preoccupations of the times in which they live, on their own interests and perspectives, and on the sources available to them. These may be artefacts, buildings, pictures, archaeological sites or a variety of written sources ranging from statistics and laws to diaries and contemporary literature.

Third, in order to construct accounts of the past, historians make deductions and inferences about sources, the traces of the past which remain. Because sources are often incomplete, or because their status is unknown, it is often possible to make more than one valid supposition about a source. Validity depends on whether the supposition is likely, in the light of what else is known of the period, and whether there is other supporting evidence. These three interrelated aspects of historical thinking will be examined in more detail in Part II. In Part I, we shall consider the ways in which young children may be aware of the past when they begin school, and research in cognitive psychology related to each of the three aspects of historical thinking which suggests the extent to which they may be capable of thinking about the past in a genuinely historical way.

Chapter 1

Understanding change over time

MEASURING THE PASSING OF TIME

The measurement of time involves complex interacting concepts which emerge slowly: concepts of speed, space and number. Our lives are measured in hours and days, which depend on the rotation of the earth on its axis, in months recorded by the moon's orbit of the earth, and in seasons and years, governed by the earth's orbit of the sun.

To the Ancient Greek philosophers, the nature of space, time, matter and motion was deeply problematical. Our everyday conception of time is a product of the scientific world view created in the seventeenth century by Newton, who discovered a theory which relates these concepts. Central to Newton's theory is the hypothesis that material bodies move through space along predictable paths subject to forces which accelerate them in accordance with strict mathematical laws. Therefore, Newton wrote that absolute true and mathematical time, of itself and from its own nature, flows equably without relation to anything external. This was time told by cosmic clockwork, the time by which motion was to be gauged and events determined. This is the basis of our preoccupation with precision time-keeping. After Newton, time became more than merely our stream of consciousness; it began to play a fundamental role in our description of the physical world. Newton did for time what the Greeks did for space: he abstracted it into a measurable dimension. Journeys of exploration in the seventeenth century required accurate clocks in order to determine longitude, so the tyranny of the clock began. Three centuries later we have atomic clocks accurate to a billionth of a second and satellite navigation which can pinpoint a boat to within metres. As a result we can now see that Newton's image of time, though suitable for most human purposes and still the basis of commonsense reality, is flawed. Newton showed that time is mathematical and measurable, but time is also relative to the observer's frame of reference. My time and your time may be similar but they are not identical. If I live at the top of a high building, my time runs slightly faster than yours.

Piaget (1956) investigated children's developing understanding of the measurement of time. He showed how developing concepts of speed, space and time interact. In one experiment children were asked to draw a succession of pictures showing water pouring from one container into another container below. He found the first competence to emerge was the ability to match pictures of water in the upper and lower containers and to put the pictures in order showing an understanding of events occurring in ordered succession. Next, children understood that the drop in one container and the rise in the other took the same amount of time to occur; they could understand a scale for measuring the passing of time. At the third stage Piaget found that children could understand that events can occur at the same time, and also that units of time can be added together. Only then could they understand the measurement of time in equal intervals. In other experiments he showed that children had to reach a certain developmental level before they could understand that if two trains enter tunnels of different lengths and emerge at the same time, the train travelling through the longer tunnel must be faster, or that if two snails take an equal time to move along tracks which begin and end at parallel points the snail moving along a bending path must move faster than the snail on a straight path.

Children only learn gradually that time can be measured using standard scales of equal intervals: minutes and hours, days, years and centuries. It has often been assumed that young children are not interested in the past because they cannot measure time. Yet their ability to understand that time can be measured develops, piecemeal, through relating their subjective experience of the passing of time to standard scales of hours, days and years. In fact, children are immersed in concepts of time. They are part of their developing identity and must be nurtured. Days have patterns, passing years are marked by birthdays, seasons remembered in relation to festivals, holidays and weather.

However, concepts of time are subjective and cultural. They depend on children's experiences, on language and opportunities to listen to and talk about stories and rhymes concerned with the passing of time and with other times, and to relate events in their own lives to the passing of time: 'When I am 5 I will go to school', 'When I was 2 our baby was born', 'My birthday was in June, last summer', 'The bus will come in half an hour.' Awareness of past times depends, too, on the family unit and on where the children live and how long they have lived there. Few children today live with adults extending over several generations, or among furniture and ornaments from previous generations. Often they have recently moved to new estates, or from another part of the world. Bernot and Blancard (1953) showed that people who have lived all their lives in a community where the people and way of life have changed little have an awareness of time which goes beyond their personal experience; they remember older people's shared tales of events, buildings, occupations and folk memories from before their own times. People who have moved into the community from different places have less sense of the past because they do not have shared memories which are related to their present environment.

Not all children are surrounded by physical remains of the past which are also part of their present in the way that George Mackay Brown so poetically describes in Orkney.

> There are stories in the air here. . . . These islands are a microcosm of the world. They've been continuously lived in for about 6000 years, and the layers of cultures and races are inescapable and unavoidable wherever you go. . . . History has not been parcelled up into Heritage in Orkney. The past is the present.
>
> *(The Times, 25 July 1992)*

Understanding of the relationship between subjective time and measured time develops through understanding other dimensions of the concept of time – chronological sequences, duration, changes over time, similarities and differences between now and past times – and the vocabulary of time.

CHRONOLOGICAL SEQUENCES

Piaget (1952) traced children's ability to place objects in numerical sequence and to recognise ordinal numbers. If this competence is applied to an historical context, before they start school children are becoming able to sequence events in their own lives, and possibly artefacts and photographs related to their own experience, and to retell stories in chronological sequence, recognising conventions such as 'once upon a time' and 'they all lived happily every after'.

In *Curriculum Guidance for the Foundation Stage* (DfEE/QCA 2000a: 58), the language guidance section says that children should be encouraged to use talk to rehearse, reorder and reflect on past experience, linking significant events from their own experience and from stories paying attention to sequence and to how events lead into one another. They should enjoy listening to stories, respond with relevant questions and comments (p. 50), learn to retell narratives in the correct sequence of events and show an understanding of character (p. 62). In the Reception year, children should 'recount the main events of stories in sequence' and be aware of 'actions/reactions, consequences and predictable patterns' (DfEE/QCA 1998a: 18–19). When Susan Mead read her nursery class a story in which the teddy said, 'You have to come from somewhere to have a family,' 4-year-old Adam spontaneously remarked, 'Everyone has a life story. It means when you're a baby it starts.' She followed this by suggesting that the children made their own 'family snakes'. She wrote the name of each family member on a flag and asked the children to stick them into plasticine snakes, in order, from the oldest to the youngest. Although the flags had no clear order, Adam, for instance, grouped the 'nanny' flags together and insisted on a flag at the other end of his snake for the unborn baby.

Holdaway (1979: 62–3) showed how pre-school children, through shared bed-time reading, try to repeat and retell the sequences of events in a story with increasing self-conviction. They develop the ability to follow a plot describing events over time and learn to create images which have not been experienced in sensory reality, perhaps because they belong to other times: city gates, cinders, pitch-forks, pumps. Waterland (1985) described a sequence in children's ability to retell stories which precedes decoding text. At first the child listens to the story and watches the pictures, then listens to the story and observes the text. Next, the child tells the story with the adult. When children know a story well, they will 'make up' the story, at first without accurate recall, then with more accurate retelling and finally with complete accuracy. Children can also relate, poetically, the passing of time to standard units of time through nursery rhymes.

A sunshiney shower
Will last half an hour.

Rain before seven
Fine before eleven.

March winds, April showers
Bring forth May flowers.

Monday's child is fair of face . . .

Solomon Grundy, born on Monday . . .

Old nursery rhymes are part of our heritage – a primary source – and in a rapidly changing world it is satisfying to hand them down. 'We feel part of human progression as we see our children swept into the dance as we were before them' (Butler 1988: 70).

Beryl Kingsbury (1998) has indicated the variety of picture books which will help children to understand that people, things and places change over time. *Rachel's Roses* (Christenson 1995), *This Quiet Lady* (Zolotow 1992), and *The Old, Old Man and the Very Little Boy* (Franklin 1992) are concerned in different ways with growth and change. *Remember Me* (Wild 1995), *Wilfred Gordon McDonald Partridge* (Fox 1987) and *My Great Grandpa* (Waddell 1991) are all concerned with memories of close family members, and *The Hidden House* (Waddell 1992) and *The Little House* (Burton 1978) are about houses and what can happen to them over time.

Karen Salter (1996) explored the use of story with her class of 4-year-olds during their first week in her Reception class. She decided to go into role to tell them the story of how Grace Darling, the Victorian lighthouse keeper's brave daughter, rescued shipwrecked sailors – an ambitious beginning!

Karen told them that she was a visitor to the school from a long time ago; she found that they accepted this and even those who normally found it difficult to listen sat perfectly still. They were not able to formulate any questions afterwards (so this was a skill to be developed), but they drew pictures for 'newspaper reports'. When a non-teaching assistant asked them to tell her about their pictures two weeks later so that she could scribe their written reports as an assessment, they all remembered the main events of the story, some in more detail than others, although one child's picture revealed that he had not known what a lighthouse was. Only one child's account was dominated by her own visit to a beach.

DURATION

The Foundation Stage Guidance for mathematics in *Curriculum Guidance for the Foundation Stage* (DfEE/QCA 2000a) says that children should learn to count to five, then ten and recognise numbers in familiar contexts (p. 74). They may recognise numbers on their birthday cards and badges, count their candles and sequence photographs linked to their age (p. 95).

Pat Hoodless (1998) read Nursery children stories in which a child's experiences in 'imaginary time' are told on one side of the page and parents parallel experiences in measured 'real time' are told on the opposite page, then asked them what they thought was happening (Burningham 1992; Sendak 1970). She found that these 3- and 4-year-olds seemed to understand what was happening. Some of them referred spontaneously to clock time. They tried to be specific about the actual time of day in which pictures were set. They referred to light and dark and night and day in trying to estimate durations and seemed to recognise the need to measure time.

Smith and Tomlinson (1977) found that children of 8 could not compare intervals of time in the past because they did not recognise the need for an independent calendar scale. They had little understanding of what is meant by 'a long time' or 'a short time' and would equate an interval of time with the number of events, wars or kings and queens linked to it. However, more research needs to be done. It seems likely that much younger children can compare intervals of time if they are given a time line marked in equal intervals, particularly if their first experience of time lines is linked to events in their own lives.

CAUSES AND EFFECTS OF CHANGES OVER TIME

Curriculum Guidance for the Foundation Stage (DfEE/QCA 2000a) says that children should learn to make patterns of their own experiences, to link cause and effect, to sequence, order and group, to clarify their thinking about ideas, feelings and events (p. 74). From 3 years of age, children should show an interest in why things happen and offer explanations (p. 50).

Crowther (1982), investigating concepts of change in children between 7 and 11, found that they regarded change only as a result of a direct action or as the substitution of one thing for another, taking little account of the time factor. But again the focus of the research was on older children, and the material they were asked to respond to was unlikely to produce a refined analysis of very young children's understanding of changes over time: of cause and effect, of motive or of different kinds of change. More research is needed. However, young children's understanding of stories shows that they are able to discuss how people's behaviour influences events. They ask questions and make predictions; they learn grammatical structures (if . . . then). Children between 2 and 3 years old learn about cause and effect, motives and rules through stories with consistent and dependable characters which move steadily towards a predictable outcome. Peter Rabbit is told in precise Victorian parlour language not to go into Mr McGregor's garden, and ignores the advice with predictable consequences. Rosie the Hen (Hutchins 1973) is almost overtaken at every point on her walk through the farmyard by the fox but, in her case, behaviour which ignores the rules just avoids the predicted effect in the end. By 3 years old, many children enjoy more complex stories and enjoy shades of meaning. They use the word 'perhaps' and they ask why people did things. They may begin with stories in which rigid rules apply and those in peril ultimately emerge safely ('The Three Bears' or 'The Billy Goats Gruff'). In these stories, motive is important; Goldilocks is curious and the billy goats go up the hill 'to get fat'. Between 4 and 5 years old, children begin to see things from points of view other than their own and to share the hopes, joys and fears of others. Gradually they develop greater insights about people. Although fairy stories are not about historical characters, they develop in children the ability to consider motives, causes and effects, which can later be transferred to myths and legends, heroes and heroines and to stories about people who really lived and events which really happened.

Harpin (1976) showed how growing maturity in children's syntax reflects their increasing ability to use conjunctions related to time, and to cause and effect, instead of 'and'. 'Autumn came and the leaves fell' becomes 'because the autumn came the leaves fell'. Instead of 'he finished work and went to bed' they may say, 'after he finished work he went to bed'.

However, Donaldson (1978) showed that young children are often prepared to accept, and not question, illogical situations; they need to be encouraged to question the sequence and causes and effects of events in a story.

SIMILARITY AND DIFFERENCE BETWEEN PAST AND PRESENT

Piaget (1952) showed how children learn to form sets of objects with shared characteristics. The process will be discussed in the section on the language of time (p. 16). In the context of history it means that children can begin to sort 'old' and 'new' and to discuss the reasons for putting an object into either set.

Curriculum Guidance for the Foundation Stage (DfEE/QCA 2000a) says that, from 3 years of age, children should be encouraged to make collections, and to observe, talk about and record similarities and differences between them (p. 89). They should begin to differentiate between past and present in their own lives and in those of their families and other people they know, through talking about changes in their environment or about artefacts, photographs and stories of different times, or interviewing visitors (pp. 94–5).

When Susan Mead read her nursery class the story about an old teddy this led to a discussion about which of two dolls was the older. The children concluded that the older doll must be the one with 'the china head and a body full of fluff' because the other doll had 'a plastic head. A long time ago they didn't have plastic.'

Children from 2 years old or earlier can become curious about how the past was different through illustrated nursery rhyme books. Greenaway illustrations (1991) introduce children to worlds where people wear clothes which are different from their own: long dresses, buttoned breeches, feathered bonnets and mob caps. Their toys are different: hobby horses, skipping ropes, fishing lines and see-saws. They are gently introduced to the occupations of a rural pre-industrial society:

Down to the meadow to milk the cow

Elsie Marley has grown so fine
She won't get up to feed the swine . . .

Little Bo Peep has lost her sheep . . .

They learn about bakers, and pipers and chimney-sweeps. And they are introduced to the vocabulary of other times: looking-glass, Sabbath, scholar, parlour.

Nursery rhymes form part of the 'stepping stones' to the early learning goals for the section 'Communication, Language and Literacy' in *Curriculum*

Guidance for the Foundation Stage (DfEE/QCA 2000a: 50, 53) and *The National Literacy Strategy* for Reception classes (DfEE/QCA 1998b: 18–19). *A Nursery Rhymes Resource Pack* (Hampshire Inspection and Advisory Service, 1999) gives many suggestions about using nursery rhymes to teach history.

THE LANGUAGE OF TIME

The Foundation Stage Guidance in DfEE/QCA 2000a stresses the importance of extending children's vocabulary and exploring the meanings and sounds of new words (p. 52). Children should also be encouraged to use the language of time, for example, yesterday, old, past, now, then (p. 95). They should talk about last, first, next, before, after, in discussions about life events and sequences of photographs or stories (p. 53).

Learning about the past involves learning vocabulary which is to some extent specific to history. Blyth (1990) pointed out that there is no clear agreement about what is meant by 'historical concepts'. Some are concerned with recording the passing of time (year, decade, generation, century), or with changes over time (old, new, the same, different, cause, effect). Some concepts describe the shared characteristics of periods of time (Roman, Victorian). Some concepts describe organising ideas which run through all societies and which are not exclusively historical (agriculture, trade, communication, beliefs). Others describe buildings, technology or groups of people belonging to former times (castle, villa; galleon, spinning wheel; Roundhead, knight). There are also concepts concerned with the processes of interpreting sources.

A concept may be a noun or an adjective, a verb or an adverb. It is a word, a symbol, which represents groups of objects or ideas which have one or more shared attributes. Some concepts are concrete; they refer to objects which can be borne in mind as images or as specific examples (king, castle). Other concepts are abstract (ruler, defence) and depend on an understanding of subordinate concrete concepts.

Children learn concepts not through ready-made definitions but by learning, in an active, problem-solving way, through trial and error and through discussion, to abstract their shared characteristics. In this way they gradually refine their concepts. Vygotsky (1962) showed the sequence in which concepts develop. At first, objects and ideas are linked by chance (all stone buildings are castles). At the second stage, they are linked by a characteristic which can change as new information is added (all castles are built on a mound, until we see one built on a cliff; all castles have a rectangular keep until we see one with round towers). Gradually pseudo-concepts develop which are deduced from context but are still unstable (a castle is a fort; a castle is a lord's big home; a castle has a moat). Children's and adults' words may coincide, but the child may be thinking of the concept in a different way from the adult (a castle was built to keep the baddies out; a castle represents feudal social structure). At the final stage, it is possible to formulate a rule which establishes a relationship between concepts and so creates an abstract idea (a castle is the fortified home of a feudal lord).

If children sort objects into 'old' and 'new', at the first stage they may not be able to offer any explanation for their groupings, which are random. At the next stage they may make sets of worn objects and of undamaged objects, but the defining attribute will have to change when a pristine object, which is known to be very old, is introduced. They may redefine the sets as 'things which are precious' and 'things which are not precious' until the teacher explains why her old threadbare teddy is very precious to her. Finally, the children may agree on a shared attribute for the 'old' and the 'new' sets, such as 'the old things are all older than we are', and 'the new things were made in our life-time'. Concepts of time are particularly difficult to engage with because they are relative and subjective. People of different ages have different concepts of an old person, a long time or long ago. Yesterday and tomorrow can only be defined by an abstract rule.

Klausmeier *et al.* (1979) showed how concrete tangible concepts are learnt through verbal labelling and through storing images; children become increasingly able to recognise similarities and differences.

They may, for example, increasingly extend and refine their concept of a castle by first visiting a castle, then collecting pictures of castles built in different places and in different periods, and discussing the similarities and differences between them. They may explore the concept of 'prince' by listening to stories, true and fictitious, about good princes and bad, strong and weak, powerful and powerless, who lived in different times and places.

Children may be introduced to the abstract, organising concepts which run through all societies, and to the subordinate concepts related to them, through myths, legends and folk tales, for these stories revolve around central ideas: power and social organisation, beliefs, trade, journeys, communication, agriculture.

Research has shown that children learn new concepts best when they are selected, used and discussed (Vygotsky 1962). Language is the tool for unlocking the past. Children need to discuss, explain and justify with each other and with adults the reasons for the chronological sequences they form, to suggest the causes and effects of changes the sequences represent, to explain and refine the categories they form and the similarities and differences between examples – between a windmill they have visited and other examples seen in pictures. They need to discuss vocabulary used in stories. Donaldson (1978) found that young children rarely question new vocabulary; what is meant by 'fair' or 'brave'? In their play, too, they need to explore and use the new concepts they have been introduced to in stories.

Virginia Hunt, a student, described how her son, aged 2 years and 8 months, enjoyed *Bill and Pete Go Down the Nile* (de Paolo 1988). He repeatedly asked to have it read to him and questioned the alternative meaning of 'mummy'. On each reading he remembered and identified the sarcophagus and the sphinx. Given a selection of books about the past, he chose a book on Ancient Egypt and searched for a sarcophagus, then pointed out sarcophagi and sphinxes in other books! This is an excellent example of how to use children's experience of stories as a familiar foundation from which to explore new concepts related to other times.

As children get older, language becomes increasingly important in refining concepts. What kind of soldier is he? What type of wood, or metal or fabric is it made from? What was it used for? If it was used to make work easier it is a tool. If it was used for fighting it is a weapon.

THE CONCEPT OF TIME

In helping young children to be curious about and to find out about the past, how important is a concept of time? Certainly, children's understanding of the relationship between subjective and measured time develops slowly. Their knowledge of the past and experience of time is limited. The measurement of time involves complex concepts. Concepts of time change with age and circumstance.

However, Lello (1980) argued that a grasp of chronology and the fixing of events in context and time are not synonymous with developing an understanding of past times. Certainly, many games devised to teach children about chronological sequence would not seem to develop their understanding of the past at all.

> This game will not a little contribute to make the Players acquainted with the Genealogy of their own kings. We hope the young Player will not think much of Exercising his Memory to Acquire a Perfect Knowledge of it.
>
> ('The Royal Genealogical Pastime of the Sovereigns of England', published by Edward Wallis, London, 1791)

Marbeau (1988) argued that a child of 6 has a very narrow and discontinuous grasp of his own duration: 'History at first is historicisation of a child's own existence.' Children build continuity into their existence by reciting it to others (and to themselves). However, difficulty with the measurement of time does not impair children's interest in history. Marbeau saw this as a reflection of their interest in 'the problem of origins'. One 6-year-old, Lisa, constantly asked her mother, a student history teacher, to repeat the order in which their household had come together (mum, cat, dad, dog, Lisa), but remained confused by the fact that dad was clearly older than the cat. A time-line helped, but Lisa continued to believe that she would eventually be the same age as her mother. She still talked about things she did quite recently as 'When I was a baby', but told stories about things which had happened some time ago as recent events. A video recording of all her birthdays helped her to sequence events in her own life.

Penelope Lively, who is a history graduate as well as a novelist, wrote poetically about how a child's sense of time is different from that of an adult.

> He [the father] perceived in an instant the perpetual flow of childhood, the interminable present from which, eventually, we escape, and which we can never retrieve. We cohabit with these mysterious beings who occupy a different time zone, who share our days, and move with us through them, but whose vision is that of aliens.
>
> (Lively 1991: 183)

Yet even for adults, time is not always best understood on a chronological, equal interval scale, and it is sometimes possible to feel closer to people long dead than when they were alive.

> Time present and time past
> Are both perhaps present in time future
> And time future contained in time past.
>
> (from 'Burnt Norton', in Eliot 1986)

A fascination with time runs through all Shakespeare's writing. In different ways, time permeates all cultures. The Jamaican poet Dennis Scott (1986) wrote:

> Uncle Time is a spider-man, cunnin' an' cool,
> him tell you: watch de hill an' yu se mi.
> Huh! Fe yu yi no quick enough fe si
> how 'im move like mongoose; man, yu tink 'im fool?
> . . .
> Watch how 'im spin web roun' yu house, an' creep
> inside, an' when 'im touch you, weep . . .

Or, in the words of a popular Bengali song:

> This bank erodes
> Another bank emerges:
> Such are the whims of the river.
> You are a wealthy *Amir* in the morning
> A penniless *Fakir* in the evening
> Such are the whims of the river.

It is not surprising that children get confused. Of course chronology and dates and measured time are central to history as a discipline, but for young children whose understanding of time is embryonic, a curiosity and excitement about other people, other lives and other times are more important than dates.

STUDENT TEACHERS INVESTIGATE FOUNDATION STAGE CHILDREN'S CONCEPTS OF TIME

A Nursery class

Janet Liddle, a fourth-year BA (QTS) history student, wanted to find out what understanding of changes over time 4-year-olds had when they first came into her Nursery class. In groups of four she read them a nursery rhyme book with nineteenth-century illustrations, and they talked about 'the past', stimulated initially by the pictures. She recorded their conversation. She found that 85 per cent of the children spontaneously used basic time vocabulary: a long time ago, old, new, olden days, old fashioned. They were developing some sense of chronology: Lauren: 'My Dad is old but Oscar my rabbit is new.' Rebecca decided to draw her mum and dad getting married: 'That was a very long time ago.' Sally had a nanny 'who is old, and she is my daddy's mummy' while Vicky's grandma 'lived in India when she was a little girl'. Sam talked about 'inventions', Hannah was aware that Jesus lived 'a very long time ago', and Thomas that pterodactyls lived long, long ago, but Ben knew this was 'after the sun got made'.

These children also used concepts related to history which they had heard in stories: castle, king, church, prince, queen. The children said they knew about the past mostly from their parents, from visits to castles and churches, but also from television and videos.

During the conversation they talked about changes: the invention of electricity and television, changes in shops, clothes, houses. Sam made some very complex comments about himself in relation to past and present: 'I don't wear clothes like that because I'm not in the olden days' but 'I've seen an old-fashioned car racing up a hill and I've seen it not in the olden days.'

A playgroup

Debra Vickers, another student teacher, said that in the playgroup where she worked the children did not see her as a teacher who expected 'right answers'. She listened as they talked freely about a collection of 'old things' she had brought in: a flat iron, an old typewriter and a wooden toy. James said that he would like to 'go back in time' and see what it would have been like to use them. When his friend said he felt sorry for the people who used them, James explained that the people who used them would 'have felt lucky because they would not know anything different'. He went on, with amazing insight, to explain that his children will have new toys to play with and 'will look at my toys like things from the past'.

Chapter 2

Interpretations of the past

Historians write different accounts of the past. They differ because of the preoccupations of the age in which they live, because of their own interests and perspectives, and because historical evidence is frequently incomplete. There is no single correct view of the past. We all reconstruct our own views of the past, depending on our knowledge, political stance, class, race, gender and interests. Doing so enables us to reflect on our own position in relation to the present and to the past.

Selecting, piecing together and interpreting evidence in order to construct an account of the past requires imagination. Trevelyan (1919) said that at bottom the appeal of history is imaginative; truth is the criterion of historical study but its impelling motive is poetic. Elton (1970) saw historical imagination as a tool for filling in the gaps when facts are not available. Lee (1984) defined it more precisely as the disposition to make a range of valid suppositions based on evidence. Historians do not aim to identify with people in the past or to project themselves into the past because this is not possible, but they attempt to understand and explain on the basis of likely possibilities the thoughts and feelings which underpinned the actions and behaviour of people in the past. This is difficult because people in the past had attitudes and values different from our own, because of their different knowledge bases and the different political, social and economic constraints within which they lived.

Young children can begin to understand why there may be more than one version of a story about the past. In order to do so they need opportunities to create their own interpretations, based on what they know, and to see how and why they may differ.

UNDERSTANDING INTERPRETATIONS

Piaget (1956) suggested that young children are incapable of holding more than one perspective at a time. This implies that they cannot compare two different versions of a story. Others have said, however, that their ability to see a situation from more than one viewpoint depends on how involved they are, and on their understanding of a situation.

Donaldson (1978), Borke (1978) and Flavell (1985) found that children are capable of seeing more than one viewpoint but that they do not often see the need to do so. Recent research has differentiated between visual perspective-taking, conversational role-taking and pictorial representation, and in each instance young children appear to be underestimated. Cox (1986) said that in their verbal interactions, young children do develop inferences concerning the points of view of others, although more research is needed. It will be interesting, then, to investigate to what extent they are able to recognise different versions of a story, different illustrations of the same story, or a story told from different perspectives, and whether they can explain what is the same and what is different. Two-year-olds can learn that there are different versions of stories and nursery rhymes. A traditional *Mother Goose Treasury* with Victorian-style illustrations (Hague 1984) contrasts strongly with the purples and scarlets of Brian Wildsmith's (1987) *Mother Goose,* and with the meticulous dignity and quiet colour of Katherine Line's *Lavender's Blue* (1989). Nursery rhymes translated into different languages can be compared (Chinese nursery rhymes, translated into eight languages, from Haringey Multicultural Resource Centre, see p. 218), or different versions in bilingual books (e.g. Wasu 1986). In *Mother Goose Comes to Cable Street* (Stones and Mann 1987) English nursery rhymes are brilliantly illustrated in the context of contemporary East London street scenes; traditional pictures of 'I do not like thee, Dr. Fell' can be compared with amusing pictures of a doctor's waiting room today. In *The Baby's Catalogue* (Ahlberg 1984) the babies illustrate the similarities and differences in the lives of five different families. Young children could make comparisons between the experience of a baby in their own family and in their friends' families.

Thomas (1993) showed how nursery-age children can detect contradictory meanings in books. She introduced children who had previous experience of browsing and talking about illustrations to books which explicitly invite the reader to find meanings in pictures which are different from those in the text, for example, *If at First You Do not See* (Brown 1982), *Lights On, Lights Off* (Taylor 1988). Then they progressed to books where text and pictures do not conform: *Time to Get Out of the Bath, Shirley* (Burningham 1985), *Not Now Bernard* (McKee 1980), *Rosie's Walk* (Hutchins 1973), *Never Satisfied* (Testa 1982). In the text of *Never Satisfied,* children constantly restate how boring everything is while the pictures show all kinds of incredible happenings: a woman tightrope-walking on a washing line and monsters appearing over walls. The seven children listening to the story all insisted that there *were* things happening but the characters did not appear to notice. Cameron said that much of the story was unseen. The children only paused when the pictures became ambiguous, showing the characters' eyes apparently directed at unseen events. This caused Thomas to re-examine her own preconceptions; is the story about people who do not look, or about looking but not seeing, or about seeing but not being impressed? Thomas found that the children could recognise and discuss contradictory meanings irrespective of their ability to decode the text, that being able to read between the lines includes the recognition of different possible interpretations of meaning, and that adults should be wary of imposing their own presuppositions on children. She concluded that children need to hear alternative versions of the same story in fiction and later to be aware that different newspapers may present conflicting accounts of 'the truth', as do different historians and different scientists.

> Nursery-aged children are not too young to be offered play and literary experiences that will help them to develop the ability to look for alternative views and viewpoints later in their development, and to start to think about character and motive.
>
> (Thomas 1993)

The guidance given in *Curriculum Guidance for the Foundation Stage* DfEE/QCA 2000a says that children should be encouraged to talk with each other about similarities and differences, and to understand and respect that people may have different views (pp. 42–3) and to have a developing awareness of their own views (pp. 34–5).

CREATING INTERPRETATIONS

Through 'let's pretend' imaginative play children, alone or together, can create their own interpretations of past times, based on stories, visits and pictures. There is no single, all-embracing explanation of what or how children learn through play, but each theory suggests different ways in which play can help children to interpret the past.

At the beginning of this century play was seen as a way in which a child reproduces the early experiences of humanity: wandering tribes, hunting, war, building shelters and fighting. Certainly shelters, tree-houses, tents, caves, defending the 'hide-out' and preparing food often feature in spontaneous play.

Bruner saw play as a means of exploring the uses of basic technology. Free play often involves, for example, making castles (making moats and dams and bridges, moving loads with carts and pulleys), sailing boats, exploring materials central to human societies (wood, stone, metal, wool, leather, synthetic materials), and taking things apart to see how they work and what they are used for.

Others have stressed the psychodynamic nature of play. This may involve exploring relationships changing over time within the family unit, for example, as a new baby is born, or coping with the loss of a grandparent. It may involve exploring motives, a family decision to move house for example. Such play could explore stories told about what life was like when grandparents were young, or re-enacting stories from other cultures. These may all be ways of relating what children find meaningful and significant in their own lives to changes over time, and to life in other times and places.

Erikson (1965) found that if children were asked to reconstruct exciting scenes from folk tales through 'let's pretend' play, the stories they acted out seemed to be metaphors for their own lives, concerns and interests. Such play, he said, helps children to engage with the mainstream of human emotions in the context of times and places other than their own.

Winnicott (Bruce 1991: 77) suggested that adults are able to relate to powerful events, hero figures, music and paintings as part of the external world if they have related to them and merged with what is important to them, through play. Singer and Singer (1990) traced a continuum between such childhood play, fantasy in adolescence and creativity in adult life.

In imaginative 'let's pretend' play, then, children reconstruct their own versions of stories (Warlow 1977: 93). Play about stories from the past involves experimental dialogue about materials, places and people in other times (Garvey 1977: 32). It allows children to explore emotions, attitudes, relationships and situations outside their direct experience. They can make 'suppositions' about alternative worlds which are imaginative, creative and innovative. Such play brings together what children already know, feel and understand and allows them to explore situations which they will not meet in their real lives until later.

Moyles (1989) suggested that play in the context of a pretend castle, an old kitchen, a Victorian classroom for dolls, a palace or a workplace helps children both to understand themselves and their own self-worth, and also explore what it might have been like to be somebody else. The ability to pretend helps children to learn about something without experiencing it for themselves. Through role-play children can wear different 'hats' in different situations, imitate gestures, movements and expressions, and explore what it might have been like to wear a hooped skirt or knee breeches, to milk a cow or ride a horse. They can investigate what it might feel like to use a flat iron, scrub a floor, sight a new land from a crow's nest or keep watch from the battlements. A child looks in the mirror and fits, in manner and gesture, the picture in the mirror. Garvey (1977) found that re-enactments are created from concepts of appropriate behaviour and are most likely not direct imitations of people.

Children who have heard stories about the past spontaneously reconstruct them in play. A student described how a 3-year-old who had seen a film about Robin Hood on television continued long afterwards to re-enact whole scenes in solitary play quoting verbatim and with great relish such phrases as 'Seize the fat one!' Younger children in a group often find themselves in the play without knowing too much about it but the older children negotiate in advance a general script or statement, then 'tell them the story'. Bruce (1991) described how a group of 5-year-olds heard stories about the Black Prince and about King Arthur which led to extensive play about princes and princesses. On another occasion, Hannah, aged 5, and Tom, aged 3, used a rough script based on the story of George and the Dragon as an agenda for play. Children's toys can stimulate stories about the past which will extend their play. Bruce (1991) showed how one teacher added wings to 4-year-old Sukvinder's 'My Little Pony' and used it as a prop to tell children the story of Pegasus. Although the children were under no pressure to take up the myth, they were enthralled by it and it re-appeared in free-flow play and in their paintings. From the age of 2, children, in their play, can take on a role, create a context, use symbols and negotiate a narrative. They are able to exist in two worlds, the real and the imaginary, at the same time, by creating symbols which are the pivot between the two worlds: a table may become a cave or a horse.

Play stimulates language development, clarifying new words and concepts, motivating language use and encouraging verbal thinking, for language cannot occur in a vacuum. It is about the reconstruction of meaning. In play children can make inferences about behaviour, consider alternatives and probability, and use different tenses and complex sentences related to causes and effects. Such language is essential in the development of historical thinking. Sources can tell us nothing about the past until we know how to interpret them and how to communicate our interpretations.

Of course children's imaginative play, stimulated by stories about the past, or by a visit to a sailing ship or a castle, has very little in common with the processes by which historians construct accounts of the past. Genuine historical imagination depends on careful consideration of what seems likely in the light of known evidence. This requires both the maturity to consider how adults in the past may have felt, thought and behaved, and extensive knowledge of the times in which they lived. Historians do not project themselves into a past time, or identify with people in the past. They can only try to explain the past with circumspection and humility (Cooper 1992: 136–7). Young children have neither the maturity, nor the knowledge, nor the circumspection to do this in a way that is historically valid. Links with evidence, with what is known, are slight and play is dominated by fantasy rather than by genuine historical imagination. However, in play children do attempt to identify with people in the past and to project themselves into past times. In play set in an historical context, children are, in an embryonic way embarking on the process of finding out about and trying to understand and reconstruct past times. This can be the beginning of a continuum in which, with maturity, fantasy will gradually diminish and a search for what is known will become increasingly important.

PLAY, THE PAST AND PRE-SCHOOL SETTINGS

Curriculum Guidance for the Foundation Stage (DfEE 2000a) emphasises the importance of extending and supporting children's learning through play and the role of adults in creating and resourcing challenging contexts for play. Stories, pictures, CD-ROMs, videos about the past, visits to old buildings, dressing-up, or collections of 'old things' help children to explore and develop their own imaginative and creative interpretations of times beyond their own experiences. Such play may be boisterous outdoor play, with imaginative use of large equipment and open spaces: making shelters, scaling castles, defending forts, building bridges, being hunters and explorers. Through such play children are also learning to negotiate space, move with confidence, co-ordination, control and safety (DfEE/QCA 2000a: 104–8). An area of rough ground in an outside play area can enable today's children to create their 'special place' such as Donald MacIntosh (1999) describes in his rural childhood in Galloway, where he was always Bonnie Prince Charlie and his younger sister was Flora MacDonald – when she was in the mood – although 'there are few things more unsettling to a Prince on the run than to find that the lady who has elected to join him in his hour of need is made cantankerous because her hair is full of midges and her knickers infested with ticks'.

Indoors, through making models of windmills, castles and ships children learn to handle tools and materials correctly (DfEE/QCA 2000a: 102–14). Through helping to develop a role-play area (an old kitchen, a castle or a shop), children can learn to make connections between one area of learning and another. With support they may include art, music and dance in the imaginative play (DfEE/QCA 2000a: 116–27). They develop language and communication skills. Dressing-up will even help them to dress and undress independently (p. 40).

Many early years practitioners assume that play is implicitly valuable in encouraging language and social skills. However, it has been found that, although young children do not always find free play as easy and natural as theories suggest, cognitive development, subject knowledge and assessment are rarely seen as important aspects of play (Bennett *et al.* 1996). This study suggested that to improve the quality of play it is important to make time for quality interactions to enhance learning through play, to allow children extended time to play with teacher participation and use of ancillary help, to recognise opportunities for teaching through play by integrating play into the curriculum with clearly specified aims and interventions, and freeing the teacher to observe, interact and assess. The following examples give a flavour of how this may be done.

FOUNDATION STAGE CHILDREN'S INTERPRETATIONS OF THE PAST THROUGH PLAY

A shelter

Gordon Guest (1997) suggests how Littlenose stories by John Grant (e.g. 1990), for example, could provide a starting point for collecting twigs, stones and branches to build a 'Stone Age shelter', which could help children to explore life in the distant past and to develop their technological skills. Can they make eating tools from twigs, containers from leaves or stones, a soft bed, a waterproof roof? And do not forget to explain that there is archaeological evidence that four-fifths of the average cave-family's diet was grubbed from the earth by women with pointy sticks, not by macho male bison hunters! (Miles 1989).

A castle

Catherine Garside, a fourth-year BA (QTS) history specialist student, described how she helped a group of children in a Nursery class to create a castle play area in an urban, multicultural school, how she supported their play and assessed new learning.

First she asked them what they knew about castles ('old, big'); who might have lived in them ('Kings, Queens, Princes, Princesses, spiders, witches, frogs, old people'); what might have happened in them ('the King tells people what to do, soldiers fight'). Then she read them two stories about castles: *Meg's Castle* (Hissey 1990) and *The Story of a Castle* (Goodall 1986). They discussed characters, events and new vocabulary, and immediately wanted to draw pictures. Later in the day Catherine read them *King None the Wiser* (McNaughton 1991) and they looked at *The Story of a Castle* again. When Catherine returned to the three questions she had asked initially, the children's answers were extended: castles have battlements, a drawbridge, towers, flags, moats. Cooks, knights, horses, blacksmiths might have lived in them. When they were asked if they would like to have lived in a castle and why, one child wanted to be a knight, 'to do things for the King'; one wanted to be a King, 'I would own the castle and give orders', and one to be a blacksmith, 'to look after the horses'. All the girls wanted to be queens, but not because they felt subservient. They wanted 'to give orders and be rich'.

The following day the children arrived early, eager to 'build a castle'. They looked at photographs and illustrations. Catherine helped them to make battlements and fireplaces out of cardboard boxes, to suspend a cardboard portcullis from a beam, to make a crown and shields. This sustained an extended period of free play. Catherine observed that the children all took on the identity of someone from the stories; throughout they frequently changed roles, assuming new roles and announcing who they were. They tended not to all play together in the castle but to play individually or in pairs. Some of the events in their play resembled some of the events in the stories; killing a dragon so they would be safe, for example. Constantly as they played they talked about what they were doing. However, events from the stories which had been read did not appear in sequence: the children's make-believe play appeared to be a creative blend of events from different stories – their own interpretations.

On Thursday Catherine played alongside the children for a while. In the role of King she summoned all the children and told them of an expected attack, based on events in the story of a castle. Then she withdrew and watched as children discussed their roles and what they would do. She found that they now played a lot more as a group; one child took the role of leader, which others accepted. They acted out the story (which was a true story of an event in a castle), sequencing the incidents correctly, but they also added new incidents.

On Friday the children continued with their free play. Catherine observed unobtrusively and noted what they had learned. They talked about reasons why the past was different.

> I'm cooking the food over a fire because a long time ago, when people lived in castles, there was no electricity – they didn't have ovens . . .

> Pass me the candle. It's too dark in here. I will light it so we can see what we're doing. Put it on the table so we can see the food.

Sometimes in the make-believe play, children corrected each other.

Sarah   Knights, attack your enemies. Get them and shoot them.
Usman   We don't have guns. Knights in battle use swords and spears and bow and arrows.
Sarah   Well, attack them with your sword then.

Catherine noticed that the more time the children spent in their make-believe castle, the more they used 'special vocabulary' learned from discussing the stories.

> We need *armour* to protect us . . .
> We've got to *defend* the castle.
> Quick, put the drawbridge up and the *portcullis* down.
> Let's check what the enemy are doing through the *battlements*.
> Watch where you're walking. You're going to fall into the *moat*.
> You need to go over the *drawbridge*. Let me lower it . . .
> The *drawbridge* is up so the enemies can't get in.

An old shop

Julie Woodward introduced 'an old shop' into her Nursery class. They looked at photographs of grocers' shops in the 1930s, and asked an elderly visitor about shopping in those days. They compared advertisements now and then and discussed old artefacts: butter pats, old money, an old till and balance scales. Then they discussed how they could make 'an old shop'. They had noticed that most things were loose, not packaged, so they filled jars with old-fashioned 'play-doh' sweets. They made a slab of yellow 'play-doh' butter for moulding with the butter pats, and they cut grease-proof paper for wrapping it. They filled old biscuit tins with loose biscuits, collected a sack of potatoes and a tin of tea (sand). They used an old wooden table for the counter, on which stood the old till and scales, and they put the old posters advertising cocoa and Bovril on the walls behind, and a chair and wicker basket for the customer.

At first the children played freely in the shop but there was no evidence that they were imagining it was an old shop: 'I'll have a tin of coke and a pizza, please.'

Julie showed how she gradually helped them to imagine they were in a shop in the past and to extend and develop their play by participating periodically herself over several sessions. For example:

First teacher participation

J.W.   I'd like 2 ounces of butter, please.
        [R. hands her a slab of play-doh.]
J.W.   Oh, that's far too much. I only want a little bit.
H.   Yeah – use those pat things.
J.W.   You mean the butter pats.
H.   Yeah. That's what they used for butter.
J.W.   That's right. Use the butter pats to shape my piece of butter, then you can weigh and wrap it in greaseproof paper.
        [R. took great pleasure in doing this.]

Second teacher participation

R.   We'd like some sweets.
        [J.W. weighs sweets on old scales and puts in paper bag.]
A.   Can I have some ice-cream?
J.W.   I'm sorry. I'm not sure what you mean.
R.   Yeah, silly. We forgot they had no frozen food – it would all melt. Yuk! . . .
A.   We could buy some teabags and have a nice cup of tea with our biscuits.
J.W.   I only have loose tea. How much would you like?
R.   Not a lot.
        [J.W. weighs tea, puts it in a bag and places it in R's basket.]

A.   Yuk, my Nanna gets tea like that. You get bits in it.
J.   Can we have some butter, please?
J.W.   How much?
J.   Just a little bit.
        [J.W. takes play-doh, weighs, pats it into shape and wraps in greaseproof paper.]

Free play next day

R.   Can I come shopping with you today?
A.   Yes, but you'll have to wear this because it's what they used to wear.
J.   I'll be the shopkeeper . . .
R.   I'd like 4 ounces of butter, please.
        [J. pats, weighs and wraps the butter.]
R.   And six ounces of tea, please.
        [J. pours sand onto scales, weighs and bags the tea.]
J.   That's one pound, please.
        [J. gives change and puts tea and butter in basket.]
R.   Thank you. Good morning.

Julie concluded the term by taking all the children who had played in the old shop to a local supermarket so they could talk more about the differences between 'now' and 'then'.

The old kitchen

The following term Julie returned to the same Nursery class and set up 'an old kitchen' role-play area, complete with a range made from cardboard boxes with a rag rug in front of it, two flat irons, an old hot water bottle, scrubbing brush and carpet beater. In the corner there was a dolly tub and butter pats were on the table. Again, she wanted to investigate the effect when she occasionally participated in the children's free play. This time she introduced another variable. One group of children talked about the artefacts before they played in the kitchen, what they were called, how they were used and why. Another group did not. She participated at intervals in the play of both groups, but found that her participation was much more effective in extending the play of the children who had first spent time discussing the artefacts with her. Here are more examples of how she developed their understanding of the past through joining in their play.

J.W.   . . . can you pass me the posser . . . no, that's a dolly-peg – that's the posser . . .
B.   Here you are, let's swish the clothes around to get them clean . . .
H.   I'll do some ironing.
J.W.   Put the irons in front of the range then to warm them up . . .

H.   They're warm now.
R.   Make sure you get all the creases out . . .
A.   I'll make some bread and we can have bread and butter for tea.
J.W. That's a good idea. But is that iron hot? Do you want to swap it for the other one by the range?
B.   I think I'd better get it.
H.   I'll get it, it's heavy.

A Victorian police station

Gill Bicknell (1988) felt that her Nursery class visit to a local memorial to Robert Peel (p. 36) had been so successful that she repeated it with her Reception class as part of a history/geography project on 'People who help us in the community'. After a visit from the local policeman, followed by pictures of Victorian policemen and stories of pickpockets from an elderly visitor, she set up a role-play area as a Victorian Police Station complete with top hats, truncheons, handcuffs and bars at the windows. A key objective was to develop children's language.

Later, she found the children using the Police Station play area to act out a version of the 'Billy Goats Gruff' with the troll cast as a pickpocket (having made a descriptive 'wanted' poster of the ugly troll!). She built on this to encourage them to write carefully observed descriptions of lost or stolen Victorian artefacts and to use Victorian photographs to create a collection of police record cards of pickpockets. Parents were brought in to see the Victorian Police Station. Gill felt that the considerable knowledge of Victorian times which the children displayed was largely attributed to the high amount of oral work, both in and out of the role-play.

Pirates

Two vivid examples of students supporting a 'pirates' theme in Nursery classes developed from ideas in the first edition of this book spring to mind. In one class, I was given a pirate hat and eye-patch and invited to look through the porthole of the play area as children described the desert island backdrop they had painted, and to suspend belief as we tracked an approaching galleon. In another class, the whole room was converted into a pirate ship with flags suspended from the beam, maps on the walls, hornpipes being danced and decks being scrubbed. This project lasted several weeks. It was exciting and encouraging to see how suggestions made in the first edition of this book and explored in student workshops in college have been developed in very different, but equally vibrant ways in classrooms.

Chapter 3

Deductions and inferences from sources

Historians find out about the past through asking questions and making inferences about sources which remain: buildings, sites, pictures, artefacts and written sources. How was it made? Why? How was it used? What did it mean to the people who made and used it? Sources are often incomplete, and their status may be unknown. (For example, was the bone pendant in a bronze age grave an ornament or symbolic object?) Therefore it may be possible to make a number of different and equally valid inferences about a source. Inferences are valid if they conform with what else is known of the period and if they assume that people in the past acted rationally. It is necessary to support inferences with arguments and also to listen to the arguments of others. To what extent, then, are young children able to make valid inferences about historical sources, to support their inferences with arguments, and to listen to each other's suggestions?

INFERENTIAL THINKING

According to Piaget's posited sequence in cognitive development, the thinking of young children is dominated by trial and error and by their own experiences and feelings. Gradually they take in more information about the tangible and visible world, sometimes needing to adjust their own mental patterns to accommodate new information. Piaget (1951) traced the development of children's increasing awareness of what can be known and what can be reasonably supposed. Through his work on language (1926) and on logic (1928) a pattern in the development of argument can be traced. At first the child is not concerned with interesting or convincing others and leaps from a premise to an unreasonable conclusion in one bound. Next the child tries to communicate intellectual processes which are factual and descriptive and show incipient logic, but these are not clearly expressed. This leads to a valid statement of fact or description. From this follows 'primitive argument' in which the statement or opinion is followed by a deduction going beyond the information given, but the explanation for the deduction is only implicit. At the next stage, the child tries to justify and demonstrate the assertion using a conjunction ('therefore' or 'because'), but does not succeed in expressing a truly logical relationship. Eventually, through frequent attempts to justify his or her own opinion and avoid contradiction, and also as a result of internal debate, a child is able to use 'therefore' or 'because' correctly, and to relate an argument to its premise. Others have found that children's capacity for deductive and inferential thinking is influenced by their interest and involvement, and by their understanding of what kind of thinking is required.

Donaldson (1978) examined the dichotomy she recognised between children's capacity for deductive reasoning in informal, everyday situations and Piaget's conclusion that children under 7 have little reasoning ability. She found that young children are capable of deductive reasoning, that their problem-solving depends on the extent to which they can concentrate on language, and that language development is related to other non-verbal clues which are also brought to bear on problem-solving. She found that children find reasoning difficult because they rarely spontaneously discuss the meanings of words, they are easily distracted and they do not always select relevant terms in problem-solving. She concluded that their level of deductive and inferential thinking depends on whether the reasoning stems from the children's immediate concerns, or whether it is externally imposed. It also depends on the child's expectation of what the questioner wants.

Wright (1984) found that 7-year-olds could draw their own conclusions from pottery finds and there is evidence that 8-year-olds can learn to make complex inferences about artefacts, pictures, archaeological plans, maps and written sources (Cooper 1991).

So far, however, there has been no systematic study of younger children's ability to make inferences about historical sources. But there is increasing awareness that young children can ask questions about artefacts from everyday life in the past which involve looking, listening, touching and smelling. *Under Fives and Museums* (Ironbridge Gorge Museum Trust) gives useful suggestions about how the Ironbridge Gorge Museum site can be used to help pre-school children make deductions and inferences about the past. Donaldson (1978) argued that they must be helped to make inferences, and to understand the nature of different disciplines, as early as possible, in order to recognise the abstraction of language.

DISCUSSION

Dialogue which allows children to make deductions and inferences, to speculate, to consider possibilities and accept that there may be no single right answer, to discuss causes and effects and to retell stories is essential for the development of historical understanding. Lee (1984) suggested that the capacity to generate a number of suggestions makes mature historical imagination possible.

Some pre-school children have more opportunities for interactive dialogue than others. Much has been written about the importance of spoken language and social interaction from birth (e.g. Bruner 1983). Doise (1975, 1978) saw cognitive growth as the result of either conflict of viewpoint or of interaction at different cognitive levels, although no sensitive measures for assessing the effect of social interaction on cognition have been achieved. Light (1983) concluded that there will be rapid development in our understanding of these issues.

Most children have more opportunities at home than they do in school to talk to an adult one-to-one, to ask open-ended questions and to initiate discussion, because in school there is a different ratio of children to adults and different social relationships. Maclure and French (1986) found that children are more likely to correct their parents than their teachers. However, there is more continuity between patterns of language interaction at home and in school than has sometimes been assumed. Both parents and teachers sometimes ask closed questions to which they know the answers in order to monitor children's understanding: 'After spring it will be . . .?' After summer it will be . . .?' 'So how many seasons are there altogether?' (Wells 1986). But in school, children are also encouraged to make suggestions. Maclure and French (1986) found that teachers are more likely than parents to want children to offer alternative interpretations, rather than to correct them. Often they do this by making a general statement, then asking individual children a series of questions related to it. This requires on-going attention in order to participate and so to share ideas. They may begin with a question about the physical environment which will produce a positive response, then extend the discussion. Or they may begin with a shared experience: 'Did you look inside?' 'What did you see?'

Children need to learn the kinds of questions to ask and appropriate ways of answering them, and to take turns. There is evidence that if they do, their talk among themselves may be more dense, discursive and reflective than when an adult is present (Prisk 1987).

Open-ended discussion in the school, then, can build on and extend patterns of interactive language at home, so that children gradually learn to talk to each other in a purposeful and focused way, without continuous adult support. They learn to share ideas about how artefacts or buildings may have been made and used, and how they may have affected people's lives, and to make up and compare stories which may explain pictures, photographs, artefacts or statues.

USING SOURCES: THE FOUNDATION STAGE

Talking about appropriate artefacts, pictures and photographs, visiting historical places or talking to older visitors can encourage children to observe, to question, think critically and discuss their ideas with others in order to begin to understand the past (DfEE/QCA 2000a: 82–3). They will learn to be confident in making suggestions about how things were made, what they are made of, why things happen and how things work (pp. 86–8). They will find out about the place they live in (p. 96), how old things were used and why (p. 32), learn to take turns in discussion (p. 36), and to understand that people may have different views (p. 42). They learn to develop language using the past as well as the present tense and extend their vocabulary, exploring the meaning and sounds of new words. They can help to create their own display of 'old things' and begin to write labels and captions.

SITE VISITS WITH FOUNDATION STAGE CHILDREN

A local monument

Gill Bicknell took her Nursery class in Bury, Greater Manchester, for a picnic to nearby Peel Tower, a familiar feature of the local landscape built 150 years ago in memory of Robert Peel, the Prime Minister. They found his name engraved in the stone (Bicknell 1988). During the following days, as they reinforced their experience by making pictures and models of the tower, Gill listened to the talk. They used time language, 'longest ago' and causal language, 'it is called the Peel Tower because a man started the police and that was his name'.

A mill

When Joanne Reeves (with plenty of other adults) took her Reception class for a walk along the river near their school, they 'discovered' an old mill. They decided that it was a watermill because from the bridge they could discern the position of the old waterwheel, and there were steps leading down from the mill to the river. They worked out from these two facts why the mill was by the river, what the wheel was for, why it was no longer needed, and how wool and cloth was lifted into and out of the mill by the hoist which remained over the big arched doorway. They took photographs and continued to talk about the mill which they had never noticed before, all the way back to school. They found the site of the mill on a map; they found pictures and diagrams of watermills in books, mounted the photographs with captions and made a working model of a hoist for their display.

A 'Living History' Museum

Alison Coleman walked around Beamish Open Air Museum with her group of Reception class children, looking at the dentist's surgery, the fairground, the town street. They had many questions for her and the staff on site. She felt that, although it was an 'old-fashioned world', it was still a real situation to them and they thought the staff really did live in Beamish and in these conditions. It needed some discussion to help them to separate the 'real world now', the 'pretend old-fashioned world' and the notion that the 'pretend world' was once 'real'!

Pictures

Penelope Harnett has shown how skilful questioning helped Reception class children to move beyond making inferences about pictures of Queen Elizabeth II, based on their own limited experience, to explain then adjust their views and consider alternatives (Harnett 1998). At first, although all the pictures showed the Queen involved in ceremonial duties, children described her work as cleaning the house and making the beds. The teacher listened to and valued these inferences, but also encouraged children to justify their views and made suggestions to help them to think of alternatives. 'Does she do anything else?' 'Have you seen the Queen on television . . .?'

PARENTS AS PARTNERS AT THE FOUNDATION STAGE

There are many opportunities to work with parents as partners to support children's learning in the context of history: sharing traditional tales at home and in nursery and playgroup and, where possible, drawing on the experience of families from diverse cultures and building on these in developing imaginative play; allowing children with English as an additional language to develop their home language and their English through such play; encouraging parents to talk to children about changes in their own lifetime, and older adults to tell them about their own childhood; creating opportunities for children to talk about and further explore experiences at home, birthdays, celebrations, family visits. Parents may bring in 'precious old artefacts' from their home or childhood and talk to children about them, or grandparents bring in music or clothes from their youth – platform shoes and flared trousers – or demonstrate traditional crafts: even sewing, knitting, cooking and gardening are becoming a novelty for some children! Involve parents in the creation of play resources. Knitted chainmail sprayed in silver is very successful!

So, by the age of five, many children will have had experience of talking to their families about past and present events in their lives, an awareness of cultures different from their own, listening and responding to stories, songs and rhymes set in the past, taking part in role-play, exploring objects and looking closely at similarities, differences, patterns and changes, comparing, sorting, matching and sequencing everyday objects, talking about their observations and asking questions to gain information about why things happen and how things work (DfEE/QCA 1998b: 6).

Part II

History during the first three years of school

Part I considered the ways in which 3- to 5-year-olds are already capable of embryonic historical thinking. They have some awareness of the passing of time, of causes and effects in sequences of events and of differences between present and past times. They are able to recognise and construct different interpretations of stories and are capable of deductive reasoning in informal situations. We saw how these strands of historical thinking could be developed in playgroups and Nursery and Reception classes, drawing on *Curriculum Guidance for the Foundation Stage* (DfEE/QCA 2000a) and correlating aspects of the five areas for learning in a coherent way. Case study examples illustrated how this can be done.

In Part II we shall consider how teachers can build on this embryonic capacity for historical thinking in structured ways. Each strand of historical thinking introduced in Part I will be examined in turn, although it is important to remember that they interact; they are not discrete and need to be learnt through coherent activities related to particular themes. (Discussion of how this may be done is in Part III.) First, we shall consider how we may develop children's understanding of concepts of change, then how we can help children to learn how and why accounts of the past may differ, and finally we shall consider how children can learn to find out about the past from sources – the traces of the past which remain.

Chapter 4

Teaching children to understand concepts of time and change

History in the National Curriculum (DfEE/QCA 1999a: 104) requires children at Key Stage 1 to learn to sequence events and objects chronologically and to use language associated with the passing of time; to identify differences between ways of life at different times and the causes and effects of events; and to consider the reasons why people did things. They should do so in the context of changes in their own lives and those of their families and others around them and of people who lived in the distant past, in their own locality, in Britain and in the wider world.

Yet it was argued in Part I that understanding standard measurements of time and relating them to subjective understanding is complex and piecemeal. It is a broadening rather than a hierarchical process. The National Curriculum level descriptors can only be crudely hierarchical. Children gradually build up a map of the past which is constantly changing as new information and new processes are added. It is a map which children carry in their heads just as they build up a map of their locality in their heads. This militates against the easy view of a chronological map as a framework of facts. The more a chronological framework becomes merely a framework of 'basic facts', the less it will be used and remembered. If children are to be genuinely equipped with a chronological map, they also need a set of themes and concepts for handling the past.

A television programme made to support the introduction of the National Curriculum for history at Key Stage 1 illustrated how 6- to 7-year-olds can learn procedural concepts of history, cause and effect, continuity and change, similarity and difference in the context of a theme they could assimilate into their own, existing chronological maps ('Watch, Forty Years On', BBC TV 1990). The film showed evidence of changes typical in many localities since the 1950s: bomb sites replaced by new flats, Victorian schools by modern buildings, the corner shop by the supermarket. West Indians were seen leaving their Caribbean islands to look for work in Britain. The *causes* of these changes were explained: new materials and inventions led to new styles of building and of home decoration, and to new household appliances. The 'baby boom' after the war led to more schools being built.

West Indians came to Britain because they were needed to work on trains and buses and in hospitals. Children had the opportunity to consider the different *effects* of these changes. Gran explained why she did not think the new supermarket was an improvement while mum appreciated the benefits of the washing machine. Two West Indian women talked of their contrasting feelings when they first came to Britain. Children, too, reacted to change in different ways; when a girl discovered a book called *Electricity for Boys* she said with incredulity, 'Surely they would share it?' The programme ended with a question which challenged the children to continue to discuss *continuity and change, similarities and differences*: 'Holidays are still the same, aren't they?'

Research has suggested that understanding historical time is dependent on an understanding of personal, clock and calendar time. Jahoda (1963) and Friedman (1978) suggested that children of about 4 years old become aware of time through events specific to themselves and to people in their immediate surroundings; the past and present are differentiated by words such as 'before', 'after', 'now' and 'then'. At about 5, events are ordered into earlier and later ones, and the succession of events becomes apparent. Harner (1982) showed that understanding these words depended on an understanding of the varied linguistic structures for the past tense, and also of adverbs such as 'yesterday', 'before', 'already', and 'last week'. Thornton and Vukelich (1988) found that between 4 and 6 years old, children begin to order daily routines chronologically, from early morning until bedtime. Bradley (1947) identified a third 'time distinction', beginning at 6 or 7 years when 'clock' time skills appear to develop from larger to smaller units (hour, to minute, to second), while 'calendar' time appears to work in reverse (from days, to weeks, to months).

Recent research, however, has shown that sometimes young pupils can demonstrate quite sophisticated understanding of the concepts of cause and consequence if the context and questions are meaningful to them.

Seven-year-old Tom, for example, explained that 'the fact that the Romans wanted tin and pearls from Britain' did not explain why they took over Britain, 'cos, you see, just because they wanted them doesn't mean they're going to be able to take it over' (Lee *et al.* 1998). Throughout years 1 and 2, *The National Literacy Strategy* (DfEE/QCA 1998b) provides good contexts for sequencing stories, discussing causes and effects of incidents, and understanding why people may have behaved as they did.

The activities in Box 4.1 will help to develop children's understanding of the measurement of time and relate this to chronological sequences, to the causes and effects of changes they represent, and to similarities and differences between now and past times. Concepts central to investigating changes over time are discussed. However, since there is little research investigating young children's understanding of historical time, the numerous questions arising in planning activities will be discussed in the hope that teachers will approach them in a spirit of genuine enquiry, rather than simply regard them as replicate activities devised as assessment tasks; this could restrict both children's opportunities for real historical enquiry and teachers' professional understanding of children's capabilities.

CHRONOLOGICAL SEQUENCES: CAUSES AND EFFECTS

Children begin to sequence events by describing the pattern of their own lives. Loader (1993) quoted a nursery child, working on a topic on 'Ourselves'.

> I could only crawl when I was tiny And I can walk when I was a bit older. And when I was 3 I was happy enough. And I didn't drink out of a bottle any more, and I didn't play with rattles any more, and I didn't cuddle toys any more (sometimes I do).

Salma, in year 2, was able to consider not only her own recollections but how her life was linked by her family to other times before she was born, and to other places.

> My Mum's Mum is the oldest person I know. I never got to see my Mum's Dad. He lived in Bangladesh. When I first got here everyone was carrying me because I was so small. My Mum was crying because her Dad had died. I was about 3. . . . Grandads and aunts tell about how things were before you were born. They have photographs . . .

Carl, aged 6, also became aware of past times through the death of a grandparent.

> You can look in the churchyard cemetery – look at the gravestones. My Nan always goes to the cemetery because they built my Grandad a bench and his stone is by his ashes. She's always talking to him. She thinks he's alive.

Describing events in their own lives can help children to describe the sequence of events in stories, as suggested in *The National Literacy Strategy* (DfEE/QCA 1998b). This, too, is not straightforward. It depends on the complexity of the story, the number of events, on whether they are clearly sequential, on the complexity of causes and motives, and on a child's ability to recognise and describe these. The text of these 4-page books, in which two reception children retell the story of 'Snow White', record images of key events, but if they see the causal connection between them they do not see the need to make this explicit.

Box 4.1 The measurement of time

Units of time	What the children will do	Possible questions
1 Night/day	• Collect and draw or make sets of day-time and night-time pictures (use great paintings, magazines, children's books) • Read and write (picture) stories about getting up and going to bed. Read 'Wintertime' and 'Bed in Summer' (R.L. Stevenson, in Opie and Opie 1973)	• Describe each picture: colours, feelings, activity. How are they the same/different? Why? • What do you do when you get up/go to bed? In what order? Why is it candlelight in the poem? How is the poem the same as/different from what you do? Why is it dark at bedtime in the winter?
2 Day: morning, afternoon, evening	• Sets: things we do in the morning, afternoon, evening • Zig-zag book, 'My Day' • Make cards: getting up, breakfast, going to school, etc. Can you put cards in the right order?	• What does everyone do, and what things do only some people do? • Read your zig-zag book to a grown-up. Ask about their day • Does it matter which order the pictures are in? Is that true for all the pictures? Why not?
3 Days of the week	• Talk about/look at class timetable. Make pictures sequencing activities during a day showing 'Us in PE, assembly', etc. • Rhymes (e.g. Solomon Grundy)	• Are the days all the same? What is different? (Learn days of the week.) What happens today / tomorrow/yesterday/next week/last week? • Make up your own rhyme for days of the week

4 Months of the year	• Make a bar chart or time-line for birthdays each month
	• Learn Victorian rhyme:
	    January brings the snow,
	    makes your feet and fingers glow.
	    February brings the rain,
	    thaws the frozen lake again
	    (Sara Coleridge in Opie and Opie 1973)
		• How many birthdays in, e.g. June or in summer?
		• Make up a couplet for this month

	Activities	Questions
5 The four seasons	• Look at calendars from different cultures (e.g. Muslim, Chinese and from different times (e.g. Medieval agricultural calendar) • Make devices for measuring sun, rain, wind. Keep records • Collect paintings from different periods showing summer, autumn, winter, spring (e.g. Breughel and Monet snow scenes) • Collect poems about seasons • Make a spinner game • Make a picture showing seasons (four groups?), e.g. make a picture of a familiar tree in each season • Make a collection of clothes for each season • Design dolls' clothes for each season	each month. What is the same/different about calendars from other cultures? Why was the 'agricultural' calendar important? • Are all the pictures of winter the same? How are they the same/different? What comes before/after/next? • How do you know which season this is about? • When it lands on summer, say a word to do with summer before the count of ten. Collect words for word bank • Make up music to go with your picture. Can others match the picture and the music? • Do some things belong to all the seasons? Which? Why? • How do we keep warm/cool?
6 Measuring time	• Make devices for measuring time (sun sticks, sand clocks, water clocks. candle clocks, marble and bagatelle clocks) using non-standard units • Collect instruments for measuring time (digital and analogue clocks, chronometer, sundial, egg-timer)	• Use them to measure time taken, e.g. for a child to wash hands for lunch. Compare them with an egg-timer/stop-watch. Are they reliable? Why not? • How do they work?
7 Standardised units: seconds, minutes, hours	• Devise games: how many times can you run across the playground, jump on the spot, say a word, in 30 seconds? Can you be quiet for 1 minute? Keep records	• Can you guess how many times? Who was fastest, slowest? By how many seconds?
8 Telling the time	• Make timetables and clocks showing times for let's pretend play: house corner shop; bus journey play; doctor's waiting room and surgery time; timetables for pretend police or fire station or for any workplace	• When does it open? Close? How long does it take? When will it be open again?

Snow White, by S.J.
Snow White is in the glass coffin.
The wicked queen is in the castle.
Snow White and the Prince got married.

Snow White Got Married, by S.G.
Snow White ate an apple and fell to the ground.
Snow White is in a glass coffin.
Snow White and a prince got married.

Children in a year 1 class were helped to consider the structure of the story of Cinderella by discussing causes and effects of changes in the story: how did she change? Into what? Why? Was she happier? They wrote a storyboard as a class. Then they worked in groups on each stage of the story and made a Big Book. From this they frequently retold and shared the story. This led to discussion about how they would like to change and whether they thought the change would make them happier, and why. This led to work involving other curriculum areas: discussing Cinderella's shoe size, then sequencing their shoes in order of size; dancing at the ball, with a partner, to music; happy and sad role-play; drawing pictures of Cinderella and the Prince in modern clothes and comparing the drawings with traditional illustrations; designing clothes for different occasions; testing the fabrics used for appropriate durability!

Lynn Clarke, a PGCE student, investigated the ability of a group of year 2 children, who were beginning to speak English, to explore the passing of time in relation to family history and to their own lives through story. First, they looked at the pictures in *Once There Were Giants* (Waddell and Dale 1989). These pictures show in sequence the life story of 'me', who is seen as a baby at the beginning of the book and at the end of the book is seen looking after her own baby in the same room, surrounded by the same members of her family, all altered to some extent by the intervening two or three decades. At the end of the story, the children, after some confusion about whether 'me' was the teacher, since she had introduced the session with a picture of herself as a small child, realised that 'me' was both the baby at the beginning of the book and the mother at the end. The extract from their discussion which leads to this conclusion shows how the children gradually focused on the fine details in the two pictures of the 'me' as a baby and as a mother, and discussed the similarities and the differences between them.

Teacher Are these two pictures the same?
Aminur Yes.
Teacher Are you sure?
Aminur No, there are different people in them.

Teacher	Who is different?
Sehrish	The mum. She had a red jumper and her hair is tied back.
Teacher	Is it the same mum?
All	Yes.
Sehrish	No, it isn't. It's 'ME'! 'Me' is the baby's Mum.
Group	Oh yes – she's grown up hasn't she? [etc.]
Koiesur	That's Uncle Tom. He's still got a beard.
Teacher	That's right. Is there anything else you recognise in the picture?
Aminur	The carpet.
Ayesha	It's a bit pink [faded] now.
Koiesur	There's a mirror on the wall, but it's a bigger mirror.

They went on to discuss the differences in clothes and in hair styles and hair colour; the replacement of cloth nappies by disposable ones, of frilly pants by leggings; and the different styles of lighting. However, Sehrish noticed that the baby's toys, the teddy bear and the rabbit, were still the same.

In a second session, the children read 'Jill's history' (Shutter and Reynoldson 1991). Each page they turned showed Jill as a progressively younger child until in the final picture they saw her mother when she had been pregnant with Jill. This led the children to identify with Jill on each page, and to discuss their own similar experiences, moving sequentially back in time. They talked about their birthday parties, the sequence of teachers since they had begun school, their first day at school, their nursery school experience, shopping as a toddler and playing at home as a baby. Their sense of duration varied; Aminur correctly sequenced all his teachers, the rooms they had been in and the kind of work he had done, from the nursery school to year 2:

> In the nursery we did scribbling and played with water. Now we do writing and read books and do puzzles and play nicely. We did paintings then and we still do painting, but now we do close drawing.

Ayesha condensed two years of schooling into one day!

Ofsted (1999) found that at Key Stage 1 teachers tend to neglect the distant past and places. Stories can provide an excellent approach. Bage (1999) has explained ways in which young children can analyse causes and effects of changes through historical stories set in distant times. Kath Cox and Pat Hughes (1998) show how they used *Seeing Red* (Garland 1996), a picture narrative set in the Napoleonic Wars dominated by a strong female character, with a year 2 class to clarify differences between now and then (clothes, warships, weapons) and to develop chronology. Each child took it in turn to retell a section of the story, what happened and why. Why, for example, did 'Old Boney' want to bring his soldiers to England? Answers included: 'He didn't like the English; he wanted power; he wanted to take land; to make the English soldiers fight for him; to get hold of their money'.

Silvera and Cawood (2000) show how the story of Mary Seacole used as a shared reading text was used to develop key elements of both the History Curriculum and of the Literacy Framework with year 1 children.

Vass (1999) has undertaken more extensive research into how teachers use story to teach history at Key Stage 1. He believes that historical skills integrated through story make the past understandable to children. His study identifies thirty-eight different approaches to telling stories about people and events in the past, including reading, retelling as first- or third-person narratives, and acting out in role. A surprising 80 per cent of the Key Stage 1 teachers said that they regularly told stories drawn from their own lives.

Children can also learn about chronological sequence by ordering photographs or artefacts, or listening to oral accounts. Selection of the sources which children are given raises a number of questions which it will be interesting for teachers to investigate. It will also be interesting to consider the best questions to ask children in order to examine the reasoning by which they arrive at their sequence.

Are some aspects of change easier than others to illustrate or to understand (technological, social, aesthetic)? What is the best mode of representation for sequence of change (artefacts, photographs, stories, oral accounts)? How should sequencing activities be structured to involve different periods of time (from the child's own life-time, to living memory and beyond, to the distant past; from family to impersonal affairs)?

How should sequences be extended from the simple and obvious, with limited examples, to larger numbers of objects, photographs or sequences which are ambiguous? How can simple stories be extended to stories with more events, with more complex causes, involving greater understanding of human behaviour? What knowledge do children bring to bear on their reasoning in these contexts? How do children read pictures, in order to compare similarities and differences? What sorts of pictures and how much detail do children of different ages enjoy? What reasons do children give for changes, and how do they suggest that changes affected people's lives? Teachers need to consider such issues in planning activities and, through observation and discussion, to discover the kind of thinking which children bring to bear on these tasks.

Loader (1993) found that Reception children, asked to sequence photographs of themselves, had idiosyncratic ways of doing this. Clare put her 'now' photograph (of her in school uniform) first, then the picture of her at 1 day old, then the rest chronologically. Séan arranged his in a circular pattern in chronological order.

A group of year 3 children in Joanne Edwards' class, given five of her family photographs to sequence, dating from 1880, 1912, 1946, 1960 and

1970, could all put them in chronological order, but they used different reasoning to do so. One child sequenced them correctly on the basis of quality and technology. Another child recognised the same person at different ages in four of the pictures. Three children used other clues in the pictures, particularly clothes.

Clearly, helping children to sequence photographs or artefacts will not be an isolated activity, but part of a broader topic. Boxes 4.2 and 4.3 contain suggestions for sequencing activities and questions related to typical Key Stage 1 themes.

Scott (1994) described how year 2 children were able to put a toasting fork, an old electric toaster, a new toaster and a sandwich-maker in chronological order, although they were predictably unclear about the last two items. One child, Jane, then chose to draw and number the sequence in a circular, clock-wise rotation. (This led to a subsequent discussion among the students working with the children about the possibility of reflecting with them on the need to show some sequences in linear form – since we do not return to using a toasting fork at regular intervals – whereas it may be appropriate to record months, seasons and years in a circular form.) Jane was able to say confidently that the object she labelled 'one' was the 'oldest' and 'four' was the 'youngest'. With much prompting and encouragement, she was able to say that 'two is a bit younger than three' and 'three is more younger than two and one'. She explained the changes in terms of efficiency.

> The toasting fork takes longer than the toaster, because you have to turn the toast over. The new toaster is quite like number two. The sandwich-maker can cook more toast, so a family can all eat at once and it can make a sandwich.

Routh and Rowe (1992) have identified picture books which provide experiences of the many facets of time: night-time, day-time, special days, week by week, festivals, the year round, time and change and astrological time. Cox and Hughes (1990) showed how concepts of time and other aspects of historical thinking can be developed through story, and list examples of stories about childhood, grannies and more distant times. Stories are a traditional way of involving children in other places and times, of exploring other people's minds and encouraging children to decentre. They stimulate the imagination and the emotions, and help children to reflect on their own experiences and on the way they view others. Narrative underlies both story and history. It holds children's attention and provides a framework for asking 'Who?' and 'Why?'

Box 4.2 Chronological sequences (1)

Theme	What the children will do	Possible questions
1 Personal history	(a) • Children bring photographs of themselves when they were babies and a recent photograph • Make a book of 'Things I can do', and 'Things a baby can do' • Collect and sort sets of baby clothes and 5-year-olds' clothes • Collect and sort sets of baby toys and 5-year-olds' toys (b) • Bring in photographs for each year, 1–5. Read stories about birthdays, e.g. *Happy Birthday Bini* (Bhatia 1988) • Write a questionnaire for parent about what you were like, etc. Write about each year of your life based on the questionnaire results • Make a time-line for years 1–5 and put writing and photographs on the time-line • Collect photographs of children of 1–5 years from old newspapers and magazines (e.g. Royal Family)	(a) • Who is it? What are they doing and wearing? How big are they? Where are they? Who is with them? How have they changed? Are all the baby photographs the same / different? Why? • How have you changed since you were a baby? (b) • Can you put them in order? Put each other's photographs in order. How do you know if you are right? • e.g. When did I have my bike? My grommets? When was my sister born? Where did we go to . . .? Move house? • Can you explain or suggest why events described on time-line happened? Is this photograph earlier or later? Is it newer or older? Are you older in the new photograph or the old photograph? • Can you put these in order? Why do you think this is the right order? Can you put them on a time-line? Is the child older in this photograph than that one? Why do you think so?

	• Draw pictures (make sets) of what has stayed the same in your life and what has changed since you were a baby
2 Living memory	(a) • Children are shown photographs of a child of 1–2 years old and of its mother at the same age (e.g. the teacher as a 2-year-old and the teacher's mother as a 2-year-old) • Compare two toys or books belonging to each of the children in the photographs • Interview mother in photograph about when she was little. Ask her for more 'evidence' of her past	(a) • How old are the two children? Who are they? Has the mother changed since then? How old might she be now? Which photograph was taken first? How do you know? • Which belongs to which photograph? Why? How are they the same/different? • Write an article for a newspaper or make a tape-recording for a radio programme about this mother's life story
	(b) • Make a class museum. Collect photographs, books, toys, belonging to 'great grandparents', 'grandparents', 'parents'	(b) • Write labels for the exhibits. Find out their dates • Which photographs belong to each generation; can you sort them to find out? Does this tell which things are oldest? Can we use the dates to put them on a time-line? (This illustrates the need for a standard measure)

Box 4.3 Chronological sequences (2)

Theme	What the children will do	Possible questions
1 The locality • Shopping street	• Choose a shop. Find out from interviews and local history library what it was like/sold in past times. Write/draw the history of the shop for display by present owner	• Sequence and explain changes in what was sold, in display, advertisements, packaging, work conditions, customers' needs, ways of paying
	• From old photographs find out about transport: horses/buses /cars/lorries/vans in the street in past times. Put the photographs in order	• Describe, explain the sequence. How would the changes affect people's lives?
	• Visit a supermarket and a corner shop. How are goods and jobs organised in each? Draw a design for a supermarket layout and a corner shop	• List advantages of supermarket layout and a corner shop. Why were supermarkets 'invented'?
	• Street furniture: collect and identify initials on postboxes	• Can you put them in order on a 'kings and queens' time-line? Can you find the stamps for each king and queen?
	• Collect street lamps/coal hole covers, horse troughs	• Can you sequence these? How would they affect people's lives?
• Farm	• *Tools* Visit a farm: collect hand tools. Find out how same work is done today	• Move a load (e.g. of fodder) by hand on a barrow/cart. Compare with how much a tractor can move in the same time
	• *Buildings* Sort into old and new. Look for clues • *Maps* Look at old map(s) and contemporary map	• How are materials, structures, purposes different? • Look for and explain change in name, paths, field size, crops

• Seaside	• What changes can you see in entertainments, clothes, food, buildings, transport, station?
• Collect and sequence seaside postcards	• In three groups pretend you are a person in one of these pictures. Make up a play about what you are doing
• Compare three views, e.g. eighteenth-century or early nineteenth-century painting or engraving before holiday industry; early seaside holidays; recent	
• Listen to popular seaside music from three periods, e.g. nineteenth century ('I do like to be beside the seaside'), 1950s and today	• How have the words, sounds and means of playing music (e.g. piano, 78 record, CD) changed?
2 Clothes	• Why do you think this is the right order? Describe/explain changes
• Collect old photographs/paintings/advertisements/dress and knitting patterns. Can you put them in order?	
• Collect pictures of sports clothes, wedding clothes, work clothes, hats or shoes. Order them	• How have they changed? Why? What can we work out about how people's pastimes/attitudes have changed?
• Sort fabrics into natural (fur, wool, leather, cotton, linen) and synthetic	• Find out about methods of spinning, dyeing, weaving in the past and now. Describe/explain changes
• Experiment with natural dyes and man-made dyes	
• Borrow children's clothes from local amateur dramatic club or drama college for children to try on, or buy replicas or make them for play corner	• Can you match the style to pictures in books and put them in order? What could you do/not do wearing these clothes? How do they feel different from your own clothes?

(continued)

Box 4.3 Chronological sequences (2) (continued)

Theme	What the children will do	Possible questions
3 Homes	• Collect pictures of houses and order: new, old, very old • Draw or photograph three houses from locality (e.g. 1980, 1930, 1880) • Collect old domestic appliances or ornaments from families, junk shops	• Why have you put 'this house' in this set? Did you have to change the sets when you found new pictures? • What is different? Why? Find out about the families who lived in each home when it was built (census or street directories). Use books to find out about heat, water, light, games, music, their clothes, furniture. Make up stories, plays, pictures about each family • Can you put them in order? What changes in people's lives do they show?
4 School	• Collect pictures of your school. Can you put them in order? Can you link other evidence to each picture (oral history, school log or punishment book, old school books or exercise books, timetables)? • Collect and sequence old children's books • Sequence, e.g., slate, steel pen, felt tip, word-processing disk	• Describe changes in building, furniture, display, way children are organised, what they are doing/ wearing. What can you work out about changes in schools, in how children felt, behaved? Can you explain the changes? • Describe and explain changes in type, text, pictures • What difference would each make to children's life in school?

SIMILARITIES AND DIFFERENCES

Virginia Hunt, a student, examined children's understanding of similarities and differences between now and past times, through text and illustrations in stories. When she read a group of bilingual year 1 children *Bill and Pete Go Down the Nile* (de Paolo 1988), the Museum of Ancient Egypt illustrated in the story led them to discuss what they knew about the past. Ayodele said that, 'History [referred to in the text] means "a long time ago" or "the olden days".' 'In the olden days', she said, aeroplanes were 'not like they are now', they were 'funny and flapping around'. (She went on to say that her granny was old and lived in Africa and was born 'before the war came'.) She thought that the crocodile in the picture might be old because it was crinkly like her gran, but Shellie thought it was more likely crinkly because it had been too long in the water! There is evidence of reasoning here, although the children's limited knowledge prevents them reaching a correct conclusion. Ayodele's next remark though, was subtle and accurate because her reasoning in this case was supported by knowledge. The Sphinx, she said, was very old, but it looked new because it had been cleaned; she knew this because she had seen a television programme about it. This led Shellie to talk more about the way buildings changed colour as they aged; she, too, had seen a programme about this on television. Aaron knew about the olden days because he had visited 'a dinosaur museum'. The group displayed rudimentary maps of the past based on incidental knowledge they had acquired. Egyptian mummies were from a long time ago, before Shellie's mum was born, but dinosaurs lived in the olden days before even people were here, but they 'got killed off'.

When these children were read *Joseph and His Magnificent Coat of Colours* (Williams 1992), they again related the story to knowledge acquired from television. Shellie knew from a programme she had seen that the pyramids were built a long time ago and that they still exist, and Theodore developed her point to add that they were in Egypt because the River Nile was mentioned. He thought that probably Canaan was therefore a real place too. From evidence in the pictures, the children thought that the story happened a long time ago in Egypt, 'before I was born; before everyone was born', because 'there are chariots – you don't see them today' and because of the furniture – 'you don't get those things no more'. However, the circumspection of their reasoning was surprisingly sophisticated: 'But people in Africa might still wear clothes like this. I've seen them on telly.'

When the children were read a story about the more recent past, about *Princess Victoria* (Mitchellhill 1991), they again used their limited knowledge, from their own experience and from television, to consider the possible differences between 'then' and 'now'. Theodore thought the king was old, 'like my Grandad and my friend Jack. He's 70 and has got a stick.' However, he decided that the king had probably lived before his grandad and worked out why he thought so.

> The coach is from the olden days, like in cowboys. I saw a coach like that on telly. You don't get cowboys now, only on the telly. They lived about two hundred years ago. Also the globe in the picture is different from my teacher's globe.

He tried very hard to support his argument and this led to the rest of the group finding many other differences in the illustrations, between then and now: the clothes, the furniture, the chalkboard and the toys, including wooden dolls. Again, they tested their conclusions. 'You don't get a lady to teach you now, you have to go to school.' 'But you might get one if you were a queen.' Focused observation like this shows how year 1 children, some with little English and with very limited knowledge, supported their statements with arguments, and both developed and questioned each other's ideas. It would be interesting to find out the level of sophistication they could have achieved if they had been taught in a coherent way about the past.

Warton (1993) asked year 2 children to compare two pictures, to encourage them to discuss similarities and differences between the milkman today and in the past. This was part of a project on 'where we live'. Their discussion illustrated how children need to learn the kind of question they are being asked and the type of answer that is expected in an historical context.

Matthew and Colin were confident that they knew what was required:

Matthew   That's easy. The old one's black and white.
Amy   Did people used to have cars and horses because electricity wasn't invented?
Matthew   The milk's not in bottles. It's in big metal pots.
Colin   And there's no roof on the cart. That's why the milkman's wearing a hat.

Amy, however, was less sure!

Amy   Both milkmen have got moustaches. And our milkman hasn't, but he's got a dog and it's called Bones.

Children can learn to consider similarities and differences between past and present times by sorting pictures and artefacts into sets of very old, old and new, for example. This again raises questions which it will be interesting to investigate. What reasons can they give for their choices? What vocabulary do they use or need to? Do they concentrate at first on evidence of ageing: if it is worn or dirty it must be old? Do they consider reproductions as old and if so, why? Can they sort pictures better than artefacts? Are they prepared to listen to the arguments of others and change their decisions? Do some categories overlap? Do they consider materials or technology? Do black and white pictures appear older than coloured ones? Can they discuss the effects of the changes on people's lives? What sort of changes are easiest to perceive?

Hilary Croft, a student, began to investigate some of these questions, while working with a year 2 class. She found that when they were asked to sort into very old, old and modern they were at first hampered by the terminology. They did not understand modern, and when this was replaced by 'new' they assumed that this meant straight from the shop. They thought at first that 'old' was the equivalent of worn; therefore they classed relatively new trainers as old. However, they refined their understanding of the concept as they took clearly older things from the box, and as they did so they also resorted the artefacts into different categories.

The teacher explored the children's reasoning as she observed them by asking them questions: 'Why do you think it belongs there?' 'What made you decide that it was old?' 'Do you think this is older than that?' She recognised the need to extend the children's thinking, but not to intervene too much, because she noticed that the children did not contradict her and were very anxious at first about giving the right answer. Carl expressed this initial anxiety: 'But how do we know if it's right if you don't tell us or help us?' Children need to *learn* to accept uncertainty, to make possible inferences, to support them with arguments and to listen to the arguments of others.

The following extract, in which they were discussing a sepia photograph of the teacher's family dressed up as American pioneers, shows how they gradually learned to revise their categories.

D   It's a very, very old photograph because it's black and white, and
         they're wearing funny clothes.
Teacher Let's look at it more closely. Do you recognise anybody?
S   It's you, Hilary!
E   It can't be old then.

They all agree that it is not *very* old, but could be either new or old.

Similarly, the children at first thought that lace underskirts they were shown were new until they found similar clothes in old photographs in which people were wearing very long skirts. They decided that the underskirts must also be very old because they were very long and similar to the skirts in the photographs.

S at first said, 'I don't think they would have had hats like that in the old days', but then she found similar hats in old photographs and decided that they did. Children also began to give reasons for their suggestions and to use 'because'.

E   It's old because it's wrinkly.
D   It's new – they didn't have plastic in the olden days.
S   Yes it's old, because, look at the buttons – they're made of bone.

They began to consider alternative possibilities. In discussing a pair of new platform sandals which were similar in style to platform shoes of the 1960s and 1970s, E said, 'they're old fashioned'. But D said they were similar to those currently worn by 'Betty Boo' (a 1990s singer). This led them to examine the bottoms and find that they were clean and so to agree that 'they are probably new'.

Gradually the children were learning to form hypotheses, to reason, to look for supporting evidence, to discuss alternatives and so to change their hypotheses and to refine their understanding of concepts of very old, old and new.

In a second session, the children chose an old hat or a new hat, or an old or a new shoe, to draw. This gave rise to further discussion of 'old' and 'new' while they were drawing. In the final session, they brought their own 'old things'. The teacher found that they talked far more extensively about their own artefacts and pictures than they had about the things she had brought in previously, because they had background knowledge about them which they could share with others and use to answer questions. She concluded that although children need to learn to accept uncertainty, some knowledge and personal experience made them more confident in asking questions and considering possibilities.

CONCEPTS RELATED TO UNDERSTANDING CHANGES OVER TIME: ORGANISING CONCEPTS

It was said in Part I that there is no clear agreement about what is meant by historical concepts. Some concepts, which have already been discussed, are concerned with changes over time, with similarities and differences, continuity and change. Others are organising ideas which run through all societies: conflict, beliefs, agriculture. Some special vocabulary relates to particular periods in the past: Roman, Medieval. Other concepts are concerned with the process of interpreting sources. We shall consider in turn ways of introducing each type of concept to young children.

First, we shall consider those concepts which are central to all societies. Children need to learn to understand such key concepts in order to place detail in a structural pattern so that it is not forgotten. This enables them to compare similarities and differences between times and places (Bruner

1966). Concepts such as trade, communication, power and government are abstract and complex. But young children can be introduced to simpler, concrete concepts, selected because they relate to and will eventually lead to an understanding of the over-arching, abstract concepts (Vygotsky 1962; Ausubel 1968; Gagne 1977; Klausmeier 1978; Klausmeier *et al.* 1979). Vygotsky suggested that concept understanding is promoted by careful use of language. He found that concepts which are specially introduced because they belong to a particular discipline and are not acquired spontaneously are learned more consciously and completely, and that the significant use of new vocabulary promotes intellectual growth. Bruner (1966) suggested that children need opportunities to learn new concepts through physical experience and sensation (handling and using an old artefact, for example), through images (pictures and models), and through relating these to language (in stories and poems, and by labelling). There is evidence that if young children are introduced, in these ways, to selected concrete concepts, they gradually learn to use the more abstract over-arching concepts related to them.

Furth (1980) traced children's growing understanding of concepts such as government, social roles, money and community. He found that at 5 years old children had an image of government as a 'special man' (sic). From this they developed the concept of a ruler, then of a job-giver or owner of land, until at 9 or 10 they understood that a government provides functions and services in return for taxes.

Suggestions in Box 4.4 show how subordinate concepts related to key concepts may be selected and introduced through traditional topics.

CONCEPTS RELATED TO PARTICULAR PERIODS

The second type of historical concept to which young children may be introduced through visits, pictures, stories and imaginative play is associated with different periods in the past. Young children relish using 'special words', such as 'portcullis' or 'gargoyle', usually accompanied by appropriate body language, although refined use, as Vygotsky showed, develops piecemeal, through trial and error. A group of 5-year-olds, sharing their knowledge about castles, confused me by describing the Spitfire they were adding to their model, until I saw it demonstrated, rotating a paper ox over the fire; and the parents of a Reception child were mystified by a lusty rendering of 'wind the poppy up' accompanied by wild twisting and pulling gestures, until the teacher explained that a visitor had brought a bobbin to school and taught the class an old weavers' song! Examples of labels used by historians to describe society in a particular time and place are shown in the first column of Box 4.5. Words describing characteristic aspects of that society are in the second column.

Box 4.4 Concepts and topics

Organising concept	Related concepts	Possible topic
Agriculture	Farm: farmhouse, barn, dairy Crops: yams, corn, tobacco, coffee, groundnuts, cassava, maize, rice, barley Animals: horses, sheep, pigs, chickens, buffalo, oxen Tools: sickle, plough, windmill, tractor, watermill, combine harvester Sow, reap, winnow, thresh, store Milkmaid, goose girl, shepherd	Farming A farm visit, or visit to a reconstruction of rural life. Folk tales about crops, farming, e.g. *The Village of Round and Square Houses* (Grafoni 1989) (Cameroon villages); *Shaker Lane* (Provensen and Provensen 1991); *Mufaro's Beautiful Daughters* (Steptoe 1992); *Where the Forest Meets the Sea* (Baker 1991) Stories about real people
Manufacture	Cloth: tailor, weaver, spinster, loom, spinning wheel Pottery: potter, kiln, clay Metalwork: mine, smelt, mould Leather: cobbler, cordwainer Buildings: carpenter, stone-mason Energy: machines, tools, weapons, water power, wind power, steam power, (nuclear) factory	Jobs people do Buildings Visits to sites, workplaces, e.g. windmill, watermill Visits to a reconstruction of an industrial site or workplace (the Tin Smith, the Mine, Foundry, Candle Factory at Ironbridge Gorge Museum) True stories about real people Folk tales (e.g. *The Tailor of Gloucester*, Beatrix Potter)
Trade	Exchange, buy, sell, weight, money, price, fair, market, merchant, rich, poor	Jobs people do Visit to local shop, shopping street, market, other workplace Visit a reconstruction, e.g. The Bank, Blists Hill (Ironbridge Gorge Museum) or Black Country Museum, Dudley Stories about real people Folk tales (e.g. Dick Whittington), *The Emperor's Dan-Dan* (Agard 1992)

Communication	Transport: track, road coach, car, steam train diesel, tram, bus Ship: oars, sail, steam Oral: folk tales, stories, laws, proclamations Writing: glyph, wax, quill, print, fax, disk Media: radio, record, film, television Symbols: religious symbols, logos, paintings	Folk tales and true stories about journeys, inventions Stories about real people (e.g. King Alfred, The Highwayman, Mary Seacole (Blyth *et al.* 1991) or consult local history library for journeys made by people from or to your locality (Collicott 1993) Visit to printers, toll house, canal at Blists Hill (Ironbridge Gorge Museum)
Power/social structure	Attack, defend, conflict, weapons Ruler: king, queen, prince, princess, government Rich, poor, peasant, knight, lord, servant Laws, obey, fight	True stories Folk tales (e.g. Robin Hood)
Beliefs, values, attitudes	Religious buildings: church, mosque, synagogue Religious writings Symbols of belief systems Ceremony: festival, faith, prayer, praise, worship, good, evil, hope, fear	Festivals Stories related to belief systems Stories related to statues, stained glass, religious paintings Folk tale

Box 4.5 Historical vocabulary

Roman	Villa, fort, centurion, legion, standard, toga
Medieval	Monastery, cathedral, castle, knight, battlements, portcullis, moat, tournament, spinning wheel, bow and arrow, tunic, hose
Elizabethan	Explorers, galleon, treasure, pirate, ruff, wig
Victorian	Carriage, coalman, flat iron, hotwater bottle, oil lamp, button hook

While Lynn (1993) and Harnett (1993) found that 6- to 7-year-olds felt threatened when asked to identify and sequence pictures using 'period' labels, by 1998 Stow found that children of this age were able to identify and categorise pictures according to some periods, particularly Roman, and tackled the task with confidence.

CONCEPTS ASSOCIATED WITH MAKING DEDUCTIONS AND INFERENCES ABOUT SOURCES

A third group of concepts which children may learn is concerned with describing historical sources and with recognising different levels of validity and certainty in interpreting sources: I am sure, I think, I can guess; probably, perhaps, maybe; because, therefore. Box 4.6 shows activities through which children may explore, discuss and use probability language.

Box 4.6 Activities which allow children to become conscious of levels of
probability

Activity	*Possible questions*
• Piece together broken tool, pot, plate, with parts missing. Draw possible original. This could be deliberately broken, or a genuine fragment	• What shape do you think it was? Why? Who do you think used it? What do you think the writing/picture was like when the pot/plate was complete?
• (Photo)copy a complete (old) artefact. Cut it up into a jigsaw with pieces missing and ask your friend to put it together again	• How many ways could you remake the jigsaw? Why do you think this is the best answer?
• Class museum. Collect old things. Research, using books, asking adults questions, making reasonable guesses about what cannot be known. Write labels, or a guide for the museum or make an oral tape	• What do you know about this? What is it made of? How old is it? Who used it? What for? What difference did it make to their lives? Are there others?
• A class dig. Measure off a square metre of rough ground. See what you can find. Measure and draw finds, put them on a time-line. Draw a plan to show where they were found	• Label finds. What can you work out about the people they belonged to? Can you find out more? Why were they buried?
• Make a stratified model in a fish tank by burying a few objects every day in layers of soil, sand, gravel, etc. Put a dolls' house on top	• Can you make up stories for each group of people who lived on this 'site' before the dolls' house was built?
• Extend a photograph: attach it to a large sheet of paper and draw what the camera did not record	• Why have you added this? Why do you think it is certainly/probably true?
• Read extract from account in old newspaper of interest to children	• Why do you think this happened?
• Participate in an excavation. Harrison (1993) described an infant archaeology project at Battle Abbey in which children mixed colours to match the shades of the stone, did wall rubbings, observational drawings of pottery shards, measured walls, doors and keys, decorated tiles and looked for layers and gargoyles	• Can you draw the whole pot from this piece? Can you draw the building when it was new? How was it built? Can you make up a play about building the abbey?

Chapter 5

Interpretations

Historians' accounts of the past may be different but equally valid if they conform to what is known, if they are reasonable, and if there is no contradictory evidence. Historians construct accounts by selecting and interpreting sources which are often incomplete. Accounts differ, first because they reflect the values and preoccupations of the times in which they are written. Historians in Ancient Greece and Imperial Rome were preoccupied with the idealised views of glorious conquests. Victorians were concerned with the origins of common law and parliaments. In the twentieth century, the emphasis has been on the perspectives of 'ordinary people' and most recently on the role of women and on non-Eurocentric history. Second, accounts vary according to the interests of the writer. History today encompasses all aspects of human activity: industry, religion, arts, literature, folklore, great individuals, key events and groups and movements, in-depth studies and broad brush strokes. Third, history is rewritten as new evidence is discovered.

We are also surrounded by reconstructions of the past, of varying status, which were not produced by historians: historical drama, fiction, theme parks and re-enactments.

Our view of the past is dynamic. It is constantly being reinterpreted, just as we continually reappraise our personal histories throughout our lives. History is many faceted; no simple framework or perspective or truth is possible. For this reason, it is important to learn history in order to develop a questioning understanding of values and attitudes and of our own place in a changing society (Jenkins 1991).

There are many ways in which young children can begin to learn that there are different interpretations of the past. They hear different versions of stories set in the past. Their families have their own histories and views of the past. They come from different parts of the British Isles and of the world; they come from different social backgrounds; they consist of men and women. Children can learn from the beginning to be aware of, to build on and to evaluate these perspectives, for this is what history is, and they need to find their place in it. Fryer (1989) quotes Ayi Kwei Armah ('The Healers' 1979):

The present is where we get lost
If we forget our own past and have
No vision of the future.

In the section on History in the National Curriculum at Key Stage 1 in *The National Curriculum for England and Wales* (DfEE/QCA 1999a: 104), children are expected to be 'taught to identify different ways in which the past is represented'. Pictures, plays, films, reconstructions of the past, museum displays, television programmes and fictional stories are suggested contexts. This strand of historical thinking, although often neglected (Ofsted 1999, Harrison 2000), is of vital importance and can be fun to teach. Learning that the past is represented in different ways is a protection against the exploitation of history, and is also central to the understanding of the nature of history. Any study of the past will lead to an interpretation, but this will change as perspectives change, and according to how one period in the past is represented by a subsequent period. Children will eventually learn how and why historians' accounts differ if, from the beginning, they are given opportunities to: (1) develop awareness of different ways of representing past events, for example: pictures, written accounts, film, television programmes, plays, songs, reproductions of objects in museums, museum displays; and (2) distinguish between different versions of events, for example: different accounts by pupils of the same events. Children can learn that stories may be about real or fictional characters, that different stories about the past give different versions of what happened.

Interpretations of events and of behaviour, and different versions of stories, are part of everyday life. Young children may begin by discussing different versions of events in their own lives during the day or week (different accounts of their shared experience of the morning, of the concert, of a playground squabble) before they consider different accounts of family events, of oral history, or events in the distant past. Children may go on to learn about different interpretations, both by considering existing reconstructions of the past and by constructing their own versions of a place, event or person.

COMPARING INTERPRETATIONS

Physical reconstructions

There are many exciting opportunities for children to see reconstructions of past times. They are made for different purposes and have differing levels of validity. Museum 'still life' reconstructions, for example of an air-raid shelter, a Roman kitchen or a neolithic site, or replicas of museum exhibits, are based on evidence and research. They may well raise questions such as: 'How did they know?' 'Are there others?' 'What might it have felt like when . . .?' Reconstructions of sites, homes, streets and workplaces, such as West Stowe Anglo-Saxon village in Suffolk, Butser Iron Age Farm in Hampshire, the Yorvik Viking Centre, Ironbridge Gorge Museum and Morwellham Quay Copper mine at Tavistock in Devon, have an educational purpose and a foundation in serious academic research. They can inform, but will also stimulate questions for children as well as for researchers: how do you know what crops the Iron Age people grew, or how Saxons made their homes? How do you know how a Viking village smelt? Why do you think a maid may have talked or dressed like that? Would the streets and the air really have been so clean? Reconstructions of events, made primarily for entertainment, are, to differing degrees, authentic. The National Trust and English Heritage Events diaries list exciting historical re-enactments and demonstrations: mummers, tournaments, feasts, dances, music, parades of Roman Imperial troops, civil war battles, archery and falconry.

Other reconstructions are made predominantly for commercial reasons: cartoons such as *Asterix* or *The Flintstones*, musicals and films such as *Oliver* and *Robin Hood*. Young children who have learned to ask 'Why?' and 'How do we know?' can begin to discuss why reconstructions have been made, whether it might really have been like that, why, why not, and why they think it might have been different.

Different versions of stories

Stories are important. They are as central to everyday life as they are to historians. 'There is conflict of characters, the natural likes and dislikes, loves and hatreds . . . the conflicts, the irrationalities . . . the divided loyalties, complexity of motive . . . drama and tragedy' (Rowse 1946: 47).

Young children are comfortable listening to stories. They broaden their experience and their knowledge. Stories affect children's intellectual growth, for they do not listen passively; they are called upon to create new worlds through powers of imagination. Holdaway (1979) described how stories enable children to escape from the bonds of the present into the past, and to explore emotion, intention, behaviour and human purpose. Stories extend first-hand experiences of the world, giving access to more experiences than any one person can have in their life-time, and so extending perceptions of the world.

In listening to stories about other times, children are required to react, to confirm, to modify or to reject their existing ideas. Listening to different versions of stories, then, helps children not only to learn about times and places and people outside their own experience, but also to understand that there is no single 'correct' version of the past. Alternative versions of stories may battle with one another, marry one another or mock one another in the listener's mind (Bruner 1986: 7). They represent models of our world which we carry in our mind and which allow us constantly to redefine our views of the world. Until recently, the only history in many societies was oral history and, in some cultures, the oral tradition has remained alive to the present day. A society with no history would be like an individual with no memory; the oral tradition perpetuates stories of a people's past, shared folk memories, beliefs, values and social customs. But unlike the story in a written text, the story in oral tradition is ephemeral and elusive because it is created by a particular teller, for a particular audience, in a particular place and time. Therefore, stories change their form in response to different audiences. Philip (1989) recorded twenty variations of the Cinderella story which illustrate its development through the centuries, from ninth-century China to the seventeenth-century French court. Children can also compare versions of the same story told in different languages: 'The Hare and the Tortoise', for example, in English, Hindi, Gujarati and Turkish (Douloubakas, 1985).

Anthony Enahoro described his own experience of the living oral tradition, as the son of a schoolmaster in West Africa in the 1930s:

> Women were ever our historians. Singing, spinning, now one, then another, now in parts, now in unison, they told of the old days before the coming of white men, of the founding of the clan, of tribal wars, of families, of the great deeds of our forebears, in their small world.

He told how,

> Those young children of the very large family, who were not already asleep lay on mats listening to stories told by the women of the household. Such stories might be folk lore, myth or history, and such themes had been enacted thousands of times in every family in the Ishan sub-tribe of the Binis, from time immemorial. This was the story of the tribe of the clan, of the family, passed on from generation to generation, from the time when the Ishans settled in that part of Nigeria . . .
>
> (Hutton 1989: 83)

West African stories analyse the problems as well as the advantages of communal living and the extended family; they describe the buildings and the compound of the universal family village, an institution which has existed in West Africa since time immemorial. Osoba (1993) has collected folk tales and legends from his oral tradition in Edo State which blend fact and fiction, and keep alive and share the values and history of the Bini people who live there. In Thailand and in Indonesia, through Nat Yai shadow puppets, stories pass on the religious mythology of the people, the community's shared wisdom and values, their explanations of the world and of the behaviour of the people in it.

In native American oral culture, stories tell of journeys of nomadic progress, the cycle of time and the rhythm of the seasons. Australian stories deal with family patterns, government and tribal organisation. When stories from the oral tradition were finally written down, a variety of different versions was recorded.

In Europe, the oral tradition remains only in 'fairy stories', the stories of the peasant and the nurse, written down in the nineteenth century by, for example, Perrault, the brothers Grimm and Hans Andersen. The European oral tradition, therefore, became part of the nursery by historical accident. Children's understanding of history cannot be assessed through fairy stories because they have become divorced from real events and contain elements of fantasy. But fairy stories introduce children to powerful perennial ideas and emotions which run through the oral tradition. Evil is not suppressed, but is omnipresent with virtue, and children are offered new dimensions of imagination which they could not discover on their own. Such stories help them to examine the relationship between fantasy and reality, to recognise what is likely or possible and what is not, based on their own experiences, and to look for causes of events and reasons for behaviour. Fairy stories, because they come from an oral tradition, can also help children to see that there may be more than one version of a story. (For a brilliant analysis of fairy stories, see Warner 1994.)

Versions of fairy stories

Some would argue that many fairy stories are not suitable for children starting school because they are still not able to differentiate between fact and fantasy. Susan Isaacs (1930) thought that they might therefore be damaging to children under 7. However, Tucker (1981) argued that stories which are in tune with modes of thought which are not logical may in fact help children to examine the relationship between fantasy and reality and so build their intellectual confidence. Stories which explain natural phenomena in terms of human intervention long ago reflect Piagetian levels of autistic thought in which everything in the Universe is made for the convenience of man, and human thoughts and feelings are attributed to most things in the Universe. There is also often a Piagetian concept of 'immanent justice' in fairy stories: the bridge broke because it *knew* the boy crossing it had stolen the apple. When they listen to stories which reflect this stage of thinking, children may *expect* success for the good and doom for the bad because at this stage a child's view is subjective and is constructed around what he or she thinks ought to be true rather than what is. Nevertheless, the stories encourage them to begin to question and ask *why* things happen as they do. Applebee (Tucker 1981) found that 41 per cent of 6-year-olds had firm expectations about characters and predicted the outcome of situations.

Children observe deductions being made in stories, and these deductions are based on concrete, logical analysis of the evidence. Children also identify with characters making deductions in the story based on their own level of experience – either with those who are, or those who are *not*, in control. For example, the story of the 'Three Little Pigs' mirrors the progress of a child's own thinking, and children identify with the pigs according to their own level of learning from experience. This process is interesting for those who have arrived at this level of inductive reasoning and those who have not can begin to see what it is about. Thus the little billy goats went up to the high pastures *because* the grass was sweet; the pigs perceived *from the rough voice* that it was the wolf.

In this way, the bridge between fantasy and reality is gradually crossed. Applebee (Tucker 1981: 70) found that at about 6 years old children thought that Cinderella existed, but few thought that she could be visited, either because she lived too far away or too long ago. Some stories reflect this intermediate level of thinking. Inanimate objects cannot *always* talk; in some stories only animals can talk; in some stories only some animals can talk. This intermediate level is shown by a 5-year-old who, asked if he thought 'Jack and the Beanstalk' was a true story, said that he knew the giant was not real because he knew there were no giants, but that he thought Jack's mother was real 'because my mum talks to me like that'!

After experience of different texts, one teacher found that her 6-year-olds were quite confident in sorting books into 'reality' and 'fantasy' sets: 'The Knights and Armour books are about what happened long ago. *Willy the Wimp* – that's not true. The knights and the racing car books are true. . . .' As Meek (1988: 18) pointed out, you cannot be given a rule in advance. You learn by joining in.

Cook (1969) argued the need for the reinterpretation of fairy stories for a modern audience. Since then there have been many 'modern versions' telling the same story but with inverted gender roles: the competent, combative princess rescues the vain, passive prince. In other reinterpretations, the story is retold from the point of view of the villain; or the essential story is retold in a modern context. Sometimes the traditional version is illustrated in different styles.

Shelley Moore, a PGCE student, investigated the ability of her Reception class to decentre and so to differentiate between, and account for the differences between, two versions of a story. She was attempting to teach these 4- and 5-year-olds the rudiments of historical thinking by going with the grain of their interests. First she read them *The Pain and the Great One* (Blume 1988), two stories of an ordinary day told from a brother's and a sister's perspective. The children were spontaneously very interested. They appeared to empathise with one or with both of the characters and tried to explain how two contradictory interpretations were possible. Next they were read a traditional version of 'Little Red Riding Hood' and a second version told from the wolf's perspective ('Little Red Riding Hood', in Wilson 1988). She was careful in her choice of language when she introduced the second story and did not refer to it as 'a different story' or 'another story'. The children appeared to be operating on two levels at once, on the one level recognising that it was the same story about the same wolf told from different viewpoints, and at the same time thinking that there were two wolves, a 'good wolf' and a 'bad wolf'. Jordan said, 'He told us his own story because the two was different', but then went on to say later, 'There was one wolf in each story, a good wolf and a bad wolf.'

Brogan also at first seemed to think that the same wolf was telling his own version of the story, 'I think the wolf's good. He didn't eat her.' Joanne accounted for the alternative version by explaining that there was one wolf, who had lied to create the second version, while Lan produced an alternative, sophisticated argument, 'Little Red Riding Hood was lying; she made her story up.' Jordan then made the amazing remark, 'They might be different because they're reported differently.' However, as the discussion continued, it revealed two powerful influences which changed the children's fragile attempts to explain the two versions: first teacher intervention, then peer group pressure. In the middle of the discussion, the teacher asked if they thought it was 'the same wolf in each story'. On listening to the tape-recording of the discussion, the teacher decided that this 'leading question' caused the children to lose confidence in their own reasoning. Joanne and Brogan went on to make statements apparently contradicting their previous arguments and to accept that there were two different wolves. They contested Lan's argument that Little Red Riding Hood had made up her story, and Lan, possibly because English was her second language and she felt unable to explain or defend her view, gave in to peer group pressure.

In a second session, the teacher therefore tried to eliminate peer group pressure by talking to the children individually, and to eliminate teacher influence by asking open questions. In this session, she confirmed her original impression that both Joanne and Jordan understood that they had heard two versions of the same events. Both the children were more confident, and began to identify motives, and looked for possible reasons for the different versions and to develop arguments.

Jordan   They were the same story because the last one was the real one, because the wolf didn't want to eat her and the granny lied.

Joanne   The wolf isn't bad. I believe the wolf. The wolf told us his own story. The wolf did want to eat granny. He was hungry. Granny lied.

These discussions are a good example of how a perceptive teacher can look for the reasoning and complex thinking that children are often struggling to clarify and express. It shows the significance of the questions teachers ask, in influencing expectations, as well as the influence of peer group pressure on children's fragile reasoning. These 4- and 5-year-olds were operating at two levels, but one of them was a very sophisticated level which they could not quite achieve. It shows, too, the limitations of assessing children's thinking on the basis of one example.

In a third session, Shelley Moore read the children a traditional version of 'The Three Little Pigs' and a second version which was clearly stated to be 'the wolf's version of events' (Sciesczka 1991). She wanted to see if this quite explicit statement would make it easier for children to understand that there were different versions of the same story. It was interesting that Jordan again understood initially that these were different versions of the same events and began to develop arguments as to why. But when Joanne again insisted that there were two wolves, one good and one bad, he again became uncertain and ended up saying, 'No, yes, I don't know . . . got no idea.' This seems to reinforce the idea that the qualitative differences in children's inferential thinking occur gradually through constant opportunities to reason and to discuss in different contexts.

Susan Jarvis, another PGCE student, told her year 1 class the traditional story of 'Little Red Riding Hood', then read them 'newspaper interviews' which she had written, telling the story from Red Riding Hood's point of view (at first she had assumed it was Granny in bed), from Granny's perspective (the wolf locked her in the cupboard), and the wolf's story (he had popped in for an aspirin because he had a headache, then fallen asleep on the bed). The children were able to select one of these stories and draw an appropriate picture and caption. Most of the girls identified with Red Riding Hood because they 'liked her cape'; Jamie concluded that Granny's story must be true because 'Grannies don't tell lies.' But the children's discussion of their pictures showed that they understood that there were three explanations of the story.

Claire Turnbull's case study illustrates the considerable difference between the groups of 4- and 5-year-olds described above, and her group of 7-year-olds, in their ability to differentiate between fantasy and reality and to understand that there may be different versions of a fairy story.

The 7-year-olds said that as 'babies' they probably thought fairy tales were true but that now they realised that they had been made up a long time ago. They contrasted them with true stories and with cautionary tales, as told by the visiting policeman. They offered sophisticated insights as to what is meant by real and by fantasy. Ryan said that he liked fairy stories because: 'They're *more* like real than real life. They're about really important things.' They thought that *Prince Cinders* (Cole 1987) was *not* like real life 'because it was modern'.

The 7-year-olds had no difficulty in extracting the common moral theme from different versions of a story and thought that the moral is the reason why people enjoy them. In the story they had been read, Ryan defined the moral as: 'Never boss other people around and make them do all the work.' Jason said the story meant, 'don't be unkind'. And Laura added: 'Don't be unkind because you'll probably get it back.'

Because they could extract the common theme in different versions, the children were also able to understand the differences between versions. *Prince Cinders* is not the same as the traditional story of Cinderella because: 'It's about a man instead of a girl.' Laura liked *The Paper Bag Princess* (Munsch 1988), which is not a version of any particular fairy tale, but differs from the traditional genre because the princess *tackles* the dragon. 'Normally in the books I read, when someone gets captured, it's usually the girl', she said. However, when the adaptation was more subtle, as in 'Little Red Cap', the Grimm version of 'Little Red Riding Hood' (in which the wolf dies), and in 'Little Red Riding Hood' (Ross 1991) (in which the wolf repents, the woodcutter has a 'quiet smoke', Gran drinks stout and Little Red Riding Hood rides a bike), the children seemed unaware of the details in the modern version; the similar story line was what they recognised as being important.

Myths, legends and folk tales

The distinction between myths, legends and folk tales is not clear. A myth is defined in the *Oxford English Dictionary* as purely fictitious narrative involving supernatural persons, actions or events and embodying some popular idea concerning natural or historical phenomena. Legends depend more on folk memories of events which have really happened although there is clearly overlap. In Medieval times, legends were the life stories of saints, but later came to mean stories, histories or accounts which were not authentic but were handed down by tradition from early times and regarded as authentic. They are therefore folk tales; the *Oxford English Dictionary* defines folk as a people, a nation or a tribe.

When children are able to distinguish between what may be real and what is fantasy in fairy stories, they will find a fresh challenge in understanding the complex dual role of fantasy and reality in myths, legends and folk tales. These stories were not created for young children, but they are important to children who are already used to fairy stories. First, they are full of metaphor, symbol, imagery and oblique meanings which express the complex interaction of 'pretend' and reality. Bruner (1989) suggested that such stories offer the opportunity of reconciling 'here and now' reality with the reality of the imagination. Second, myths and legends help children to look outward, to value differences between now and past times, and between different societies in the past. They learn new ways of thinking about the world, to change perspective and, as Booth (1985) put it, 'to try on other lives for size'. By questioning traditional stories and trying to resolve issues, children learn to speculate and hypothesise about behaviour and beliefs. Third, myths and folk tales from Africa, the Caribbean, India and China are most important for children who have no experience of cultural and ethnic diversity, because they open up to them values and attitudes other than their own (Klein 1989).

Finally, myths in particular are important because they grapple with the big matters of existence: life and death, the after-life and other worlds. Often they deal with morality and the relationship between the supernatural and everyday life.

Myths, legends and folk tales may need to be challenged and this can draw children into a discussion of alternative versions of stories. First, because they are rooted in the oral tradition, there is often more than one version of a story – of a Greek myth or of creation stories in different cultures, for example. Second, folk tales in different cultures often have a common theme. This may be because of communication between societies. Aesop recorded in Greek the allegories about jackals and lions which belonged to his own culture in Africa, and versions of the West African Anansi stories are well known throughout the Caribbean and Britain. In other cases, there is no known link between the places. The idea that knowledge of a person's name gives power over the person is found in stories in the Kalahari Desert, among the North American Indians, the Vikings, in Celtic Britain and in Germany. Third, folk tales are often found in dual language books (or in the language of the country the story comes from). A child explaining it in one language, and another child retelling it in a second language, may provide two versions of the story which can be discussed.

Most importantly because folk tales flowed through the oral tradition, they evolved around the key organising concepts which lie at the heart of all societies. They deal with values and beliefs: heroism, compassion, self-sacrifice, jealousy courage, betrayal, rough justice, creation stories and spiritual power. They describe social structure. Kings, princes, blacksmiths, tailors and peasants may occasionally change status, but rank itself is not challenged. They are concerned with agriculture and with economic systems; markets in West Africa are full of yams, cassava and sweetcorn, and in Europe there are turnips, potatoes, cows and pigs. Stories tell of threats to society from wind, fire and flood. They tell of journeys, of communication systems, by sea and land. These central organising concepts – values and beliefs, social structure, economic and communication systems – provide a framework. Within this conceptual framework children can compare similarities and differences between societies. Do they all have rich and poor people, rulers and subjects? Do they all grow things and make things and buy and sell them? Do crafty people, jealous people, compassionate people exist in all societies? Do they all have hopes, fears, gods? How are they different in their rules, the things they grow and make and in their daily lives?

Myths, legends and folk tales offer opportunities for comparing different versions of a story or similar themes in stories from different cultures. They provide a framework for seeing similarities (and differences) in attitudes, values and behaviour, and in social and economic systems, in different societies. 'King March's Secret', for example (History Box, National Language Unit of Wales, see p. 218), is the Welsh version of Midas and his ass's ears. Different versions of the same folk tales have been collected by folklore societies. The Folklore Society at the University of Edinburgh School of Scottish Studies and the Nigerian Folk Lore Society, Ibadan, for example, publish versions of myths, legends and folk tales for use by teachers.

Virginia Hunt, a student teacher, investigated the reasoning of a group of year 1 children who were discussing whether, and in what ways, myths, legends and other stories which she read them were true. They all thought that *The Turtle and the Island*, a creation myth from Papua, New Guinea (Ker Wilson 1990), was made up, apart from Ayodele, who thought it might be true because Papua, New Guinea, was on the globe and 'therefore it's a real place, so you could go there, and you might see the turtle – but you wouldn't get purple crabs!' But Theodore argued that the purple crabs, 'and the other colours', showed that the story was not true. He supported this argument by adding that he had seen a turtle in Granada, 'and it couldn't carry a woman or make an island'. Shelley accepted this, and added that 'if it tried, the shell might crack and the person would fall off'. These 5-year-olds were reasoning logically, based on their own experiences and knowledge, and were listening to, considering and developing each other's points. They used similar arguments in discussing whether *Joseph and His Magnificent Coat of Colours* (Williams 1992) was a true story. Shelley said that she thought it was not true because of the colours of the pyramids and the trees, 'so they must be made up'. But she recognised the subtle distinction that Egypt was a real place because she had seen it on television, and that part of the story was probably about Egypt because 'it said about the Nile'. Therefore Canaan, also mentioned in the story, was probably a real place too. Aaron and Ayodele decided, on the basis of their own experience, that the bit about Joseph's brothers would not be true because brothers would not be that horrible to each other.

The children again made reasoned distinctions about the parts of *Bill and Pete Go Down the Nile* (de Paolo 1988) which might be true, and the parts which they thought were not. Aaron knew 'the sphinx and pyramids are true', because he had seen them on television, and in pictures, 'so you *could* probably see them in a museum'. Theodore agreed; he had learnt about sphinxes from his mum. So, as Ayodele concluded, 'parts are about real things, but crocodiles and birds can't talk!'

Princess Victoria (Mitchelhill 1991) was generally agreed to be 'true', and the children were able to explain why. Ayodele had seen a picture of Queen Victoria which looked like the one in the book and she had been to a museum about Queen Victoria; she thought it was the 'Victoria Museum'. She had also noticed the word 'history' on the cover: 'That means it happened a long time ago?' Shelley thought you could find out more about whether the things in the pictures were 'true' by 'going to an old-fashioned shop where they had things from the olden days'.

These year 1 children were able to differentiate between degrees of probability in different aspects of each story and in different types of story. They could support their views with arguments based on their existing knowledge and experience, and listen to, endorse or disagree with each other's arguments.

Different versions of stories in pictures and artefacts

Barnes (1993) showed how he helps Key Stage 1 children to discuss different interpretations, through looking at different representations of Christian festivals and of Christian saints. His workshop for teachers took place in the Medieval Rooms of the Victoria and Albert Museum, but he also takes his children to Canterbury Cathedral. Many children already know the stories of the Nativity and the Crucifixion, and can look for different images of these stories. They may also be introduced to and become familiar with stories about St George and other Christian saints, and learn the symbols associated with them in Medieval images. For example:

- St Michael has wings, a shield, a dragon.
- St John is young and beardless, with a book.
- St Peter has a beard, a book and the keys of Heaven.
- Mary, mother of Jesus, has a halo, covered head, long clothes and a baby.

When they arrive in the museum or the cathedral, children can see how many different images they can find of the Nativity, or how many examples they can find of their chosen saint. They can then compare the way the scene, or the saint, they discover is depicted in different poses and in different media. In the Victoria and Albert Museum there may be examples in wood, stone, ivory, metal, stained glass or embroidery. Close observational drawing, using the 'view finder' (a small piece of card with a rectangular hole cut in it) to isolate their chosen example, will encourage children to look very carefully at detail. Back in school, children can discuss similarities and differences. With very young children, it might be best to select just two examples, an altarpiece carving and a stained glass window, for example.

Older children could note the dates of their images and where they come from. In school they could display them in chronological order and find the places on a map. This would help them to recognise and explain differences between styles and periods, between austere early Medieval, Byzantine and Baroque (even if they did not use this terminology).

Powerful images in metal, ivory, glass, wood and stone taught people in Medieval Europe, through symbolic stories, about the Gospels and the lives of the saints. These were embodied in an oral tradition. For this reason, different images tell different stories, and tell stories in different ways. By collecting different examples of dragons, or of the Nativity, or of a particular saint, children become aware that there may be many versions of the same story. This stimulates them to begin to ask questions which will help them to understand the complex relationship between fantasy, reality and symbolism; they will begin to discuss whether characters may be real or fictional and to be aware of the difference between a fact and a point of view. There are lots of dragons in the Victoria and Albert Museum, in the Medieval and the Chinese rooms, so did dragons really exist? Is this story likely to be true? Were the saints from the Gospels white? Why do they look white?

Different versions of stories in comics

Children enjoy comic strip stories, and they can be as important in learning history as they are in the reading process. They are important in reading because they are easy to read. You can tell the story with the bubble voices. They offer children choice in styles of reading. They make the experience of reading meaningful and purposeful. Seven-year-old Chris said of a comic strip of 'Maid Marion and the Merry Men': 'I like the way you can see the writer . . . his hand with his pen . . . and they climb out of the pictures when they escape with the knight.' He liked the humour and the colour. Comics are important because they do not rely on an adult to reinforce the meaning.

Such comic strips can be important in beginning history too, in helping children to understand that there are clearly different versions of stories, and that these are of varying status. Chris used the word 'proper' to show that he noticed the different status and level of acceptability of comics and 'proper' books: 'The people aren't rich. In the *proper* story they don't eat *that* much!' Meek (1988: 27) felt that there is a danger that if children are taught to pay attention only to words in books, 'This particular kind of multi-consciousness, apparently so natural in childhood, yet culturally and specifically learned, is passed over.'

Discussing the captions in a humorous cartoon book such as *The Normans are Coming; The Truth About 1066* (Clements 1987) could help older children in a zany way, to begin to see how accounts of a period may be written through the anachronistic blinkers of another age. The Normans, depicted in Bayeux tapestry style, refresh themselves with frogburgers and snail sorbet at William's wine bar in Hastings! Certainly, *The Truth About Castles* (Clements 1988) combines lots of graphically shown factual information about how castles were built and defended, and about the lives of people living in a castle, with humorous speech bubbles; this would make a wonderful comparison with the images of life in a castle in *Sir Gawain and the Loathly Lady* (Hastings 1992) which is illustrated with rich, elegant and detailed pre-Raphaelite-style paintings.

Comparing interpretations in illustrations

It is important to help children to explain how different illustrations can express different ideas and feelings about a story. They enjoy talking about what an illustration means and go back to their favourite pictures again and again, searching out details and constructing and reconstructing meanings (Doonan 1993). In order to explain why different pictures express different ideas and feelings, children need to talk about how colour, shape, composition, scale, pattern and the rhythm of lines convey different feelings. They can also begin to understand that styles change with society and with technology, and that they reflect society's values. Nineteenth-century illustrations in children's history books are different from those of the early twentieth century, and from those in modern books.

Different versions of stories about real people

There are recently published stories for young children about real people (Shuter and Reynoldson 1991; Blyth *et al.* 1991) in response to the requirement of *History in the National Curriculum* (DES 1991) that children should learn about famous men and women and events. However, it seems doubtful whether stories about complex events, told in necessarily simple language, are as suitable for young children as stories about the lives of 'ordinary' people.

The Women's History Network Key Stage 1 Biography Project (see p. 219) has involved teachers in researching biographies of well-known women which involve more than one interpretation and they have been tried out with Key Stage 1 children.

The biography of Mary Anning, for instance, has raised some very interesting issues about the way that she has been presented. She has been remembered for the fossil discoveries she made as a child in the early nineteenth century, while playing on the beach at Lyme Regis. Stories about her childhood exploits appear to be untrue, while her very real achievements as an adult appear to have been seriously undervalued.

Fictional stories set in the past

Many stories explore changes over the generations in family life. *Minnie and Ginger* (Smith 1990) tells, with beautiful illustrations, of the lives of Minnie, who began work as an assistant milliner, and Ginger, who worked in a soap factory, and how they had married before Ginger was called up, fought in and survived the Great War. *Timothy's Teddy* (Harrison 1992) describes Teddy's life over two generations; Great Grandpa's memories are humorously treated in *My Great Grandpa* (Waddell and Mansell 1991), and Burningham's *Granpa* (1984) interprets ideas simultaneously through the eyes of a little girl and her grandfather:

> 'If I catch a fish we can eat it for supper.'
> 'What if you catch a whale, Granpa?'

In the end, we are left with the empty chair. The life and death of another Grandpa is sensitively told in *Grandpa's Slide Show* (Gould 1990). Grandmas seem blessed with greater longevity. *When I Was Little* (Williams 1991) tells, in beautiful, humorous, detailed strip cartoons with speech bubbles, of Granny's rosy recollections of her childhood when 'ice cream tasted of cream' and 'babies never cried'.

Such stories are a wonderful way of making children aware of changes over time, within living memory in their own lives and families. This can lead to investigating the lives of their own grandparents and great grandparents and finding that there are many versions of the past.

Children could make their own books about their Teddy or Grandpa, or when Gran or an older person comes to visit, then compare their books. Gran, Grandpa or older friends could help to draw things for the pages 'We didn't have these' and 'We did have these.'

Children could sort statements written on cards about things Granny says which may be true and things which may not be true: 'we did sums on the blackboard'; 'the sun always shone'. There may be all sorts of opportunities for cross-curricular extensions: science – how many days will it rain *this* summer, or snow *this* winter; how long *do* lollipops last? When *did* the first man land on the moon? Sorting materials – Granny didn't have these, but she did have these. Maths – 'We walked four miles to school.' Is this true? How far is this? Do we do our sums differently from Gran? How far do we walk? Geography – what food do we have that Granny didn't? Why?

CONSTRUCTING INTERPRETATIONS OF THE PAST

Children can begin to learn how and why interpretations of the past differ by constructing their own accounts. They may do this through play both in 'let's pretend' play, model making and drawing, and by telling and writing stories. Their interpretations must be based on evidence, on what is known. This could be learnt through a story or a visit to a site. 'Story-telling at Historic Sites' (see p. 218, English Heritage entry) is a selection of myths, legends and folk tales told on audiotape, which are linked to sites. Children's own interpretations could be stimulated by a museum or living history reconstruction, by discussing artefacts or pictures, or by talking to older people. Nevertheless, with very young children, there will be a greater emphasis in their reconstructions on imagination than there is on evidence. Their imagination will involve more fantasy than historical validity if we take validity to mean conformity with what is known of the period (Lee 1984; Shemilt 1984), because they are immature and their knowledge is limited.

Yet it is important that from the beginning children have the opportunity to develop their imagination about past times. As they get older and their knowledge increases, they can rely more on finding out what is known. Through the process of making a variety of suppositions about the past, children can gradually, with increasing maturity, learn valid histori-cal imagination. This may lead eventually to the achievement of historical empathy, to understanding in a coherent way that people in the past may have thought, felt and behaved differently from us, because of their different knowledge bases and the different social, economic and political constraints of the societies in which they lived (Cooper 1992: 137). Generating hypotheses cultivates multiple perspectives, and possible worlds to match the requirements of those perspectives. This process lies at the heart of history from the very beginning. The eventual aim is that hypotheses will be 'true to conceivable experience: that they have verisimilitudes' (Bruner 1986: 52).

Constructing interpretations through 'let's pretend' play

Children need to explore the world in which they live and their relation to it through play. Yet if play in school is to be valued and justified as central to education, we need to be articulate about how it can be related, in an embryonic way, to the disciplines which constitute a broad curriculum, and about the role of the teacher in supporting such play. Tough (1976: 79) believed that imaginative play enables children to think in an historical way. O'Toole (1992) showed how Dorothy Heathcote's model for distance framing can be developed by teachers in historical contexts.

First, we shall consider how historical thinking can be developed through play and why play is an important way of introducing young children to history, then we shall consider the role of the teacher in interpreting, observing, structuring and extending such play.

Historical thinking can develop through play about people, places, events and stories from the past, because such play involves making inferences about how artefacts (a candle, an old mangle, a bow and arrow) were used, and how they influenced people's lives. This will involve considering how the past may have been different from the present (in the things people did, the way they dressed, the situations they found themselves in); it will involve constructing and explaining sequences of events and the reasons for actions. Through such play, children can explore the difference between what is known, what might be supposed and what cannot be known; they learn that stories may be about real or fictional characters and that there may be different versions of what happened.

Play is an excellent way of introducing children to history. First, it helps them to make sense of what they have learned, to explore and develop it, and to integrate it with what they already know. Before new knowledge can be used it has to be integrated into existing knowledge, and young children find it difficult to integrate 'impersonal' information. Stories about the past have a structure which children can reinvent through play and so recreate and internalise their meanings. Second, play allows children to explore the boundaries between imagination and reality, which are, in any case, blurred for young children. This is particularly so in history, which is concerned with reconstructing, from incomplete traces, a past reality which no longer exists. In play, children are able to live in several worlds at once, the everyday and the imaginary. By recreating myths, legends and stories about the past, children can explore and speculate; wonder what would happen if. . . . 'Through metaphor, chairs and tables can become mountains and caves and a young child can become a powerful adventurer' (Bearne 1992:147). Children find it difficult to deal with abstract information, but in play they can move from the anecdotal to the formulation of hypotheses. Third, play can allow children to reject what they are not able to internalise and make sense of. Rosen and Rosen (1973) thought that sliding from reality thinking to fantasy may be an intellectual stage, or that it may be a device for cutting off when the information given by adults is inappropriate or unacceptable. Chukovksy (1968) believed that a child is armoured against thoughts and information that it does not need, which is prematurely offered by adults.

Research has shown that the role of the teacher is essential to ensure optimum value in play (Sylva *et al.* 1980; Bateson 1985), and that the most effective teachers are those who involve themselves as well as the children in problem-solving. Free-flow play does not just happen; the adult acts as the catalyst (Singer and Singer 1990). First, the adult needs to provide materials ('props') and construct an environment related to a story, a visit or a living history reconstruction which children have been to see. The 'props' may be costumes (a mob cap, flowing skirts, breeches, caps, a parasol or walking stick) and old artefacts (a scrubbing board and wash tub, a candle, a besom). Constructing the environment may mean turning the play corner or climbing frame into a castle with a flag and a drawbridge, a ship's cabin, a cave or a Victorian kitchen with a cardboard-box range.

Adult interaction needs to be sensitive, for play and language arise from within the child. It is important that the play is not teacher-dominated and geared to 'let's pretend this story'. Intervention should be based on observation of the children's play, and initiated by the children so that it builds on their own ideas. Children between 4 and 5 years old may, for instance, ask for confirmation of events and experiences through the questions they ask. Teachers should contribute their own ideas and avoid giving brief functional answers. They may ask, for instance, to 'tell me one thing you know about it. Now tell me more . . .' and encourage children to think about hypothetical experiences. Through the context of play, the teacher is freed for real and meaningful discussion, possibly in role as the play develops: 'What do you think Stone Age people would be frightened of?' 'Where is your ship sailing to? Why?' 'Why have you built your castle there?' 'What are you going to cook for dinner?' Older children may sustain play over a longer period and the questions they raise could lead to discussion and use of information books as a basis for further play, or picture-making and story-writing which is more closely related to evidence and to what is known.

'Let's pretend' play about the past can take place in a museum as well as in the classroom. Tullie House in Carlisle has a 15-foot replica of Hadrian's Wall, replica crossbows which can be fired and Roman silver mines to explore. At the National Waterways Museum in Gloucester, you can build bridges and haul canal boat pulleys; at Madame Tussauds, a £10 million 'Spirit of London' ride whisks you through London's history. In 1988, the National Maritime Museum in London established two temporary interactive history centres, in collaboration with the staff and students of Goldsmiths' College, University of London (Anderson 1989). Their aim was to develop historical thinking: an awareness of evidence and its incompleteness, of primary and secondary sources, of similarity and difference between past and present, awareness that 'causes' are the product of interpretation and that events have many causes. They wanted children to understand how historians, in attempting to reconstruct the past, reconstruct not only the externals of life and behaviour, but also the thoughts, feelings, motives, values and attitudes of people in the past. The Armada Discovery Centre was designed for children from 3 to 8 years old and the Bounty Discovery Centre, which followed it, was for 3- to 14-year-olds and their parents.

In the Armada Discovery Centre, children's play was stimulated by stories and by the construction of the play area. Initially sitting in a rocky corner of a darkened room (7 m × 12 m), children heard the story of the *Gran Grifon* which was wrecked off Northern Scotland in 1588. At the point in the story when the ship was about to be wrecked, the lights went up and the children were invited to explore a 10 m-long reconstruction of part of the upper deck and the captain's cabin, standing out from a painted seascape, complete with replica artefacts, including a gun carriage which could be loaded with canon, a barrel of salt fish, and rations of dried biscuits and chickpeas. The play session ended with the story of the Spaniards' rescue, or with folk tales of shipwrecks.

The Bounty Discovery Centre presented the *Bounty* in Tahiti in 1789, a few months before the mutiny. It was recreated against a painted background. The sounds of Tahiti, of children, chickens, pigs, birdsong and the sea, were recorded. There were replicas of a Tahitian house and its artefacts. These contrasted with a 3 m × 3 m reconstruction of Bligh's cabin and part of the lower deck of the *Bounty*, complete with hoists, hammocks, scattered sailors' belongings and barrels of malt vinegar and salt fish. Student teachers who had specialised in Early Years education interacted with the children. It was decided that they could help to interpret the experience for the children in a way that was more historically honest, and arguably with greater diversity and sophistication, if they did not wear costume. The role of the adults here was not to stimulate play with stories, as in the Armada Discovery Centre, but to respond to questions.

It was interesting that parents and students played a crucial role in the children's play. Most parents and grandparents of either sex joined in the children's play activities with enthusiasm. However, when the student interpreters were not present, learning and enjoyment suffered noticeably, and visits were shorter. When the students were present, children and adults readily appreciated the frame within which they participated. It was concluded that the role of the students was to establish rule structures for imaginative play. Once these were communicated, children showed remarkable ability to move confidently and creatively between play and reality.

Classrooms cannot provide such elaborate reconstructions, but children's play does not require this. A play area can easily be transformed into a ship, a castle, a cave or a Victorian kitchen with a few 'props' and dressing-up clothes. Fairclough and Redsell (1987: 34) give basic patterns for eighteenth-century and twelfth-century costumes. Each of the following play reconstructions was set up in a Key Stage 1 classroom. If teachers set play objectives and provide a framework for children to explore, so that they take responsibility for their own learning, the teacher is free to observe the children's learning in a more incisive and focused way. Unfortunately, Tizard *et al.* (1988: 49) found that in thirty-three London schools children in top infant classes spent less than 1 per cent of their time on such 'free' activities.

The following example shows how drama was used in a more structured way to introduce historical information about voyages of trade and exploration to year 1 children, as part of a topic on transport.

Box 5.1 The ship

POSSIBLE STIMULI

- Visits to, e.g.
  - The National Maritime Museum, the *Cutty Sark*, London
  - *The Mary Rose, The Victory*, Portsmouth
  - Chatham Historic Dockyard, Kent ('living museum' with tradesmen at work)
  - Town Docks Museum, Hull (on whales and whaling)
  - Royal Research Ship, *Discovery*, Dundee (Scott's Antarctic ship)
  - Merseyside Maritime Museum
  - National Waterways Museum, Gloucester
  - Stoke Bruerne Canal Museum
- Sea shanties
- Poetry, e.g. 'Nursery Chairs' (the third chair), 'The Island' (in Milne 1979a)
- A visit by a sailor
- Video excerpts or excerpts from stories, e.g. *Treasure Island, Peter Pan*
- Fictional stories set in the past told by teacher in role as a pirate or old sailor, e.g. *Jack at Sea* (Dupasquier 1987), a story with brief text and detailed illustrations about a young boy who has run away to join his friend who was press-ganged into the navy during the Napoleonic Wars; or stories of pirates, e.g. *I wish I had a Pirate Suit* (P. Allen, Penguin, London, 1991).
- Maritime paintings
- 'Ships and Seafarers', National Maritime Museum Resource pack
- Replica posters, National Maritime Museum

PLAY

- Initial resources for free play:
  - *Outdoors:*
    - Climbing frame, climbing net, monkey run
  - *Indoors:*
    - Playhouse 'cabin'; deck outlined with benches
    - How could we make this more like a ship?
    - Broom-handle mast, tablecloth sail, flag, gangplank, wheel, telescope, (skipping) ropes, bucket and mop, life belt, compass, chart, maps

EXTENDING PLAY

(Possible questions which may arise from children's comments, from observing play or being involved in play. These could extend the play and may encourage some children to seek further information from other sources.)

Historical thinking

- *Time and change*

Retell a story Suggest reasons why people in the past acted as they did	Do you know any stories about sailing ships? Where are you sailing to? Why? What do you think it will be like there?

(continued)

Identify differences between past and present times	What jobs do you do on the ship? What do you eat/drink? Why? Where do you sleep?
• *Interpretations*	Is your story about a real ship/person? How do you know that story? Have you made up parts of the story? Why?
• *Deductions from sources*	What do you know about sailing ships? How do you know that? What else can you find out? How do you hoist the sails? How do you know which way to sail? etc.

Cross-curricular extensions

Mathematics

• Calculations, e.g. How far is it? And back?
• Shape of flags, sails
• Measures: time – how long is the journey? Keep a log
  capacity – how much water will fill the barrel?
  weight – how many apples/biscuits? How heavy?
  length – how tall/long/wide is your ship?
  money – what are you buying/selling? Bills, paying crew

English
Speaking and listening, reading, writing:

• Name of ship
• Posters advertising for crew for voyage
• List of crew's names
• List of stores, ship's log, buried treasure map and clues, rules and jobs for crew, letters home
• Reading stories and information books
• Concepts: rigging, prow, cabin, deck, gang-plank, explore, navigate, steer, anchor, crow's nest, 'land ahoy'

Science

• Investigations: wind power, sinking and floating, food preservation, waterproof materials, pulleys (sails), balance (gang-plank – walking the plank!)

Music

• Making wind/water music
• Singing sea shanties

Art

• Making 'props': fish, palm trees, flags, pirate hats, eyepatches
• Mixing sea colours: sea finger-paintings
• Looking at seascapes in different styles

Geography

- Graphic skills: make imaginary maps, treasure maps, devise symbols and key, write directions as clues
- Use globe or maps to trace route
- Find out about new country: mountains, rivers, climate
- Keep weather chart on journey: wind direction, sunshine, rain
- Learn weather lore, e.g. 'Mackerel skies and mare's tails / Make tall ships carry low sails'

PE

- Pirates (home base game)
- Shadow fence with pirates
- Swimming, diving
- Jumping into shark-infested seas
- Walk plank
- Climb rigging
- Scrub decks
- Dance hornpipe

Stage 1

In the classroom the children were shown the *Westward* poster (Maritime Museum, London) which advertised for able-bodied men to sail on the *Westward* to foreign lands in 1798. Out of role they discussed briefly what they knew about sailing ships. How did they go? What would the sailors have to take with them? The children were told that when they got to the hall the teacher would be captain of the ship and would be training them as new crew members for the voyage.

Stage 2

In the hall the first part of the lesson was like a simple movement session. The children practised scrubbing decks, climbing rigging and steering. They were taught the shanty 'Haul Away Joe' and they hauled on the heavy ropes. Detail was added at all times by comments like 'Hold tight up there, don't fall', 'How far can you see from up there?', 'Get on with it, work harder, we don't have any slackers here.'

Stage 3

In the second part of the lesson, they were declared fit to crew the ship. They built the shape of the ship from benches and blocks, loaded the ship with food, fresh water and goods to trade, and set sail.

Again, information was given by comments in role. 'We need all the fresh water we can carry – who knows when we'll see land again.' 'Stow the cargo safely, we must try and get as much as we can for it.'

They had an adventure with pirates during the voyage. But it could have been any of a dozen scenarios.

Stage 4

Back in the classroom, the children wrote up their entries for the ship's log and drew maps of their journeys. They had assimilated a great deal of detail and information in the course of one hour's session.

With all the children working at their own level, the teacher, in role, was able to challenge and extend their understanding by questioning and commenting in the course of the drama. Subsequent drama lessons can move the activity forward and introduce new learning areas. In this case, they could have dealt with being becalmed or storm-damaged, initiating trade with a foreign country or charting lands Europeans had not visited before.

Box 5.2 The castle

POSSIBLE STIMULI

- Visits to, e.g. a castle or a Living History reconstruction of tournaments, jousts, feasts and battles (English Heritage), or reconstruction of a site, e.g. Mountfitchet Castle, Stansted. This is an authentic reconstruction of Richard de Mountfitchet's castle, razed to the ground by King John in 1212 in revenge because Mountfitchet joined the barons responsible for Magna Carta. The building materials are authentic; so, probably, are the noises and smells. Telling the story as the children walk around the site can trigger an imaginative understanding of how these Normans lived, cheek by jowl with their animals, with one eye always on potential attackers from outside (the catapult and the quintain) and from within (the gaol, stocks, mantrap and gibbet)
- Video excerpts, e.g. Ivanhoe, Robin Hood
- Stories set in castles or fictional stories, e.g. *Tim's Knight* (S. Isherwood, Hamish Hamilton, London, 1987), in which a lonely boy finds he can 'magic' a Medieval knight into his own time
- Paintings, photographs, illustrations of castles (posters of castles are available from English Heritage, XR13258)
- Poetry ('Knights and Ladies', in Milne 1979a)

PLAY

- Initial resources for free play
  Outdoors: • Play fort, climbing tower
  Indoors: • Playhouse converted into keep
  • How could we make this more like a castle?
  • Moat, marked with paper, drawbridge, flags, shields, helmets and head-dresses, straw on floor, hobby horses for tournament . . .

EXTENDING PLAY

Historical thinking

- *Time and change*
  Place events in sequence
  Suggest reasons why people in the past acted as they did.
  Identify differences between past and present

  Do you know any stories about castles? What happens? Why have you built the castle here? What do people eat? How do they cook? Where does the water come from? Who might attack you? How? Why? A teacher, in role, could introduce the idea of spies in the castle ... How will you defend yourselves? How did you build the castle?

- *Interpretations*

  Is your story a true story? Why do you think that? What part do you know is true/made up? Why?

- *Making deductions from (secondary) sources*

  Are you going to have a tournament? a ball? a banquet? Can you find out what it might be like?

Cross-curricular extensions

Mathematics

- Shape and space: body size for making armour, shields, cones for ladies' hats, battlements, round towers, rectangular windows

English
Speaking and listening, reading, writing:

- Proclamations
- Invitations to the ball
- Reading stories (fairy stories, legends, stories about local castle)
- Concepts: keep, battlements, moat, drawbridge, portcullis, siege, attack, defend, tournament, jousting, armour, ball

Science

- Pulleys: drawbridge, flag, well
- Levers: bridge
- Structures: test strength of a thick/thin wall, a tall/squat tower, a long/short bridge
- Investigate spinning, weaving, natural dyes
- Design and technology: design armour, ladies' hats

Music

- Listen to Medieval music for banquet/tournament
- Compose music for banquet/tournament

Art
- Design and make shields, flags
- Collect paintings of castles in different styles

(continued)

Geography

- Look at maps of site of a real castle
- Draw pretend plans of castle for spies, with directions
- Draw pretend plans of countryside to decide where to build castle

PE

- Dancing at the ball
- Jousting at the tournament
- Climbing, scaling walls, climbing ropes, crawling through undergrowth, tunnels, passages

---

Box 5.3 Cave/shelter

POSSIBLE STIMULI

- Visits to museums, to a museum reconstruction of a Neolithic site or to a site where there is evidence of a Neolithic settlement, or alternatively modify plans to base play on a visit to a reconstruction of an Iron Age village (Butser, Hampshire) or a Saxon village (West Stowe, Suffolk)
- Slides of cave paintings, Neolithic implements
- Fictional stories, e.g. *Stone Age Magic* (Ball 1989), in which a group of children travel back in time to the Stone Age during a museum visit

PLAY

- Initial resources
  Outdoors:
    - Visit to a local site where Neolithic implements (could have been) found
    - Pretend you are Neolithic people. Where will you build your shelter? Why here? How?
    - How will you keep warm? Make a comfortable place to sleep? What will you eat? How will you defend yourself?
  Indoors:
    - Make 'cave paintings' by projecting slides on to paper on a wall. Use sticks, feathers, fingers to make 'cave paintings'. Make replica clay pots for storage and cooking
    - Collect nuts, seeds and berries to store
    - Use leather off-cuts, wood, (blunt) stone, twine; design then make a Neolithic tool or weapon
    - Cook a 'Neolithic meal' (Renfrew 1985)
    - Make a shelter from tables, covered in hessian, with twigs attached, and a pretend fire

EXTENDING PLAY

Historical thinking

- *Time and change*
Suggest reasons why people in the past acted as they did.	Why do you think Stone Age people made the cave paintings? What things do you think they might have been frightened of?

Identify differences between past and present times	What animals are you going to hunt? How? What do you eat? How do you make your shelter? Your clothes?
• *Interpretations*	Do you think this could really have happened? Why do you think that? What have you made up? Why?
• *Making deductions from sources*	How do you think people might have used this tool (e.g. pictures of arrowhead, axe, scraper)? Why? Teacher, in role, could introduce the idea of a hunting expedition . . . the teacher may be no good at hunting and afraid of killing . . .

Cross-curricular extensions

Mathematics
- Sorting collections, e.g. nuts, berries, roots, leaves; or things for shelter, food, tools, weapons; or sorting pictures of tools and weapons; or sorting into wood, stone, bone, plants
- Calculations based on sets

English
Speaking and listening, reading, writing:

- Trying to interpret petraglyphics; making up a Stone Age language and its symbols, for a friend to decode
- Ritual chants for a hunting or healing ceremony
- Stories based on play
- Concepts: power, defend, attack, tools, weapons

Science

- Materials: firing clay, spinning, weaving, dyeing
- Cooking 'Neolithic' food
- Growing wheat seeds
- Technology: design (and make) a tool or weapon
- Forces and structures: how might Neolithic people have moved/lifted stones?

Music

- Make instruments using natural materials: percussion, wind, strings (?)

Art

- Make pottery decorated with natural objects
- Devise ways of applying paint for cave paintings; mix limited 'natural' colours
- Discuss slides of cave paintings: what do they depict? How were they made? Why?

Geography
- Reasons for selecting your site (protection, drainage, water, wood, crops)
- How were flint and chalk formed?

PE
- Hunting: tracking, crawling, running, jumping, changing speed/direction, stopping and starting, transferring body weight

Box 5.4 The Victorian kitchen

POSSIBLE STIMULI

- Visit to an old house or living history reconstruction (e.g. the Squatters Cottage and The Toll House at Blists Hill Open Air Museum, Ironbridge Gorge)
- Illustrated diaries (Bradley 1974: 70)
- Contemporary book illustrations, e.g. Beatrix Potter, *The Pie and the Pattie Pan; Mrs Tiggy-Winkle*
- Artefacts, e.g. old cooking, washing and cleaning utensils
- Photographs
- Video, e.g. 'The Victorian Kitchen', BBC TV
- Recipes, e.g. jelly, blancmange, gingerbread men, jams, pickles, sweets

PLAY

- Initial resources for free play: range made from cardboard boxes, mantelpiece, table, chair, candle, enamel bowl, flat iron, scrubbing brush, mop, floor polish, carpet beater, pastry cutters, basins, boot scraper, tin bath, old ornaments, rag rug, clothes horse, flowers and vegetables from kitchen garden

EXTENDING PLAY

Historical thinking

- *Time and change*

Suggest reasons why people in the past acted as they did	Why do you think people grew their own fruit/vegetables? Why did most women only work in the home? Did you have to do all these jobs if you were rich? What if you were poor?
Identify differences between past and present	Why did they use a tin bath, beat the rugs, scrub the clothes?

- *Interpretations*   Are all kitchens we have found out about the same? How?
  How are they different? Why?
- *Making deductions from sources*   Where does the water come from?
  How was it heated?
  How do you dry the clothes, do the ironing?
  Where is the coal kept? Where does the smoke go?
  Where do you keep the food? How is it packed/stored?
  Children, as 'themselves', could 'visit' a Victorian kitchen, where they meet a person dressed differently from themselves who is trying to find someone who worked there a hundred years ago

Cross-curricular extensions

Mathematics

- Calculations, e.g. shopping lists using old pennies
- Measures: time – how long does it take to scrub this . . . clean without detergent? to polish this candlestick; scrub the floor, polish the lino?
weight – how much does the flat iron/coal bucket weigh?
cooking – weighing ingredients
capacity – how much does the jug/basin/blancmange mould hold?
shape and space – rolling out pastry to fit pattie pans/cutters
length – making paper aprons

English

Speaking and listening, reading, writing:

- Kitchen rules, maids' jobs, samplers
- Shopping lists, recipes
- Victorian parlour games

Science

- Electricity: how does it make things work? Effects on life in the kitchen?
- Food preservation, then and now
- Materials: old and new fabrics/kitchen implements

Art

- Drawing/painting old kitchen ornaments and utensils

Music

- Victorian songs: learn hymns, music-hall songs, Gilbert and Sullivan; collect and listen to records on old gramophone

Geography

- Draw a plan of the Victorian kitchen for house corner
- Draw a plan of your kitchen at home (differences?)

PE
- Gardening, polishing, scrubbing, balancing trays, lifting loads

It is possible to help children to understand why there may be more than one interpretation of a story through more structured play. Shamroth (1992) described how a teacher, in role as Goldilocks, maintained that Daddy Bear's traditional version of the story was not true, and that he had captured her in the woods. A piece of her dress, found in the woods, was produced! The children, in role as villagers searching for Goldilocks, questioned Goldilocks (the teacher) about what had happened. They compared the teacher's version and the original version. They fed back what they knew, what they thought they knew and what they wanted to find out. Daddy Bear was tried and the teacher eventually confessed to a hall full of intent 'villagers' that her version was not true. With great relief Daddy Bear was released.

In another example (Vass 1993) the teacher began by saying, 'I am going to pretend to be a little girl who lived x years ago and I want you to pretend too.' She then reconstructed the Great Fire of London as a witness, within the conventions of a simulation game. The children became part of the reconstruction and contributed to it with their questions. The key features, the hard evidence of the narrative, were combined with opinions and imagination. Out of role they discussed what was true and what was made up.

Supporting and extending play

The case studies outlined below were undertaken in order to explore in detail the role of the teacher in initiating and supporting imaginative play in ways which ensure that history and language objectives are achieved while allowing the children ownership and creativity.

A medieval banquet

A recent case study in which year 1/2 children reconstructed their version of a medieval banquet aimed to analyse the links between the National Curriculum for History and for English, and subsequently between history and the National Literacy Framework (Cooper 1997, 1998a, 1998b, 2000b).

After a site visit to Kendal Castle, children found out more about medieval dress from brass rubbings, and about food and entertainment from pictures in information books. This rich and intense 3-day project involved finding out as much factual information as they could through asking questions about a variety of sources (the site, receipts, music, brasses, pictures) in order to create their play interpretation. It also involved note-taking and making labelled diagrams and picture notes during the visit, using information books in school, and modelling a variety of types of writing: invitations, menus, fairy stories, jokes for the jesters.

A Victorian street

This 3-day case study aimed to identify precise links between *The National Literacy Strategy* and the *National Curriculum for History* and to investigate how these could be extended through other related history activities (Cooper and Twiselton 1998, 1999, 2000). A year 2 class created a Pollock's Toy Theatre for which they wrote and performed plays, made Kate Greenway replica 'little books' and Victorian peg-dolls, and devised Victorian street-sellers' cries. On the final day, they joined a year 5/6 class, which had been developing role-plays based on Victorian schools, to recreate an interpretation of a Victorian street, and to compare the lives of the 'rich children in the big house' with those of the children in the Board School.

A Victorian house

In another example of structured and supported role-play, year 1 and 2 children from five different schools worked with their teachers and student teachers to reconstruct life in a real Victorian house, drawing on what they had found out over the previous weeks (Cooper 1995). The owner of the house decided to be in role as the housekeeper. As she moved around stoking the fires she was able to keep an eye on the parlour games in her drawing room, the story-telling in her library, the maids beating her precious Persian rugs, the children in the nursery, and the lads being drilled in the garden (in preparation for the Boer War). But Victorian dress and awe of the splendid and unfamiliar environment helped everyone to stay in role, to the extent that a teacher's large hat blocked the (concealed) video camera in the library for at least half an hour, and one child explained that his dirty face was the result of cleaning the chimney.

CONSTRUCTING INTERPRETATIONS THROUGH TELLING AND WRITING STORIES: THE NATIONAL LITERACY FRAMEWORK

The National Literacy Strategy (DfEE/QCA 1998b) provides excellent opportunities for retelling and re-enacting stories through role-play, dolls or puppets, comparing characters from different stories, comparing basic story structures, and comparing and contrasting preferences and common themes in stories in year 1. In year 2, children are encouraged to compare and contrast stories, discuss story settings, express views about characters, and retell stories in different ways. Recent work in philosophy for children has emphasised how reading a story together can help 5- to 7-year-old children to understand different opinions, points of view and perspectives and to think critically and creatively about them, and has identified ways of developing classroom inclusion through such enquiries (Costello 2000; Toye and Prendiville 2000).

Telling a story is a skill which children develop gradually. To begin with, events may be linked in a chain but have no point, purpose or causal links. There may be a setting but no character or problem, or there may be action but no setting (Temple *et al.* 1982: 154). Children only gradually learn to understand the structure of a story and to see the links between problem, cause and action. They find it easier to listen to stories than to make up their own.

Anderson (1993) suggested how museum artefacts could stimulate young children to make up their own versions of stories which explain them. They could, for example, look at incomplete carvings and 'guess' the rest of the story, or make up stories about how they had been damaged. (How did St Michael lose his wing?) They could make up stories to explain what someone in a carving or stained glass picture might be saying. (To whom is Christ speaking in the sixteenth-century carving of Christ riding on a donkey and what might he be saying?)

Medieval carvings, statues and stained glass often depict different versions of the same story. (St George sometimes kills the dragon, and in others he captures it.) This is because folk tales about the saints were accepted by the church as a device for explaining to people their lives and beliefs. These stories were part of the oral tradition and so many versions existed, which became frozen in statues and carvings. Children can retell the different stories depicted. Or they could compare the dragon painted on a Medieval altarpiece with a Chinese dragon embroidered on silk (postcards W205 and FE196, Victoria and Albert Museum).

Constructing interpretations through model-making, painting and drawing is as central to the early years curriculum as stories and 'let's pretend' play. The opportunity to play with building bricks, constructional toys and a range of junk materials is clearly linked to the development of abstract and divergent thinking. In the context of history children can make models of sites or buildings they have visited, and paint and draw images of stories they have heard. They can compare them, discuss how they relate to what they saw or heard, what they have added, and why. Friends of the school may be enlisted to build models of old ships, forts, shops or dolls' houses (Honeychurch Toys Ltd; The Dolls' House Emporium), with which children could develop play about the past, stimulated by stories they have heard. Or children could make their own models based on (postcards of) a toy (shops, dolls, trains, forts, dolls' houses, an Indian Prince's carriage) in the Bethnal Green Museum of Childhood. *The Model Village* (Fisk 1990) might encourage imaginative play with their models.

Six-year-olds also draw to describe events which occurred over time. They build up the narrative as they go along. It unfolds on the surface of the paper, often showing the same characters at different points of the story. They retell their own versions of it with sound accompaniments as they record it using their own marks; lines often represent movement through space and time.

Chapter 6

Deductions from sources

THE DEVELOPMENT OF THE PROCESSES OF HISTORICAL ENQUIRY

Historians find out about the past from sources, traces of the past which remain. Gradually the range and status of the sources available to them have increased and the process of interpreting sources has developed. Medieval chronicles tended not to make inferences, and not to analyse, evaluate or reflect on statements about events. Bede was unusual in that he did list the written sources he used and attempted to evaluate the oral tradition. With the Renaissance, however, there was a new emphasis on the original documents of Greece and Rome. This led historians, from the sixteenth to the eighteenth centuries, to place greater emphasis on research, and on the use of a wider range of sources: Camden's *Britannia* was based on 'evidence', and Hume's *History of England* traced changes in prices, wages and dress. In the nineteenth century, documentation, and the particular rather than the general, became increasingly important. Documents of varying status were considered relevant: Macaulay used broad-sheets, songs, maps and party propaganda as well as political documents. For the first time the research techniques of history were taught in universities, in the Sorbonne and in Berlin, at Oxford and Cambridge. By the twentieth century history involved an even wider range of sources and areas of enquiry: archaeology, cartography, folk songs, children's games, old sayings, folklore, oral history, place names and statistics. Traditions from the past which continue into the present, such as traditional farming methods which may reflect on the past, are studied. Therefore, when children find out about the past from old newspapers, songs, games, photographs or oral history, this is not simply because such sources may be accessible to them; they are also the sources used by academic historians.

However, sources can only tell us about the past if we know the kinds of questions to ask about them, and how they may be answered. This process was clarified by Collingwood in his *Autobiography* (1939). As a young philosophy teacher he rejected the methods of the 'realists' who proceeded from logical propositions which could be proved true or false. Collingwood saw enquiry as being a complex of ordered, specific questions in the tradition of Plato, Bacon, Descartes and Kant. He said that philosophy had found it necessary to accommodate a revolution in thinking about the natural world, based on empirical observation and deduction in the seventeenth century, and that history must encompass a similar revolution in the way man is studied in constantly changing societies. Collingwood worked out his philosophy of history through constant application in archaeology. He proceeded from specific questions about the significance and purpose of objects to the people who made them. How was it made? Why? What was it used for? By whom? Where was it found? Are there others?

Sometimes a question can lead to a premise followed by a deduction. We know that these are Saxon place names, therefore Saxons settled in this area. We know that these are the laws of Aethelbert of Kent or of Ine of Wessex. Therefore we know that the Saxons made laws about homes, cattle and crops, that most people had rights as well as duties, and some freedom to move around. We know (from archaeological evidence) that certain banks indicate Iron Age fields. Therefore we know the size and shape of fields in the Iron Age and can estimate the population they could support. We know Iron Age people had coins with horses on. Therefore we know that they had horses, brass, tin, copper and used money. We know they had spindles and loom weights. Therefore they spun and wove cloth. Neolithic stone sickles, hoes and grinding mills tell us that Stone Age people grew crops. Therefore they lived in one place, in a community.

Yet often deductions cannot be made from sources. Evidence is often incomplete. Its status may also be uncertain; the walrus or whalebone pendant found in the Barnack Grave may be just an ornament, or it may be a ceremonial or cult object representing ideas or social practices we can only guess at. An account of the defeat of the British by the Saxons written by the sixth-century monk Gildas may be not so much a chronicle of events as an allegorical exhortation to the British to resist the Saxon invaders.

Diaries may be biased; they may or may not have been written for publication. Newspaper and other accounts may be prejudiced. Portraits or photographs may not be typical. The evidence of the past which remains cannot tell us for certain about the thoughts and feelings of the people who made or used it.

Therefore inferences, reasonable suppositions about historical sources, are more frequent than deductions. Inferences must be supported by arguments, and they must conform with what else is known of the period. Yet often within these criteria more than one interpretation is possible. There are no fixed rules which generate a correct conclusion. For example, in the recently discovered tomb of an Egyptian pharaoh at Abydos, some of the oldest examples of hieroglyphic writing were found. This led Dr

Vivian Davies to think that the components of later Egyptian writing were present several centuries earlier than previously supposed. However, Dr John Ray disagrees, because the writing does not have phonetic values. However, they both agree that the new evidence suggests that the idea of writing came from Sumer or Elam, and reopens the questions as to what extent Egyptian culture was an independent invention (Hammond 1993).

Historical imagination is the capacity to make a range of valid suppositions about evidence. 'If the pupil does the supposing with real insight and makes perceptive selections from the wealth of possibilities open to her/him, given the evidence she/he has, we may say the supposing is done with imagination' (Lee 1984).

Through suggesting how a source may have been made and used, and what it may have meant to the people who made and used it (whether it be a piece of writing, a place name, a picture or an artefact), the historian may attempt to understand and to explain the possible thoughts and feelings which the evidence represents. Collingwood (1946) stressed the importance of trying to understand the feelings and thoughts which resulted in actions and in artefacts which remain, for otherwise they are unintelligible. History, he said, is the history of thought. We cannot say how it felt to make a Stone Age cave painting or wear an Iron Age helmet or to be Eva Braun in the Berlin bunker, but we can speculate about the motives which account for the painting, the helmet and her death in the bunker. The job of the historian is not to duplicate the lost world of the past, but to ask questions about the traces of the past which remain. In the question and answer sequence, the 'right' questions are the ones which lead to a larger complex and do not draw a blank. There is no limit to the number or kinds of questions or to the relevant evidence. It is also important to recognise that some questions can never be answered.

Making inferences about sources, then, involves asking questions about how they were made and used, and how they may have affected the lives, the feelings and thoughts of the people who made and used them. It means accepting that there may be a number of equally valid inferences.

Young children, in making suggestions about historical sources, need to learn that there may be no one correct answer (and also why some inferences may be more likely than others). This gives them confidence in forming, justifying and discussing their own opinions and listening to those of others. It develops children's sense of control over their own thinking in a way that closed questions cannot.

> There are lots and lots of people who are always asking things,
> Like Dates and Pounds-and-Ounces and the names of funny Kings,
> And the answer's either Sixpence or A Hundred Inches Long,
> And I know they'll think me silly if I get the answer wrong . . .
> ('The Friend', in Milne 1979b)

Christopher Robin would have enjoyed 'proper' history. History in the National Curriculum at Key Stage 1 requires children to find out about the past from sources of information, to learn to answer questions about the past using sources, and to begin to select information from sources to answer specific questions about the past.

TEACHING CHILDREN TO MAKE DEDUCTIONS AND INFERENCES ABOUT SOURCES

Oral sources

Good story-tellers' accounts of their childhood are irresistible. Roald Dahl's autobiography (1986: 11) begins, 'this grandfather of mine was born, believe it or not, in 1820, shortly after Wellington had defeated Napoleon at Waterloo'. He then launches into a vivid account of how his father accidentally lost an arm which was 'pulled off' by a drunken doctor who arrived in a horse-drawn buggy, who had been summoned to treat a fracture. The very old and the very young often have a natural rapport, conveyed more poetically by A.A. Milne (1979b) in 'The Charcoal Burner'.

> The charcoal burner has tales to tell . . .
>
> The springs that come and the summers that go,
> Autumn dew on bracken and heather,
> The drip of the forest beneath the snow
> All the things they have seen
> All the things they have heard. . . .
>
> Oh the charcoal burner has tales to tell!
> And he lives in the forest and knows us well.

Yet teachers cannot assume this rapport. They need to create situations in which it can flourish. They need to consider:

- whom they should invite to talk about their past;
- a focus and stimulus for the discussion;
- how to help children to generate and structure their questions;
- how to organise the session; and
- how to follow it up.

Choosing interviewees

Oral history provides rich sources, because it is concerned with the unique, diverse and personal lives of ordinary men and women, from different backgrounds and cultures. Yet people may be wary of talking about their personal lives, especially to children!

> Hear, Land o' Cakes and brither Scots,
> Frae Maidenkirk to Johny Groats!
> If there's a hole in a' your coats
> I rede you tent it;
> A chield's amang you takin' notes,
> And faith, he'll prent it!
> > (Robert Burns, 'On the Late Captain Grose's Peregrinations
> > Through Scotland, collecting the ambiguities of that kingdom',
> > in Beattie and Meikle 1977: 161)

In deciding whom to invite, it is important to consider whether the person will want to talk about their personal experiences to children, and whether they are able to take account of children's interests, vocabulary and limited attention span.

Focus and stimulus

It is best to focus on a specific aspect of a history topic. 'Living Memory' or 'Family History' could focus on toys, clothes, school, games or food. A topic such as 'The Locality' may investigate the fair, the railway station, the library, shopping or occupations. A topic on stories may begin with asking older people how they learnt to read, then what their favourite books were and why. The guest may be able to bring, or the teacher to provide, photographs or artefacts to initiate discussion.

Preparation

The children

Cramer (1993) described classic interview techniques used by oral historians: a number of introductory questions of a closed nature to set the framework and establish a relationship with the subject, followed by a high proportion of open-ended questions about the area being investigated, then a closing frame to bring the subject back into the present.

Children need to be taught how to structure an interview in a similar way. Vass (1993) described how a father was interviewed as part of a local study about the recreation ground, where he had played as a boy. The first interview was dominated by closed questions which led nowhere. 'Did you go there a lot?' 'Did you like it?' 'Yes.' Before a second interview, the children discussed how their questions could be improved to obtain more information. They then found that questions such as 'What did you have to play on?' and 'What happened then?' led to a story about how the umbrella cradle had been removed after an accident, which was followed by a wider discussion about safety, vandalism and pollution.

Cramer suggested that, first, children decide, either as a class or in groups, on five initial questions to ask; for example, 'Where did you live?' 'Who lived in your house?' Then they should practise tape-recording interviews with each other, listen to the tapes, and discuss what makes a good interview. They need to discuss why an 'mmm' or a silence may be better than continuous questions, and how to follow up questions by asking what happened next, why, how did you feel, how do you know? They need to consider why listening and turn-taking are important. Children can then decide, in groups, on an area of their topic they want to investigate during the second stage of the interview, but not necessarily prepare lists of questions as they may focus too closely on these rather than on the topic they are engaged in.

There also needs to be discussion about the language used for the interview and for conveying the information to another audience. This can be an ideal opportunity for bilingual children to demonstrate their skills. The final stage, bringing the subject back to the present, can be the role of the teacher.

The interviewee(s)

An interviewee needs to know something of the age and abilities of the children, the work they have done on the topic and in preparing for the interview, the kinds of questions they may ask, and the expected length of the discussion. They should also understand the kinds of historical thinking and the oral skills the teacher is trying to develop. Vass (1993) described an interview by a class of 6-year-olds, of a mum in her late 20s who had attended their school. The interview was imaginatively prepared in advance. Stories of milk monitors and the demolition of the outside toilets led to a question about whether she had been taught in the same classroom. 'Yes', replied the mother, 'and I sat at your desk.' She told the (true) story of some spilt ink which had marked the desk. After a search, the stain was found by the enthralled children. They were unaware of the time spent by the teacher and parent finding the right desk!

Organisation of the interview(s)

Thought needs to be given to a number of questions. Will the discussion be with the whole class, with a small group or with pairs of children? Will one person talk in turn to several groups? How many adults can be invited? Should their visits be staggered over a period? Where will the interviews take place, and what are the best seating arrangements? What is the role of the teacher?

Follow-up

Children need to clarify and make explicit their findings in order to present them to others. They could, for example, draw a sequence of pictures to illustrate events described, make tape-recordings of what they found out, write labels explaining photographs or objects they were shown, or act out some of the incidents described.

Discussion of the interview after the visitor has left can also lead to considering the reliability of oral evidence. Children need to know that individual perceptions and stories do not necessarily correspond with the accepted view. This can lead towards an understanding of the relationship between story telling, oral sources, myths, legends and history. Vass (1993) described how a North Devon fisherman came every year to talk to children about life between the wars. Every year his stories became more elaborate and inventive as he got to know which stories went down best. The whale, originally a porpoise, which attacked his fishing boat, became an epic of *Jaws* proportions! After he had left, the children asked: 'Was the story about the whale true?' This led to a discussion about whether the story was true, whether the fisherman had been openly lying, whether he intended to deceive or whether he was elaborating in order to create a good story. Young children are capable of sophisticated analysis if the context interests them.

Redfern (1998) explains how many aspects of the past rarely represented in published learning resources can be understood through oral history at Key Stage 1: the cultural diversity of past societies, the experience of minorities and of ordinary men, women and children. He points out that older people can also talk about times long before they were born, through their oral tradition, and that children can interview adults from the distant past 'in role'. He shows, through case studies, how this can be done. Elsewhere, Redfern (1999) suggests how children can record oral accounts on audio or video tape and combine this with other sources, for example music, and with their findings from other enquiries. He shows how these can also be linked to text and written work at all levels to organise and communicate their work.

The National Curriculum for England and Wales (DfEE/QCA 1999a) encourages links between school and the local community. It may well be that visiting groups of people in their own environments (whether social clubs for local residents, workplaces or voluntary organisations), rather than inviting them into school, gives rise to further dialogue and greater understanding (Rogers 1995).

Visual sources

Visual sources have become increasingly important to historians since the Romantic Age when art became regarded as a magic carpet to times past, to the 'spirit of an age'. History became regarded as a means of decoding images of past events, places, personalities and emotions. Clark (1969) hoped that by studying art the historian might be involved in historical enquiry more truthfully than is possible using other sources, and Gombrich saw art as a central historical source. He said that 'between art and history there is no contest; as soon as a work of art is made, it becomes part of history'. Gombrich (1977) saw art as a key to understanding the ways in which different ages and different nations represent the world.

However, visual sources provide their own complexities of interpretation. Paintings present a particularly selective, sanitised and manipulated view of the past. The Dutch historian Huizinga pointed out that the idea which works of art give us of an epoch is often far more serene and happy than that which we find in other sources. Interpreting paintings as an historical source involves major issues. Can styles, for example, be regarded as the moral reflection of an era? Does Gothic represent a pure expression of faith and Baroque represent authoritarianism? Should primitive art be taken as reflecting a primitive society or ornate art be associated with decadence (Haskell 1993)?

Photographs have been recognised as an important historical source since the 1960s. Samuel (1993) described his discovery of photographs as a source.

> These were the first photographs that had ever impressed themselves on me as a visual document ... their unexpectedness giving to the anonymous the kind of reverent attention normally reserved for politicians and literary celebrities. . . . [They] promised intimacy between historians and their subject matter, allowing us if not to eavesdrop into the past . . . at least to rub shoulders with it.

In 1972, the National Portrait Gallery appointed its first photographic curator. Photographs are more likely to reflect the lives of 'ordinary' people but, like paintings, they are often, in different ways, selective, biased or contrived.

Visual sources also include cave paintings, whether from the Mpongweni mountains of Lesotho or from Lescaux in France. They include painted, printed, woven and embroidered textiles, stained glass and statues, advertisements, postcards and book illustrations.

Young children can learn to look at, discuss and make inferences about pictures. A picture gives form to ideas and is something to which they can attach their own ideas. Interpreting a picture involves dynamic interaction between the creator and the viewers. By playing with ideas provoked by a work of art, they create something of their own from it, and in that play they have to deal with concepts – logically, intuitively and imaginatively.

More research is needed into how children perceive images and what they can cope with at different ages; it seems that from 3 to 6 years old children prefer increasingly complex visual patterns. Once a child discovers how much there is to be gained from looking at pictures, reading a picture becomes wonderfully taxing. Looking at pictures represents a puzzle and our attitude to them must be open. There is no guarantee we can make sure of all we are shown. We have to begin with, 'maybe it is about . . .' (Doonan 1993: 11). Doonan went on to say that if we

> discover too many enigmatic details to support an hypothesis, we may have to abandon it and start looking all over again. We also have to tolerate ambiguity. We may settle for several interpretations and be satisfied with them all – or none. What is crucial, through all the sensitive testing and hypothesising, is that we remain open-minded and prepared to give the process plenty of time.

Book illustrations may be a good way to introduce children to the skills of decoding paintings and photographs. Children can first learn to talk about the ideas, moods and feelings they represent, and how they have been achieved, through lines, shapes and colour. Young children can infer from facial expressions and body language what people may be thinking, feeling and saying. Later they can use these skills in talking about illustrations in books about the past. Unwin (1986) suggested that children may prefer to see things as they may have been, in illustrated reconstructions of past times, rather than as archaeological remains. Children can also use illustrations in old children's books as a primary source; Beatrix Potter's *Mrs Tiggywinkle* contains much information about washday. Eventually they can transfer their decoding skills to paintings and photographs, and discuss the moods, feelings and ideas represented in them.

Harnett (1996) found that younger children using visual sources tended to observe pictures in minute detail, recounting everything they could see in them, but then progressed from focusing questions on particular details to general impressions. She has suggested frameworks for developing the key elements of historical understanding through visual sources, steps in developing picture reading, and ways in which teachers can help children to ask questions and encourage them to interact with each other in order to extend their thinking (Harnett 1998: 69–86). For example, two pairs of children may take it in turns to describe objects in a picture, and to comment on the descriptions. Or the teacher could help children to form open questions: 'What questions can you ask about the picture (of a Roman kitchen) to find out more about the Roman way of life?' Or children could be asked to identify significant details in the picture by labelling them and providing a caption; they could each be asked to select different features from a picture and talk or write about them.

Paintings

Paintings can provide an historical dimension to a variety of themes: folk tales, food, clothes, houses, children, pets. They can reflect a range of cultures. Paintings such as *The Negro Page* (Aelbert Cuyp 1620–91) or *Michael Alphonsus Shen Fu-Tsung* (*The Chinese Convert*) painted by Sir Godfrey Kneller (1646–1729), both in the Royal Collection and reproduced as postcards, can provide visual evidence of the long-standing links between Europe, Asia and Africa. Chinese or Indian paintings could be reproduced from books for older children (e.g. Gleisner 1992: 38–9; Goalen 1992: 12, 14; Roberts 1992), or from postcards in the Victoria and Albert Museum collection.

Children can extract information from paintings, and make deductions and inferences about events, clothes and artefacts. They can discuss the validity of a painting as an historical source. How was it made? For whom? Why? Did they always look like this? Did most people dress like this? Paintings can develop historical imagination. What might it feel or sound like to be in that picture?

Lulu and the Flying Babies (Simmonds 1988) delightfully illustrates the process of a child becoming involved in and enchanted by paintings in a gallery. Angry because she is not allowed to play in the snow, Lulu finds herself talking to two cherubs in one of the paintings in a gallery. They take her to fly with them into the snowy world of Breughel, to ride on horseback behind a king in another painting and to taste the fruit in a Dutch still life. *Smudge* (Dickinson 1989) shows how 'a very scruffy boy' finds himself part of the Bayeux Tapestry, a Greek vase and a Lowry scene.

Arnheim (1974) suggested how we can help children to look at a painting with us in a more organised way. First of all we describe the whole picture. Next, safely guarded by the structure of the whole, we try to recognise the principal features, then explore the dependent details. Gradually the entire work reveals itself, falls into place, and begins to engage all the powers of our mind with its message. Finally, we might ask whether the picture tells a story, what might have happened before or afterwards, or what sounds might be heard if we were there. We can discuss the picture as an interpretation, and whether it makes us feel happy or sad, whether we like it or not, and why.

Through the 'Images of People' project at the Russell-Cotes Art Gallery and Museum in Bournemouth, activities were developed which help young children to see that the way illustrations represent people may only be one interpretation and may not be reliable. For example, children can choose a collection of objects to represent themselves, guess the meanings of each other's displays and explain how they felt when others interpreted their objects; or a teacher can choose an object to represent the class and children can say whether they feel it represents them (Batho 1994).

Box 6.1 Looking at paintings: a possible sequence of questions

---

Find out about the past and answer questions using the source

1 Overview of the picture

- What people can you see?   Who do you think they are?
- Where are they?   Why?
- What are they doing?   Why?
- Are there any letters, numbers   What do they tell us?
  or crests?

2 The details

- What are they wearing?   Are they rich?
- What are they holding?   Are they powerful?
- What sorts of hairstyles?   Would they wear these clothes every
                                        day?
- What colours are their clothes?   Is there a special reason?
- What buildings can you see?   Why are they in the picture?
- What furniture, plants, pictures,   Why are they in the picture?
  pets, lighting?
- What is in the background?   Why?
- What do the people's actions,   Who is the most/least important?
  gestures suggest?   What might they be saying, feeling?
                                      What does the picture tell us about
                                        women, children, age, race?

This example shows how children in a year 2 class were able to make deductions and inferences about portraits of Queen Victoria and of Queen Elizabeth I. At first the children were given four pictures of Queen Victoria painted at different times of her life. They quickly recognised that the same person was present in each picture and put them into chronological order. They then guessed who she might be. One child said a queen, because she had a crown in one picture. They next tried to work out why the different pictures had been painted, using the evidence in the pictures. They suggested various important life events, including birthdays, wedding, her coronation and retirement. They used elements in the pictures to make sensible guesses as to which pictures might relate to what. They discussed why she was wearing black when she was old. Some of the children knew it was the colour of mourning.

Then the children looked at a selection of portraits of Elizabeth I. There was some debate about whether she was the present queen, then they discussed how long ago she had died. They compared the pictures with those of Queen Victoria, even though these had been removed from sight, and quickly identified the coronation painting. They made many detailed observations, looking at hair, clothes and jewellery as well as the backgrounds. They identified which pictures the crown, sceptre and orb appeared in (they had to ask what these objects were), even when they were in the background. They later said that they had been included to show that she was a queen.

The children talked about Queen Elizabeth's age in each picture. They stated that she must be youngest in her coronation picture because that was the start of her reign. They discussed why she had so many jewels in the pictures. They suggested it was 'because she wanted to show she is rich' or 'because she was greedy'. When looking at Marcus Gheeraerts' portrait, which shows the queen standing on a map of England, the children realised that she could not really have been standing on England, that it must have been only in the picture and that she was standing on the map to show that she ruled England.

When asked why she was painted so often, they suggested 'because she was queen of England', 'because she was famous', 'because she wanted everyone to know what she looked like'. They expressed various opinions about her character. The children were quite certain that she was not as thin as she was portrayed. They knew that she had 'hoops' under her skirt.

The work covered a range of levels in the National Curriculum and the discussion was recorded to make assessment possible.

The children had opportunities to consider time and change, the differences between past and present in their own lives and in other people's lives, by comparing the pictures and seeing how Elizabeth and Victoria had changed during their lives, and to recognise similarities and differences between different periods in the past, by identifying features common to more than one picture and the differences between them.

They considered how and why images of the past are created, recognising that they were working with pictures of real people and that particular messages were being expressed in the paintings. They used the pictures as sources of information about the past, talking about what they could see in the paintings and asking questions about the pictures and the people in them, looking at the pictures for the answers to their questions, and making deductions from the paintings. They selected and put together information from more than one painting to answer specific questions.

Photographs

Photographs as an historical source include personal photographs, photographs from books, newspapers, or postcard views. They may be linked to themes such as 'Ourselves', 'Our Street' (or school or village), 'Jobs People Do', 'Holidays', 'Clothes' or 'Transport'. Old photographs are also often used with young children because they are a graphic representation of 'otherness'. Dates, addresses, messages and titles often extend the visual dimension, especially on postcards which pre-date the telephone.

Teachers at Robert Le Kyng Primary School, Swindon, illustrate how they used photographs of old toys and of seaside holidays with children from their Reception class, and up to year 2, to develop key skills through historical enquiry (Tilbury and Fordham 2001). The Reception children used observation skills: 'What can you see?' Year 1 developed investigation skills and deductions: 'What can you work out from the observations?' Year 2 listed similarities and differences between now and then based on the observations. English Heritage photograph packs have been produced to support Key Stage 1 QCA Schemes of Work on toys and holidays (English Heritage 2001), based on this study.

Joanne Edwards, a student working with year 3 children who had studied the Second World War the previous term, showed them a photograph of her grandparents' wedding in 1943. They immediately deduced that it was taken during the war.

A   They've all got uniforms on. He's a pilot.
JE How do you know?
A   You can see the wings on his uniform.
K   They're wearing soldiers' outfits.
B   They didn't have much money in the war. They couldn't have new dresses. She's wearing a normal dress like you'd wear at a party. She's got a small bunch of flowers and no veil. They had short dresses so they could run down the shelters.

All the children were able to transfer their knowledge about the war to the photograph; it is interesting that the girls talked about the women's clothes and the boys about the pilot's wings and the men's centre partings.

The children were also able to make inferences about the people's feelings and motives, by drawing on their knowledge about adult behaviour from soap operas!

A   They wanted to be happy and make more out of their lives. They wanted to have happy memories in case they died. It's like *Home and Away* when Blake wanted to marry Meg before he died.
B   And Ted and Rita in *Coronation Street* . . .

In a second session these children were shown a sequence of five family photographs and the teacher recorded what they noticed about them. She found that the questioning about the earlier pictures gave them a framework for discussing the later pictures without prompting.

The synopsis in Box 6.2 of the children's descriptions, questions and deductions shows how they developed each other's points and responded to each other's questions.

Box 6.2 Looking at photographs

1880 photograph
Why is the address on the photo? So other people would go back for a photo?
You don't see ladies now with buttons from the chest to the neck.
There are beads on either side.
The dress would cling to your neck.
I think the boys' collars would be uncomfortable – it's sort of stiff material.
They got dressed up to have their picture taken. Oh yes.
And the photographer's put them in order for the picture. In the olden days they
   didn't say smile.

1912 photograph
It's winter. He's wearing his coat and gloves.
I think he was going for a walk in the park with his dog.
He's got bloomers and a dress on and socks, like girls, and frilly things on his
   shoes.

1946 photograph
This picture isn't very old because you still see girls with their hair like that.
It's an old-fashioned pram. Nowadays babies sit up in them. They don't lie down
   like in that one.
It may have been taken because they have a new baby

1960 photograph
It looks like the time of the teddy boys – you know – like in *West Side Story*.
They might be on holiday.
I don't wear *dresses* on holiday. I wear shorts and tops.
It's not far away. It's Butlins or Eastbourne maybe (both are places known to K).
It's a holiday camp or hotel.
It's summer; the flowers are out.

1970 photograph
They're sort of hippies in 1970 – you know, flower power.
They're at a wedding. You can see the church – the arch.
Are they getting married?
They all look relaxed and happy

Curtis (1993) suggested strategies for using visual sources, with low
ability and developing bilingual pupils, which could also be used with
young children to help them to understand that different sources lead to
different views of the past.

Two groups of children are given different sets of pictures which convey
contrasting messages; for example, poor and rich Victorian children or
children in a town and in the country, or leisure and work in Victorian
times. The teacher could work with each group in turn. Each child in the
group chooses a picture and tells the others what he or she thinks is
happening in it. Other children may say whether they agree, if not why
not, and whether they can see anything else in the picture. Then the group

decides what it thinks its set of pictures tells it about the period, and records this in one or two sentences of shared writing. Each group later reports back to the whole class on what it has found out from its set of pictures about the period. The teacher discusses with the whole class why the findings of the two groups were different.

Other work with photographs could examine concepts of evidence and validity

Evidence

Children could take photographs of their school, street, shop or village and work out what people in the future might know or guess from them. This would develop the idea of the photograph a a document, and that 'now' will become part of history.

Validity

To explore notions of validity, children could collect photographs of themselves and sort them into 'everyday' and 'special occasions': birthdays, weddings, festivals, first day at school, the school concert, formal group photographs of the class. They could then discuss how pictures in the two categories are different (clothes, food, place, composition), and which tell you more about everyday life. They could discuss whether people only take photographs on happy occasions. (Are you ever crying in a photograph?)

Another way into this area would be to look at old photographs, which were posed and only taken on formal occasions. Did these people always look like this? (Even photographs of Victorian working people had to be posed.) Why was the photograph taken? What did these people want us to think about them?

The following example shows how children are able to recognise that the circumstances in which, and reasons why, photographs are taken can influence the messages they convey and must be taken into account in interpreting them and generalising from them.

A group of year 3 children were shown photographs of two family groups taken at the beginning of this century; one was taken by a professional photographer and one by an amateur. They immediately noticed this difference in status:

K   This was taken by a friend or a member of the family. Otherwise he wouldn't have his head cut off! And the lady isn't ready. She's looking down. The other one was taken by a proper photographer?

B   Yes. They're all in order. It wouldn't be like that if they weren't ready.

The children recognised that therefore the photographs conveyed different messages.

B   The Harrisons are rich. You can tell because of their house behind them, and the jewellery the lady's wearing.

E   They're trying to look posh people. When we have our photograph taken we just cuddle up for it.

K   I don't think the Parsons are *that* poor. The others have got a proper photographer so they put on their nicest clothes. But this lot have just gone out into the garden. It's just a family photo.

Advertisements

Old advertisements are another good way of discussing how reliable a source is, because children are familiar with advertising. Excellent posters and advertisements can be obtained from the History of Advertising Trust. Some collections have themes, for example, advertisements tracing the changing stereotypes of women from Victorian times to the present, and related information. The clothes and situations are an historical source; their validity could be investigated by comparing them with a similar advertisement today. What does a modern advertisement tell us about clothes and houses today? Why was it made? What do the people who made the advertisements want us to think? Would advertising today give a true picture of how people live now?

The local environment

> [History] gives an interest and a meaning to things which perhaps we should not have noticed before, not only villages and towns and buildings, a church, an old house, a bridge, but even the landscape itself; prehistoric tracks, monoliths, barrows . . . the romance and pathos of industry, the mines that were once hives sounding with the activity of hundreds of men . . .
>
> (Rowse 1946: 31)

Tawney (in Rowse 1946: 42) said that what an historian needs is not more documents, but a stout pair of boots. Almost all localities have some old buildings and sites which children can visit.

English Heritage continue to produce excellent resources to support visits to important historic sites and buildings: abbeys, houses, castles. Their regional education officers are also willing to help with plans for using the local historical environment with younger pupils – a local area, shopping street, church or row of houses.

Buildings

These may be listed buildings, of which there are 400,000 in England, a local church or any unexceptional but old buildings in the locality. Children living in old houses could find out about their own homes, using street directories, and make books based on Our House (Rodgers and Rodgers 1991). This tells the story, in pictures, of different children living in the same house in 1780, 1840, 1910 and 1990. An English Heritage Key Stage 1 video (1992) shows how to prepare for, organise and follow up a class visit to an old house. It is a case study based on a seventeenth-century merchant's house in Great Yarmouth.

First, children could observe, then record in drawings or photographs:

- how the walls are made: timber frame filled with wattle, brick, plaster, stone;
- how the roof is made: thatch, slate, tiles;
- doors and hinges, windows, chimneys;
- decoration, writing, figures;
- number of rooms, upstairs/downstairs;
- fireplaces, ceilings, floors, bells, ovens, pump.

Then they could discuss questions about the past, for example:

- Has the building been changed? Why?
- How did people heat and light the house, cook, get water?
- How many people probably lived here?
- How were the rooms used?

Finally, they could follow up the visit by presenting for an audience the deductions and inferences they had made about what it may have been like to live in the house in the past, and how and why it had changed. This could be in the form of labels for photographs, a model, a slide show or role-play, and would involve explaining causes and effects of changes over time and interpretations.

Sites

These may include sites where evidence of occupation has been found:

- archaeological sites in the process of being excavated;
- incomplete structures (a Roman villa or part of a Medieval town wall);
- industrial sites (wind or water mills for grinding, drainage, spinning or weaving);
- warehouses (or a blast furnace or chainmaker's workshop);

- traces of communication systems (old tracks indicated by hedges, walls, a milestone, a horse trough);
- old streets (indicated by street names, mews, inn signs, lighting, coal holes, post boxes, plaques;
- canals (with bridges, locks, towpaths).

Children can observe clues about the site and record their observations in drawings and photographs. They can use these records later to list questions about how the sites were made and used, and why. This could lead to finding out more from books, and oral and other sources, and to presentations, in different forms, of what they have found out. This could include 'an archaeologist's talk' illustrated by slides, a display of drawings and plans with descriptions and explanations, models and play reconstructions. The processes of archaeology could be demonstrated to the audience, for example by describing a dig in the school grounds, either to see what children could find or to discover 'evidence' preselected and buried by the teacher. Alternatively, children could demonstrate to their audience how archaeologists work by burying an artefact in layers of sand/earth/gravel in a fishtank to display a section, or they could build a model and bury it in the sand tray for others slowly to rediscover, record and interpret.

A visit to a church as described in 'Church-Going Kendal' (Cooper and Etches 1996) can promote the focus for an excellent Key Stage 1 topic: reading the stories to be found in stained glass and statues and coats of arms has clear links with the local community and citizenship. Images and names on memorial stones reflect sources of local wealth (in this case, sheep-farming), and stories about famous, and less famous, local people. A church study provides links with cyclical patterns, through seasonal festivals, christenings and marriages, and a personal, social, spiritual, cultural dimension as well as links with national events. We went just after 'Poppy Day'. Children in one group, who had previously looked at photographs from World War I, were each given a poppy and asked where they could find more poppies in the church. Why? Who was commemorated in the memorials? Back in school, they designed their own memorial window and made it in tissue paper.

Artefacts

Britain has 2,500 museums. Since 1960 new ones have sprouted up at the rate of thirty a year (in Fakenham there is a Museum of Gas and Local History, while in Jarrow there is 'Bede's World'). We owe our great museums to the Victorians, but their ideas are not ours; art, relics and facts were presented in dusty cases, without context or passion, to be observed in silence. However, the museum education services which should make museums more accessible today have not been enhanced in recent years. Access to museums increasingly depends on ability to pay, on sponsorship and on cynical, spurious and snobbish assumptions about what would be popular. It is therefore essential that children learn how to observe, enjoy and ask historical questions about artefacts, both in and outside museums.

Bruner (1966) said that to explore through touch how things are made and how they work is an important way of introducing the key ideas of a discipline to young children. He called this 'enactive representation'. Children can have the opportunity to touch objects from the past in 'handling sessions' in museums, through loan collections, through sessions such as 'Mrs Tanner's Tangible History' (see p. 218), or by making their own collections in school, either temporarily in connection with a particular topic or by building up a school 'museum'. Collections of artefacts, replicas and children's historical costumes are also available commercially (e.g. History in Evidence, Articles of Antiquity – see p. 218). Tanner and Wood (1993) have written excellent books to support such Key Stage 1 collections, and children would also enjoy *My Class Visits a Museum* (Grifiths 1987) and *Me and Alice go to the Museum* (Rodgers 1989).

If a school decides to make its own collection of historical artefacts, it needs to decide on criteria for selecting these.

1   Core criteria:

- Is there a modern equivalent, which is different in several ways, so that children can compare the two and explain the changes?
- Does the object have a purpose the children are familiar with?
- What can children work out from it about how it was made and used, and how it affected the lives of the people who made and used it?

2   Other considerations:

- Will the collection include objects which relate to other curriculum areas (rocks, fossils, bones, books, etc.)?
- Will replicas be included?
- History in Evidence and Past Times Historical Gifts provide excellent artefacts and clothes (see Resources, p. 218).
- Will objects be collected only if they relate to themes the school has decided to study; if so, will they be categorised in sub-themes (e.g. Victorian kitchen, nursery, living room)?
- Will objects be collected because they represent key events or changes, so that children can extrapolate from the particular to the general?
- Is it important that the objects represent different social groups, the lives of children, men and women?

- Is it important that the collection includes artefacts which reflect religious beliefs?
- Should the collection reflect different cultures, through such themes as food, clothes, homes, possibly with the labels in more than one language?

3 Criteria for rejecting artefacts:

- Is it valuable?
- Is it too fragile to care for properly?
- Is it too dangerous for children to investigate?
- Is it too large to store permanently?

4 Storage and use:

- Who is responsible for organising the collection and for its use (a teacher, parent, friend of the school, children)?
- Is there a written rationale for the collection which can be given to possible donors?
- Is there a method of planning and evaluating children's learning from the collection which will assist future planning?

Excellent guidance on setting up a school museum for Key Stage 1 children is given in *School Museums and Primary History* (1994) published by the Historical Association.

Two recent DfE surveys found that both visiting museums and creating a school museum are important ways of introducing young children to history. Where children had visited a museum, the youngest pupils in Key Stage 1 described contrasts between life now and in the past. They could describe different features of the past and changes over time (DfE 1992a: 4). Where schools were building up a museum, 'even the youngest pupils were acquiring a sense of "now" and "then" and all the pupils were given the opportunity to develop ideas about the pace of change and to make deductions from historical sources' (DfE 1992a).

Many of the historical sources involved work in other curriculum areas. One class of year 1 and 2 pupils looked carefully at two reproductions of nineteenth-century paintings of the seashore to compare clothing then with what they wear on the beach now; they described the details and highlighted the differences between then and now. This involved both language and art. In another school, year 2 pupils' work with wooden artefacts was directly linked to an assessment exercise in National Curriculum science. They had examined the material and discussed guidelines for its display, writing instructions such as 'do not leave in bright sunlight' (DfE 1992b: 5).

Bowyer (1992) described how a cluster group of small schools produced two 'Time Boxes' with sixteen articles in each for under £200. Artefacts which were inexpensive to replace were purchased from museum shops, flea markets and replica shops. One box contained everyday objects and the other 'mystery' objects. The objects were not connected with each other except by the idea of 'time'. They included old keys, wooden toys, a button hook, Roman lamps, old coins, Tudor cutlery, an amphora, medicine bottles, a Viking game piece, Victorian lenses, a sundial, replica tin cars, pill boxes, an Egyptian charm, a needlecase, a flat iron and a candle-holder. Teachers met to discuss how the boxes could be used. They devised a structured programme of questions for those who wanted an introduction to using the boxes of artefacts with a whole class, a group or with individual children. These questions included:

- Can you draw the object? Put measurements on your sketch.
- What is it made of? Why was it made?
- What does it feel like?
- What do you think it was used for?
- What kind of person might have used it?
- Is it decorated? How?
- Which object do you think is oldest? Why?
- What else would you like to know about it? How could you find out more?

The boxes also contained a rope and pegs for making a sequence line, and lenses and magnifying glasses for close observation.

Mathieson (Batho 1994: 15–21) describes in another case study how she collected boxes of artefacts for a cluster group of first schools, and suggests good ways of introducing them to children: pretending she found an object while spring-cleaning her grandma's house, or wrapping up an object in a treasure chest, so that children first guess what it might be. She found the treasure chest worked particularly well with a mixed age range, as older children shared expertise and younger children's concentration span was extended. Mathieson is also developing a local history box for the cluster group, on such general themes as 'Local People', 'Farming', 'Transport' and 'Industry', to which individual schools add examples from their immediate locality. She then plans to add slides and videos to the boxes. This project was funded by the local education authority

Eno (1993) has pointed out how perceptions of an artefact are influenced by cultural background: Muslim children do not have photographs or statues at home, but the Sikhs do have models of their gods. What might be obviously an old Roman lamp to some people is like an oil lamp others may see at festivals today. Whereas a Morris Oxford car may seem old-fashioned to us, it is the height of modernity in some Indian cities. When she showed a replica of an English Civil War period flat metal plate to year 2 children, two Sikh boys and three Muslim girls, she was conscious that it was similar to the sort of tableware most of the children used at home. They therefore impressed her by saying it was 'something very old'; it would be interesting to know the reasons they gave, particularly since one of the boys then peered at a replica Stuart coin, trying to decide what football team it represented!

Nulty (1998) used artefacts related to a study unit on 'Famous People' (Cleopatra, Mohammed, Sitting Bull, Mary Seacole, Pocahontas and Elizabeth I), to stimulate problem-solving and debate with year 1 and year 2 children. The artefacts included replica Native American jewellery, Ancient Egyptian jewellery, Arab clothes, a steel drum and pan pipes. She shows how the children first asked questions then went on to hypothesise, conclude and support their conclusions. They used problem-solving language: maybe, perhaps, if . . . then, because, could be. They used complex vocabulary to describe colour and shape, and they responded to each other's opinions. Nulty tape-recorded these group discussions and analysed them to assess the children's speaking and listening skills using English National Curriculum descriptors.

As with play, there is increasing recognition of the importance of the role of the teacher in intervening to support and extend the process of making appropriate historical deductions and inferences about sources, which build on and extend children's prior knowledge. Wood and Holden (1997) describe how 5-year-olds investigating an enamel kettle did not know what had caused the brown stains on the lid. The teacher told them it was rust. From this they worked out in stages: 'My bike gets rusty in the rain because it's metal and metal gets wet.' When the teacher said that it is usually metal that is iron that rusts, they deduced that the lid had 'got rusty where the water gets out when it's hot' and so 'the kettle is iron'.

Drawing artefacts

Observational drawing of details, or of entire objects, in a museum or in school, encourages children to look closely, over a prolonged period. The act of drawing involves selecting the significant features and forming a personal perception of the object. In this way, a relationship with the object is created, based on internal and external ordering of experience. An image of the object is internalised and remembered. Their drawings are concerned with what they know, with what interests them and with spatial relationships rather than with perspective, but even very young children are beginning to formulate a language which is concerned with representation.

Remembering the image makes it easier to remember the discussion, the deductions and inferences made about the object, to transfer them to similar examples seen later, and to extrapolate from the particular to the general. Bruner (1966) said that this prevents a 'mental overload' of facts. Drawing historical artefacts also focuses attention on basic materials (wood, stone, metals, clay), which have been central to all civilisations throughout human history. It raises awareness of the similar and the different ways in which they have been used. Careful observation encourages children to describe objects accurately and to ask questions about them.

Strategies for questioning

Smith and Holden (1994) described a range of strategies they used to encourage children from Reception to year 3 to ask questions about objects:

- *Open-ended questions*: in small groups children handled all the artefacts, then selected one to draw. They then found out more from reference books and used the artefacts in role-play.
- *Focused questions*: children sat in small groups with one artefact per group. With no guidance from the teacher, they wrote key questions about their artefact. The groups then shared their questions and the teacher gave them further information for extending their enquiry.
- *Focused research*: children in pairs selected an object related to their history topic. They discussed its origin, use and evidence of authenticity, then planned further research.
- *Artefacts circus*: groups sat around their tables with one artefact per table. Each group wrote one question about the artefact, then moved to the next table. There it tried to answer the previous group's question and added another question. The session ended with a class discussion led by the teacher.

Here are some examples of children's deductions (information acquired from an historical source):

- *Kettle*
  This is a kettle that a Victorian would use. I noticed there was a white handle. It has a black holder and the holder is a funny shape and very bendy . . .
- *Stone hot water bottle*
  It wouldn't be very comfy. It would hurt your feet. I wouldn't like that one because it's too fat and too big. I like my own.

By year 2, children were following their deductions with further inferences about what the artefact meant to the people who used it (using historical sources to answer questions about the past):

C   They had to use horses for pulling carts. They didn't have cars in those days so they didn't go very fast.

M The milk churn was used to carry milk in. When it was empty the milk collector came to collect it to put more milk in.

Also they were considering a range of possible inferences:

D It's for storing things . . .?
K No. For carrying things . . .?
W It's to put wine in . . .
N A drinker what you drink out of?

The following example shows a sequence of work with a vertically grouped year 1/2 class. The aims were:

- to introduce the children to the idea of objects and their value as learning materials;
- to encourage children to look, and develop good concentration and observational skills;
- to introduce the notion of touching and handling objects.

In *Stage 1*, children felt and described everyday objects in a 'feely bag' then took them out to see how accurate their descriptions had been. In *Stage 2*, they compared an everyday object, a modern iron, with an iron from 'beyond living memory', a Victorian iron.

With only gentle encouragement and key questions, the discussion that followed centred around how the modern iron made steam and how it worked. The children examined and handled the iron with great interest and curiosity, pressing buttons and switches and at one point pulling it apart. Next they passed around the heavy Victorian iron and the children immediately referred to it as an 'iron from the olden days' and, without prompting, went on to state that it was probably used by a 'Victorian maid'. This was quite astounding when one considers that the children had previously done very little in the way of history topics.

They were fascinated by the iron's weight and colour, and by the words that were printed on the warmer plate. Again, they were eager to touch and feel.

The children posed questions such as 'How old is it?' and 'Where did it come from?' They were encouraged to try and answer their own questions by looking for 'clues'. They did this with enthusiasm and interest, and began to formulate opinions and to try to answer the questions they had posed. They went on to compare an old telephone and a modern one. Then they sketched the objects. They became quite enthralled at having to focus on details. A feature of all the sketches produced from these sessions was that the children drew what they could see, what they observed, rather than what they thought a telephone or an iron should look like.

Stage 3 involved work at the Museum of London with five selected Victorian artefacts. The aims were:

- to apply the handling and observational skills already practised in earlier classroom sessions;
- to look at and examine authentic historical artefacts from beyond living memory;
- for children to begin to formulate their own worksheets in order to complement and record their observations.

The adult working with each group recorded the observations on the museum handling sheet to allow the children to concentrate on using observation skills fully. Using the adult helpers in this way enabled the children to engage in free discussion and uninterrupted exploration of the object in front of them. Then the Museum Education Officer asked the children to record their findings by making a detailed sketch of the object they had focused on, drawing it as they saw it, not as they thought it should look.

The children were more than able to 'sketch as they saw' and to include the finest details. This was a marked improvement from when the work programme began and B, who regularly informs people 'I cannot draw', produced a remarkably detailed and accurate artistic impression of the metal toasting implement his group was focusing on.

It was noticeable that the children's observation and enquiry-based skills had progressed and developed over the previous few weeks. So, too, had their overall ability to concentrate and focus on the learning. Their teacher pinpointed this as a direct cause of advances in learning in other curriculum areas.

It was also significant that when the children came back together to share their views and sketches at the close of the session, they were able to sit without stirring for at least 30 minutes, listening and contributing to the ongoing discussion. This applied to all children, but again, children such as A and J, who usually had difficulty concentrating and listening, were controlled and enthusiastic throughout the session. Work in the classroom and at the museum has shown that looking at objects, and an enquiry-based and tactile approach to history, enabled all the children, including those exhibiting special learning or behavioural needs, to benefit, and, more importantly, to feel that they *were* achieving.

In *Stage 4*, five selected objects from a loan collection of Medieval artefacts were used in school. The aims were:

- to focus observational and recording skills on artefacts from a particular historical period (Medieval) and to apply knowledge already gained from topic work on 'Castles';

- for children to use their own formulated worksheets to record their observations of the artefacts used.

In preparation for this session, the children were asked to think about the sorts of question they might like to ask when examining and handling 'old' objects and artefacts. This was the first stage in getting the children to prepare their own evaluative worksheet, to be used at museums and other historical sites. The Museum of London sheet was not re-shown or discussed by the children; thus the outcome is even more remarkable as they produced a list of investigative questions which were very well structured and, from an historical point of view, extremely relevant. The children were then asked to categorise these questions into five sections, to give them some sort of logical sequence: questions such as 'What does it feel like?' or 'What is it made of?' preceded 'What is it worth?', thereby building up a descriptive picture of the object before having to formulate judgements about the object's age or worth. In this way, answers to the earlier questions could inform the later questions.

The children examined the objects assigned to their group and attempted to answer the questions from their observations. All groups had one child who acted as scribe and some groups actually shared the 'scribe' task. It was very obvious that the children were working more comfortably when answering questions they had devised than when they were using the museum worksheets, even though the objects were by far the oldest that they had examined so far and were unfamiliar. The class teacher and the museum teacher agreed that this definitely had a connection with the fact that they were working to a recording format that had come from them and was, therefore, wholly familiar and relevant.

The children were again encouraged to spend much time drawing their objects and it is significant that they were now so skilled at observing and looking closely that they sat for longer and produced some of the most detailed sketches of the whole work programme.

The final period of the session was taken up with a class discussion and by sharing answers to the sheet questions. The teachers were acting only as facilitators. It was the children who instigated, led and participated in the discussion and some of the informed guesses as to what the Medieval objects were used for, and by whom, were quite accurate.

The children had progressed from having little or no knowledge of history and, in some cases, poor concentration and observational skills to producing highly detailed sketches and a sequenced and categorised, evaluative, historical worksheet, through their work with historical artefacts.

The class teacher observed improvements, during the 6-week programme, in children's concentration and confidence, both in work related to the topic and in other areas of the curriculum.

Follow-up activities could include finding out from museum staff how they catalogue, label and care for their collection, and how they interest the public in it, in order to create a school museum or temporary class collection.

Another case study by Matthews and Shaw (Batho 1994: 22–5) describes how cross-curricular work with a year 2 class evolved from a class museum, set up as an economic awareness project; they considered problems of access, who should pay and what the money should be spent on. There were opportunities for speaking and listening, using reference material and information retrieval as children took turns as curators and guides, and for writing, keeping a visitors' book, sending invitations and making descriptive labels. In science, they considered different sources of light and heat, candles, oil, gas and electricity, then observed, predicted and set up experiments. A visit from a brewery dray led children to making their own carts, and studying 'forces'. In technology, children designed and made Victorian toys, spinners, tops, peg dolls and dolls' houses.

An alternative way of structuring work with objects might be:

Stage 1 Looking at, feeling, using and talking about one familiar object.
Stage 2 Looking at and talking about two familiar objects widely separated by time, comparing and sequencing them.
Stage 3 Looking at two objects closer together in time, comparing and sequencing them.
Stage 4 Looking at three or more objects from different times. The closer they are in time to each other, the harder it is to contrast them. But the more familiar they are to the children, the easier it is. (This is a helpful contradiction.)
Stage 5 Using other sources, e.g. old photos, old books, living memory, to date artefacts.

There are several points to remember about this scheme:

- These stages may overlap; for example, a child in year 2 working on Stage 1 may well wish to use the library to research an object.
- What is familiar to the teacher may not be so to the child and vice versa. Artefacts are an excellent way of ensuring that our classrooms reflect ethnic diversity.
- Support with questioning will enhance children's understanding.
- This diagram of progression is one-dimensional. Other aspects of progress will relate to the complexity of children's deductions, their ability to synthesise, the depth and breadth of their background historical knowledge, their experience of handling artefacts.

The third set of examples of work with artefacts comes from a school where the topic for year 1 and 2 classes was 'Our Houses'. This involved art: prints and rubbings from bricks, stone and wood, and pottery slab models of house fronts with lift-up flaps to find who lived in each house. There was science (testing the strength of model houses made with plastic bricks of different thicknesses, by blowing with straws) and mathematics (pictograms showing how many people lived in each house or flat). The teachers would not have added a history dimension had it not been required by the National Curriculum. However, they made a small collection of old domestic artefacts and were delighted by the children's responses. Some children wrote labels for a display. In some cases, the labels simply communicated information.

Bahadir The carpet beater is for beating the carpet.
Grant In olden days there was some old things.
Nikki I drew a hot water bottle and it had patterns on it.
Katy This is an old iron.
Ayra In the olden days they used a washboard.

Other labels explained what the artefacts tell us about the past.

Tainoo In the olden days there was no washing machines, so they had to use something like plungers.
Hasna In the olden days they had no rubber, so they had to use hard hot water bottles.
Deepa In the old days they had no washing machines so they had scrubbing boards. They had no electricity, so they put the cloth on the scrubbing board. The washing board was hard. It is made from wood and glass.
Sarah In the old days they did not have hoovers, so they had carpet beaters. They took the carpet up and put the carpet on the washing line and bashed the carpet and all the dirt came off.

Written sources

Frank Smith (1989) has made it clear that writing should not involve repressive discipline, deadening instruction or blind drilling, lest:

> Under a cruel eye outworn
> The little ones spend all the day
> In sighing and dismay
> (from 'The School Boy' by William Blake 1757–1827)

Fortunately, written historical sources can provide opportunities for fun! Suitable sources which communicate information and raise questions about the past include:

- a child's own documentary evidence – baby book, clinic book, birthday cards, birth and marriage certificates (although this can be a sensitive area);
- the school log book, recording why children were absent, what they were punished for in the past;
- local street names, referring to famous people (Chaucer Road) or events (Trafalgar Road), to places which have disappeared (Station Road, Market Road) or to connections which no longer exist (Jamaica Road, Canary Wharf);
- children's own names, associated with places or occupations (Smith, Patel);
- advertisements on old walls or stone lettering listing departments in now defunct stores;
- writing on street furniture – pillar boxes, coal holes, lighting;
- inscriptions on memorials, statues, brasses, plaques, gravestones;
- old newspapers, stamps, coins, letters, postcards, recipes;
- inn signs (Rotheroe 1990).

Children can also consider the nature of language as a symbolic communication system which is central to all societies. Donaldson (1978) said that if children understand the abstraction of language as an objective tool, they are helped to make inferences from an early age. Children can learn about the nature and importance of written language as a symbolic code through looking at a variety of scripts: an Arabic text from the Koran, a Medieval illuminated manuscript of the Bible, an agrarian calendar, a Roman tombstone or Egyptian hieroglyphics.

They can discuss what the meaning of the writing may be, the sorts of things that people needed to write down, and why. In the following extract, children were discussing Stone Age petraglyphics (found in *How Writing Began*, Macdonald Educational Starters Long Ago Books).

B   They could communicate. [This was a 'hard word' the children had been introduced to as a key concept in the topic.]
S   And they could talk to each other, because they could draw pictures.
N   They had signs as well, to communicate.
B   To tell each other things and to help each other.
S   They would have helped each other . . . not one person done it all.
W   They shared ideas. They left messages.
N   An 'animal' and a 'man' might have been 'going hunting'.
S   This looks like an arrow.
W   It could be a help sign . . .
B   They could use symbols. [This was another selected, taught, concept.]
S   I think the old Stone Age did very well at cave painting, but the new Stone Age thought it took too long to do a message quickly.

Even if children cannot understand examples of earlier styles of writing in English, because of difficult script and their limited reading ability, they can search for some letters which they recognise, and understand that forms change over time. Listening to brief extracts, to unfamiliar vocabulary and syntax, can help them to understand that language itself changes.

Children can also listen to extracts about childhood from contemporary diaries. *Lark Rise to Candleford* (Thompson 1989: 87, 121) describes school, play games and songs, and festivals in the 1880s. Laurie Lee (1989: 35, 53) describes his childhood in the 1920s, in the village school, in the kitchen, at outings and festivals, in summer and winter. Children will probably most enjoy Helen Bradley's illustrated account of her childhood at the beginning of this century. In *Miss Carter Came with Us*, for example, she shows preparations for Christmas, and a visit to the seaside, which they could compare with their own experiences (Bradley 1974: 22–3, 30).

Adams (1998) used newspaper accounts of the landing of Neil Armstrong on the moon on July 20th 1969 with her year 2 class as part of a topic on 'The 1960s', to explore newspapers both as non-fiction genre and as an historical source. They discussed layout, report-writing, bias, fact and fiction. They also created their own vivid front-page account and compared it with current newspaper stories about space.

Music

It is true that the appreciation of music is, of its own kind, a musical experience . . . but over and above that . . . there is always the allusion to its own time and period, of which it is the most intimate and secret revelation possible.

(Rowse 1946: 124)

Musical sources include old sheet music, records and record players, songs, instruments, and music-making depicted in old paintings. From musical sources, it is possible to find out about:

- work in the past – the tasks and rhythms of spinning, weaving, sailing and harvesting which were accompanied by work songs;
- events – described in ballads and folk music, and in military music;
- celebrations of beliefs and religious festivals;
- leisure – in folk songs and dances from a variety of cultures, and in more recent, popular, music;
- music typical of different periods (e.g. Medieval, Elizabethan).

A musical dimension can be included in any history topic. Children can listen and participate in song and dance, in a Medieval joust, an Elizabethan ball, in sea-shanties or Victorian songs around the piano.

Grandparents enjoy teaching old playground games. Parents enjoy contributing their old popular records. Bilingual children and parents welcome the opportunity to teach songs in other languages and traditional dances from other places.

Part III

Organisation, planning and assessment

CONTINUITY AND COHERENCE, 3–8

Curriculum Guidance for the Foundation Stage (DfEE/QCA 2000a) sets out clear principles and aims for the education of 3- to 5-year-olds, structured around six areas of learning: personal, social and emotional development; communication, language and literacy; mathematical development; physical development; creative development; and knowledge and understanding of the world. Clear learning goals are identified within each area, with 'stepping stones' and guidance showing how they can be achieved. A specific goal relates to history: 'find out about past and present events in their own lives and in those of their families and of other people they know' and most children are expected to demonstrate 'a sense of time' by the end of the Foundation Stage (Ofsted 2000). Further guidance provided by the QCA shows how history can be made relevant to young children through story, simple sequencing activities and appropriate sources from the past such as artefacts and family photographs, and by investigating similarities and differences, finding out about their locality and exploring cultures and beliefs (DfEE/QCA 1998a). There are key links here with the Breadth of Study content for history at Key Stage 1, learning about changes in their lives and the lives of family and friends, and of people in more distant times and places, both in Britain and the wider world. There are links too with the skills children learn to apply to this content: placing events and objects in order; using time vocabulary; understanding how the past was different; why people did things; why the past may be represented in different ways; finding out about the past from sources by asking questions.

Continuity from the Foundation Stage to the Key Stage 1 curriculum is also clear in the common principles, values, aims and purposes which underpin them: working in collaboration with families and the local community; the promotion of spiritual, moral, social and cultural development, of literacy and numeracy across the curriculum, and of equal opportunity (DfEE/QCA 1999a: 10–23; DfEE/QCA 2000a: 11–30). Personal and social education at Key Stage 1 can be developed through history by discussion and sharing opinions, discussing reasons for choices, finding out about families and communities (DfEE/QCA 2000b: 7).

There is also a continuity in the key skills which underpin the Foundation Stage Guidance and Key Stage 1 curriculum which can be developed through learning about the past: opportunities to develop communication skills through responding to historical sources, to learn to work with others and to investigate questions. There are opportunities to develop a range of thinking skills: sorting, classifying, sequencing; explaining and drawing inferences, forming opinions, suggesting hypotheses, evaluating information (DfEE/QCA 2000b: 11).

Boxes 7.1, 7.2 and 7.3 show how key skills, core values and community links, which underpin both the Foundation Stage Guidance and the Key Stage 1 curriculum, can be developed through history activities described in Part I and Part II.

However, there are difficulties in planning for coherence and continuity from the Foundation Stage to Key Stage 1 in developing children's interest in the past and in finding out what it is to be human, now and in previous times. This may be because of the tension created by planning based on areas of learning at the Foundation Stage and planning for a subject-based curriculum at Key Stage 1. It is partly because the emphasis on assessing basic skills in literacy and numeracy, both baseline testing at five years old and Standard Assessment Tests at seven years old can marginalise rather than exploit the history dimension. It is also because children experience Foundation Stage education in a variety of settings: playgroups, Nursery schools, Nursery classes. Many do not begin their education until they enter Reception classes, possibly with many basic social and communication skills still to learn.

Chapter 7 considers how these tensions may be addressed in long-term planning. Chapter 8 considers how units of study can be developed from long-term plans.

Long-term planning

The aim of the revised National Curriculum is to provide a framework around which teachers can use their professional judgement to construct a coherent and meaningful curriculum to suit the needs of their children, in their locality, in a creative and flexible way. This involves making judgements about breadth and depth and how to manage time most effectively. There is, however, a danger that history, which many teachers have begun to see as appropriate to early years education, will be marginalised if overlap with other curriculum areas is not exploited.

The first important area to consider is the relationship between the Foundation Stage and the first two years at school. It was argued in Part I that, from their earliest years, children are capable of embryonic historical thinking and are aware of the past in their environment and experiences. Part II considered how these experiences can be developed at Key Stage 1. *History for Ages 5–16* (the Rumbold Report) (DES 1990) stressed the importance of the progression showing that 'areas of experience recommended for children under 5' (DES 1989d) could be developed through stories and such activities as using the local environment and visits to places of interest as a stimulus for role-play. Suggestions for such activities based on *Curriculum Guidance for the Foundation Stage* (DfEE/QCA 2000a) are given in Part I. The constructivist High Scope curriculum (Holmann *et al.* 1979) is organised around similar key experiences.

It is important that, in spite of the differences in structure between the Foundation Stage guidance and the National Curriculum, the overlap in history context and skills is recognised in planning and assessment in order to avoid repetition and ensure progression. If the Nursery class is in the same school as the Reception class and years 1 and 2, this should not be problematical. Otherwise it is important to establish links with Nursery schools and playgroups. Case studies showing how Key Stage 1 teachers liaised with Foundation Stage practitioners in a variety of settings in order to plan together for continuity and transition in history and in other areas are given in Cooper and Sixsmith (2002).

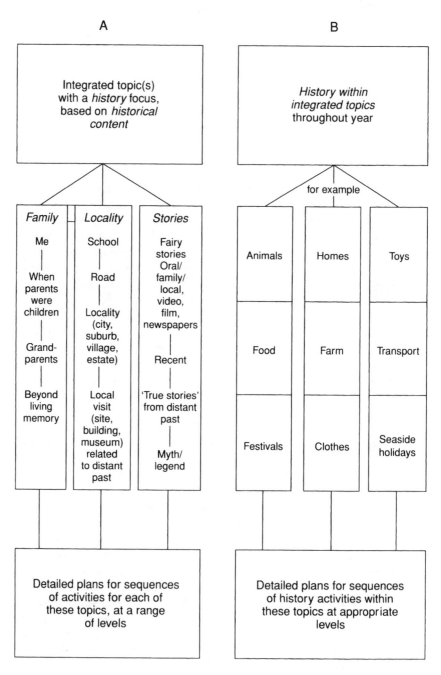

Figure 7.1 Outline of approaches to planning examined in Part III

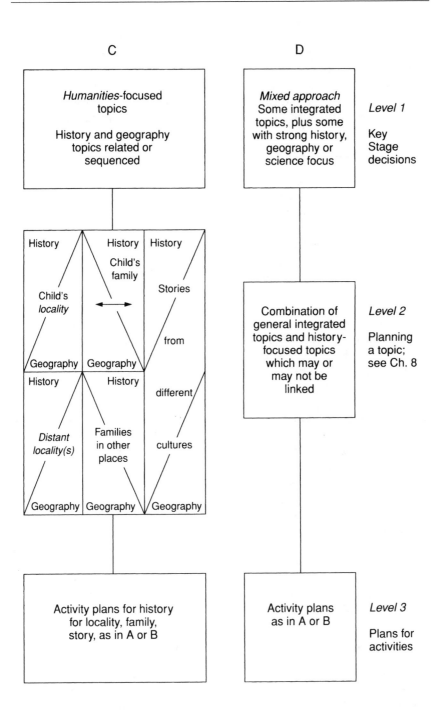

Long-term planning is undertaken in the context of the overall curriculum plan for the school. It should involve all the staff liaising where possible with colleagues working in other pre-school settings. They need to agree how to devise units of work which reflect the Programmes of Study for History and the Foundation Stage guidance, and to sequence the units of work to promote curriculum continuity and progress children's learning. They also need to agree on links with other curriculum areas.

HISTORY-FOCUSED TOPICS

- will history be taught through some topics during the year which have a strong history focus;
- or through a clearly defined historical dimension within topics such as clothes, food or toys;
- or through humanities-focused topics in which history and geography are either combined or sequenced;
- or through a mixed approach of integrated and subject-focused topics? (See Figure 7.1.)

Over each year one term, or two half-terms, could be spent on topics based on historical content, for example family history, Victorians, castles. Mathematics, English, science and technology, and music could then be related to the period studied. This approach enables teachers and children to become immersed in a period in the past, to investigate it in greater depth, ask questions and pursue investigations over a long period, to become familiar with the thinking processes which are at the centre of the discipline and to achieve a coherent understanding of another period. This would be a good introduction to a more detailed study of the period at Key Stage 2.

Mathematics and English are systems of investigation and communication which need to be used and applied in a variety of meaningful contexts, and therefore should continuously permeate all areas of the curriculum. It could also be argued that history is an umbrella discipline which involves all aspects of past societies, and therefore includes art, music and religious education. There is, therefore, a strong case for a curriculum based on a series of integrated topics, led by history, geography or science, in sequence. However, a disadvantage could be that young children may forget what they have achieved in historical thinking if it is not continuously reinforced.

HISTORY WITHIN INTEGRATED TOPICS

Traditionally Key Stage 1 topics have not been subject led; they have been based on such themes as 'Animals', 'Homes' or 'Toys'. If such a topic is planned so that it has a clear historical dimension, both in content and in

Box 7.1 Key skills which underpin the Foundation Stage Guidance and the Key Stage 1 National Curriculum, and can be developed through history activities

Key skills	Foundation Stage Activities (DfEE/QCA 2000a)	Key Stage 1 activities (DfEE/QCA 1999a)
1 (i) Communication skills; working with others	Role-play, stories, speaking and listening, experimental writing for different purposes	Play, oral history, stories, discussion, reading and writing for different purposes
(ii) Application of numeracy skills	Counting, ordering, calculating, similarities/ differences, sets, patterns, space, shape, measures, including time	Sequencing (in own lives, stories, photos, artefacts), time-line calculations, sets, similarities/ differences
(iii) Thinking skills	Problem-solving, information-processing, reasoning, enquiry, creative thinking, enquiry skills, exploration, observe objects/materials, predict, use critical thinking, awareness of differences	Deductions and inferences from sources, investigate materials/artefacts, photos

Box 7.2 Core values which underpin the Foundation Stage Guidance and the Key Stage 1 National Curriculum, and can be developed through history activities

Core values	Foundation Stage	Key Stage 1
2 (i) Physical development	Recognise importance of keeping healthy, how to do this; physical skills	Changes in diet/work/ play; imaginative play; models and constructions, using large and fine motor skills
(ii) Spiritual, moral, social and cultural education	Respect for beliefs, cultural backgrounds of others; valuing children as individuals, their ideas; art, design, dance, play, stories	Value children's ideas; biographies; stories and pictures from different cultures, understanding that interpretations may vary; cross-curricular links
(iii) Equal opportunities	Inclusion: ethnicity, special educational needs; challenging thinking about gender	(See pp. 168–71) Challenging stereotypical images; stories of influential women, women as story-tellers

Box 7.3 Links with parents and community which underpin the Foundation Stage Guidance and the Key Stage 1 National Curriculum, and can be developed through history activities

Community links	Foundation Stage	Key Stage 1
3 (i) Partnership with parents	Parents as partners; oral and family history	Oral history; parents on school visits, in school
(ii) Links with community	Equipment, displays, materials which reflect child's community/ locality/environment	Concepts related to communities, local history (p. 60)

thinking, children can see that the past is an important dimension of any theme. If the history aspect is linked to a clear chronological framework through a time-line, children can begin to build up a map of the past over a long period of time. *Teaching History at Key Stage 1* (NCC 1993: 11) suggests how history can be taught through such topics as 'Me', 'Games and celebrations', 'Places', 'People', 'Food and clothing', 'Travel and exploration'. However, 'topics' have been criticised in the past because activities have been included in a random way because they are linked to the topic by content. The thinking processes of each discipline and progression within them have not been recognised as the basis for selecting and planning activities.

HUMANITIES-FOCUSED TOPICS

There is a great deal of overlap between history and geography. Both investigate the same kinds of sources (pictures, film, artefacts, music, stories, oral and written sources) to find out how people live, their work, leisure, beliefs, homes, food and clothes. They are based on the same organising concepts which run through societies: agriculture, manufacture, trade, communication, social structure and belief systems.

There are also differences between history and geography. History focuses on interpreting the causes and effects of changes over time. Geography is more concerned with the interactions between people and their natural and man-made environment, with the influences of land-forms and climate on settlement and daily life.

However, there may be good reasons for planning topics in which the geographical and historical dimensions are either parallel or sequenced. Since societies in different places and times are based on the same organising concepts, children develop a framework for making connections, for recognising similarities and differences. The links between history and geography may be made in a number of ways.

Children might use maps, pictures and sources to find out about their locality today: its churches, houses, workplaces, transport. Next they could find out how they have changed and why. Then they could use the same categories to compare and contrast how people live in a more distant locality, in Britain, Europe or in a developing country.

- A topic on family history may lead to finding out about places where parents or grandparents were born or other family members live.
- A study of a local shop could lead to finding out more about where some of the goods came from, how they were grown there and why.
- A study of the school could lead to a comparison with a school elsewhere in the world.
- A topic on 'Me' could focus on children's personal history over five or six years, then go on to find out about children in another place.
- A visit to a workplace (a farm or post office, for example) could lead children to trace its links with other places, then to find out how it has changed and why.
- A topic on stories could trace similarities and differences between themes of folk tales from different countries: heroes, cunning, power, jealousy; stories about weather, animals, food, journeys, markets.

Bruner (1963: 10) believed that studying early societies is the best way to learn about the nature of society, the human condition and the continuity of evolution.

A MIXED APPROACH

A combination of subject-focused topics, with perhaps one half-term each year spent on a science-, a geography- and a history-focused topic, and three half-terms spent on 'themes' would allow the two approaches to curriculum planning to be evaluated. Whether history-focused topics or more general themes are planned, it is important to recognise the potential links between history and other areas of the curriculum.

The Schools Curriculum and Assessment Authority's *Planning the Curriculum at Key Stage 1 and 2* (SCAA 1997) suggests ways in which units of history-focused work can be blocked at intervals to link to continuing work in the core subjects, and also how they can be linked to other areas of the curriculum.

English

However history is taught, it provides an excellent and natural context for language development. Indeed, the National Curriculum for English at Key Stage 1 (DfEE/QCA 1999a), *Curriculum Guidance for the Foundation Stage*

(DfEE/QCA 2000a), and the *History Teacher's Guide* (DfEE/QCA 1998a: 16–17) state that children should be given opportunities for telling stories, both real and imagined, for imaginative play and drama, and for listening to nursery rhymes. They need to explore, develop and clarify their ideas, to predict outcomes and discuss possibilities, to describe events, observations and experiences, to give reasons for opinions and actions, to show an understanding of what they see and hear, to participate in drama and improved activities, using appropriate language in a role situation and also to respond to drama that they have watched. Through stories, artefacts, pictures, oral history and visits to old buildings, explored through play and discussion, history fulfils all these requirements.

These opportunities are developed in more detail in *The National Literacy Strategy* (DfEE/QCA1998b) and can be initiated within the Literacy Hour. Indeed, teaching the literacy objectives in the context of other subjects and extending the topics beyond the Literacy Hour is desirable. There are opportunities for traditional chants, rhymes and stories in the Reception year, and in years 1 and 2 for signs, labels, captions, lists, instructions, information books and non-chronological reports, accounts of observations, visits and events. Precise examples of how such links can be developed are given in Cooper 2000b: 98–119; 1997; 1998a; 1998b; Cooper and Twisleton 1998; 1999.

Mathematics

Historical enquiries may involve number calculations and data presentation. Objects can be sorted into sets according to age, materials and/or function, and recorded in Carroll and Venn diagrams. Questionnaires and surveys can be recorded in pictograms and bar charts. Calculations can be based on time-lines. Investigations may involve observing and recording tessellations and repeating patterns in windows, roof-tiles, bricks and ceilings, and decoration on artefacts or fabrics. Observing shapes in buildings, and making models, can involve the vocabulary of two- and three-dimensional shapes. Maps and plans involve direction, shape and space. There are many opportunities for measurement – of time (hours, days, months, birthdays, seasons, years), of length (the length or thickness of a castle wall), of weight (of artefacts or ingredients in recipes) – and for using money and barter (in role-play). Suggestions for links between history and numeracy are given in Cooper 2000b: 121–6.

Science and technology

History is concerned with the ways people in the past obtained and used materials: leather, wool, silk, cotton, stone, clay, wood, thatch, gold, lead, iron. It is concerned with how people grew, harvested, stored, preserved and prepared their food; how they obtained water and light and heat. Changes in tools, technology and energy sources are key causes of wider changes in society. There are many opportunities for children to investigate how people in past times kept warm, dry and fed, the jobs this involved, the tools they used, and why these changed. Stories and rhymes introduce children to cobblers, smiths, weavers, spinners, woodcutters, farmers, millers and dairymaids, markets and journeys. Through examining arte-facts, they learn about materials and about how things work. By visiting, observing and making models of old buildings, they find out about struc-tures (How tall can you build the tower? How wide can you make the arch? Can you make a timber-frame house with strips of wood or rolled paper or straws?). They can learn about energy through pictures and stories, about sailing ships, windmills, balloons, watermills, coal fires, steam trains, clockwork toys, carriages, early cars and planes. They can discuss how these worked and how they affected people's lives. Children can experi-ment, heating clay to make pots, making natural dyes, spinning and weaving, making models with natural materials (stone, wood, thatch).

Art

History provides a context for children to look closely at artefacts and paintings, to learn that they express the ideas, feelings and ways of life of the people who made them. By recording their observations of artefacts in their own drawings and paintings (possibly extended into collages, sewing and printing), they notice their shape and texture. Through making models of buildings (a castle or a Victorian dolls' house), or drawings of events in the past, children are developing their historical imagination and making their own interpretations, based on what they know.

Music

A painting, story or visit can be used as a stimulus for simple compositions. Children could make up music to accompany a story or they could investigate, select and combine sounds which describe a visit to a windmill, a steam railway or sailing ship. They could try to recreate the sounds which might be heard in a picture, for example of a Victorian street scene or rail-way station, a picture of harvest, or of a market or fair.

Children can sing together songs from other times: nursery rhymes, playground games, folk and popular songs. They could match traditional songs with folk tales from other countries. They can listen to old instru-ments and to music from other times; Medieval music, for example, can accompany 'let's pretend' play in a castle, or sea shanties can be linked with adventures on sailing ships.

Information and communication technology

At Key Stage 1, children are expected to access, enter and retrieve information from a variety of sources: databases, CD-ROMs, audio and video recordings, film and television. They should use these sources to develop their ideas, explore situations and exchange, share and review their findings (DfEE/QCA 1999a: 98–9). This provides many opportunities for developing the three strands of historical enquiry described in Part I and Part II.

Audiotape, for example, can be used on site visits to collect data for writing non-chronological reports, for recording instructions about how something in a class museum works, or explanations of how something was made and used. Parsons (1996) suggests that oral interviews are best recorded in advance, in order to keep the interviewee on track and avoid irrelevant or embarrassing questions. This also gives the opportunity to discuss validity and bias, before inviting the person to visit. Alternatively, children can visit the person in their own home or workplace, and can edit the tape themselves. Videotape may be even better. A collection of such interviews and site visit records, or a record of changes in a local area, can be built up for the school museum. Similarly, digital cameras can be used on visits and the photographs used for discussion in school, with captions added and printed as part of pupils' individual projects, or they can be produced as electronic books. Photographs can be scanned into pupil and family time-lines. With the use of a microphone, written or spoken words can be added which children can activate with a mouse.

Databases can be constructed in a wide variety of contexts. Smart (1999) describes how a database about toys allowed children to consider concepts of similarity and difference, continuity and change over three generations. It could equally well have been about food or games or street furniture. Data can be presented using a data-handling program such as *Find It*. *Front Page Extra* can be used by more able children to record and communicate findings in newspaper format.

For able year 2/3 children, *My World* provides software with historical themes. This consists of screens of pictures and captions which can be moved around, using a mouse, to construct pictures and match captions.

Wood and Holden (1995) write enthusiastically about talking programs such as Pendown and Stylus which teachers can use to create information and enable children to ask questions about the topic they are working on. More recent programs, *Textease and Talking Write Away*, enable children to write text which can be spoken back to the writer or other children. They also suggest the use of concept keyboards to help children to construct sentences using time vocabulary or, when they have limited reading skills, to sequence with information from their own family or locality.

Schools now have personal computers with concept keyboard facilities and most writing software for children has a screen wordbank or wordlists which can be created by the teacher or the children for use with specific writing. Many 'clickergrids' have a history focus (e.g. www.cricksoft.com/cgfl/index.htm).

Clip-Art can be used to provide pictures for comparison of old and new, although this needs to be supported by authentic or replica artefacts to become meaningful. In the case study on Toys and Games in Chapter 9, Nursery class children used Clip-Art teddy bears to decorate captions and questionnaires in their 'Teddy Bear Museum'.

Many schools now have their own internet websites, through which they can collect and share data with other schools, including schools in other countries and continents. They can also make community links since the internet is available to parents at home and to anyone else who can log on. Recently, year 1 at Ambleside CE Primary School asked parents questions about favourite toys and made graphs of the data they received, using the internet. And, of course, there are excellent television programmes. Hughes *et al.* (2000: 69–73) give useful suggestions about how to use television effectively.

Teachers also have internet access to national history education organisations and to an infinite variety of sources in museums and galleries, some of which are listed at the end of this book. Many programs use scanners which allow teachers to feed information into the computer (maps, documents, pictures or the children's own drawings) to create screens which operate like pages in a book and allow children to access information. However, care needs to be taken with copyright issues.

SELECTION OF CONTENT FOR HISTORY, FOUNDATION STAGE TO KEY STAGE 1

Curriculum Guidance for the Foundation Stage (DfEE/QCA 2000a) and the History guidance in *The National Curriculum for England and Wales* (DfEE/QCA 1999a) require that children should find out about the past through stories from different periods and cultures, and through a range of historical sources. They should find out about changes in life, work and leisure within their own lives and the lives of their families and other familiar adults, and in the lives of people beyond living memory. This should include learning about men and women with different backgrounds and about different types of memorable events, in Britain and in other countries.

Clearly, it is important that these areas of knowledge are structured and integrated in a meaningful way. Yet there is no evidence for a clear pattern of progression in structuring content. It may seem logical to start with a child's own history then go on to when grandparents were children, and then to a period beyond living memory. But there is no evidence that this is the best way to develop children's concept of time or of chronology; young children love stories about distant times and stories which begin 'Long, long ago . . .'. It may also seem logical to begin with a child's immediate environment, home or school, then to move outwards to the locality, the street or village, then beyond to distant places, through holidays, friends and television; but young children love stories which begin 'In a land far away . . .'. From the beginning, children create their own imaginary places and times in play.

Poster (1973) and West (1981) argued that children learn most about their own time and their own place by being confronted with stark comparisons, with dramatically different times and places, which can clearly be contrasted with their own experiences, and that recent emphasis on direct, concrete and sensory experiences has underestimated the power of this argument. However, it would seem logical to plan a sequence of units which either move outwards in time and place, from the family and school, to distant times and places, or vice versa.

Before deciding on which sequence of content, it might be helpful to brainstorm the resources in the locality, which will link the programme to first-hand experience and to children's own interests, and create valuable interaction and shared understandings between school and community. Some resources may be more suitable for a particular group, because of distance or the kinds of related activities they stimulate. For example, are there old houses or shops or a church in the immediate vicinity which young children could observe on a short walk? Is there a museum loan collection which could be borrowed for them to use in school; what period does it relate to? Would it be better to invite people from the local community or story-tellers to talk to younger children? Is there a castle, a great house, a museum, a gallery or 'living history' reconstruction which would be more suitable for older children to visit?

Figure 7.2 suggests how topics which cover a large time-span might be sequenced moving from the present outwards or vice versa, and how the range of resources available for each broad period could be noted.

PLANNING FOR PROGRESSION

Progression in historical understanding involves interaction between increasing knowledge about the past and increasingly complex historical thinking. It develops through experiencing a variety of primary and secondary sources and learning to ask appropriate questions about them. This depends on language development, on learning to say 'because' and 'perhaps', to use time language and historical vocabulary.

Historical understanding also grows with maturity because it involves understanding human behaviour. It is a broadening as well as a hierarchical process. It is particularly difficult to plan for progression in historical understanding because variables interact. It is possible to make a simple deduction from a complex source, or to develop complicated reasoning about a simple source.

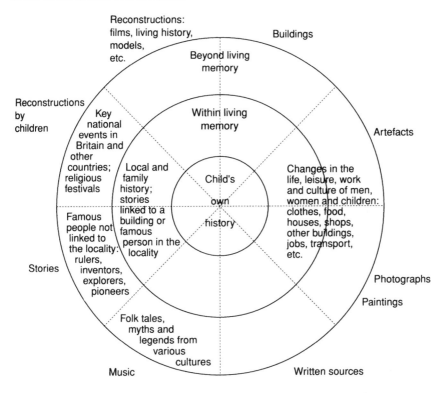

Figure 7.2 How topics may be sequenced and related appropriately to local resources

There is some commonsense progression in the things young children can do. There is a broad progression in the kinds of stories they enjoy. Simple fairy stories such as 'The Three Bears' or 'Little Red Riding Hood' can form a basis for discussing motives, perspectives and interpretations. Fairy stories with more complex motives, plots, such as 'Snow White', and myths and legends involving more powerful emotions, come later on. Stories about the life histories and families of other, familiar children may precede stories about children or events long ago. Free play in an historical context dominated by fantasy can gradually come to depend more on what is known or can be found out; it can be the basis for later role-play and hot seating or freeze-frame drama. As children's knowledge and concept of time develop they can progress from making sets of 'very old' and 'not very old' to sequencing photographs of themselves, then of their families, then impersonal photographs over several generations. They progress from sequences to standard units of time. Children may make deductions from increasingly impersonal or abstract sources; written sources may progress from a baby tag, then an old seaside postcard to Tacitus' description of

Box 7.4 Topic grid for maintaining continuity in strands of historical thinking – Foundation Stage to year 2. (Topics are those described elsewhere in this book)

		Foundation Stage				Y1	Y2
		'An old shop'	'The Peel Tower'	'Grace Darling'	FS/R 'Castles'	'Clothes'	'The farm'
ELG CLL p.52	Retell narratives, sequence events		*	*	*		
NC p.1a	Place events and objects in chronological order				*	*	
ELG CLL p.52, 54	Extend vocabulary	*	*	*	*		
NC p.1b	Use common words relating to passing of time				*	*	*
ELG CLL p.50, KUW p.88	Listen to stories, rhymes, songs; ask why things happen		*	*	*		
NC p.2a	Recognise why people did things; events happened		*	*		*	
ELG KUW p.88	Look at similarities and differences	*			*		
NC p.2b	Identify differences between ways of life at different times				*	*	*
ELG CCL p.58, ELG PSE p.42, DD p.104	Recreate roles/experiences; understand people have different needs, cultures, beliefs	*					
NC p.3	Identify different ways in which the past is represented					*	*

	1	2	3	4	5	6
ELG KUW p.56 — Investigate objects and materials	*				*	*
NC p.4a — Find out about past from a range of sources					*	*
ELG KUW p.88 — Ask and answer questions: why things happen; how they work	*	*	*		*	
NC p.4b — Ask and answer questions about the past	*	*	*		*	*
ELG KUW p.90 / CLL p.58 / CLL p.52 / CD p.124 / CD p.125 — Build and construct / Recreate roles / Retell narratives / Use imagination in art, music, dance	*	*	*	*		
NC p.5 — Communicate in a variety of ways	*	*	*		*	*
Areas of Study						
ELG KUW p.94 — Find out about past and present events in own lives/families		*			*	
NC p.6a — Changes in own lives, lives of family						
ELG KUW p.96 — Find out about environment	*	*	*	*		*
NC p.6b — Ways of life in distant past	*	*	*	*		*
NC p.6a — Significant people, events	*	*				

Key

ELG   Early Learning Goal (DfEE/QCA 2000a)

Areas of Learning (DfEE/QCA 2000a):

CLL   Communication, Language and Literacy (DfEE/QCA 2000a: 44–67)

KUW   Knowledge and Understanding of the World (DfEE/QCA 2000a: 82–100)

PSE   Personal, Social and Emotional Development (DfEE/QCA 2000a: 28–43; DfEE 1999a: 136–138)

CD   Creative Development (DfEE/QCA 2000a: 16–127)

NC   National Curriculum Programme of Study for History at Key Stage 1 (DfEE/QCA 1999a)

Boudicca. Deductions may be increasingly well argued and numerous, increasingly concerned with ideas rather than descriptive.

The whole staff then need to consider whether the long-term plan reflects the needs and interests of the children, the resources of the local community and locality, and the philosophy of the school. They also need to consider whether there is sufficient curriculum time to implement it, whether it reflects all the strands of historical enquiry and how it promotes progression in children's learning. Does it encourage children to ask increasingly complex questions, to use increasingly complex concepts and explanations, and to draw on an increasing store of historical knowledge? How do the ideas in each unit build on previous knowledge, and are the strands of historical thinking developed in new contexts?

The History Teacher's Guide Update (DfEE/QCA 2000b: 13) gives a useful grid for identifying where each strand of historical thinking and area of historical study (recent and distant past, famous people and historical events) is covered across the sequence of study units. It could be adapted for the units of study a school designs for itself. Designing study units or schemes of work will be discussed in Chapter 8. It is also useful to identify continuity across the curriculum for 3- to 8-year-olds by cross-referring the historical knowledge, skills and understanding identified in the Key Stage 1 curriculum, given the first column of the matrix, with references to the Early Learning Goals (DfEE/QCA 2000b). Box 7.4 shows how the matrix could be adapted in this way to track the historical thinking that underpins Foundation Stage topics outlined in Part I (an old shop, p. 30; a visit to the Peel Tower, p. 36; and Grace Darling, pp. 12–13) and Key Stage 1 topics discussed in Chapter 8 (castles, pp. 154–5; clothes, pp. 156–8; and the farm, pp. 158–9).

Planning a unit of study

A unit of study is a coherent sequence of activities with identified learning objectives and outcomes designed for a specified period of time. Ideally, all the teachers in a school are involved in designing a sequence of study units which will promote progression, liaising where possible with colleagues in feeder Nursery schools and playgroups. Box 7.4 could provide a basis for discussion, identifying and evaluating continuity for children from three to eight years old, in the context of whatever focuses for study units seem most appropriate for the needs of a particular school, which reflect the resources of its locality and are relevant and meaningful to its pupils. Exemplar models of schemes of work have been published (DfEE/QCA 1998a). These represent changes in family life (toys, homes, seaside holidays), a great event (the Great Fire of London), and a significant person (Florence Nightingale). They are helpful for their intended purpose, to support schools where planning was felt to be weak. Links are shown to prior learning, related vocabulary and resources. Sequences of learning objectives, teaching activities and outcomes are identified. There are three broad levels of expectations for what children are expected to have achieved at the end of the unit.

There are clear links in the structure of these schemes with the structure of the Foundation Stage Guidance – a sequence of stepping stones in learning objectives towards specified learning goals, with examples of related activities and how these may be supported. It is therefore possible, using the matrix in Box 7.4, which identifies links between the learning objectives within the strands of historical thinking at the Foundation Stage and Key Stage 1, to design pre-school units of work using the same models as the QCA schemes: learning objectives, activities and learning outcomes with practitioner support. (See case study, pp. 178–9.)

These schemes are intended as exemplar models. They could be modified to reflect children's cultural backgrounds; the famous person may not be Florence Nightingale but Mohammed or Mary Seacole (Nulty 1998, p. 116). Homes Long Ago could focus on a local house or castle (English Heritage, pp. 218–19), and the great event may be a local event rather than the Fire of London.

However, if education is to be meaningful and relevant and to meet the holistic needs of children, intellectually, personally, socially and emotionally, in line with the principles for early years education (DfEE/QCA 2000a: 11), it must be delivered by practitioners who are creative, innovative and professionally confident in planning imaginative units for the children and locality, within the generic guidance and statutory requirements. They need to take into account the resources within the community and in their school or pre-school setting. The process described in Figure 8.1 is appropriate for planning a unit of work for the Foundation Stage or Key Stage 1.

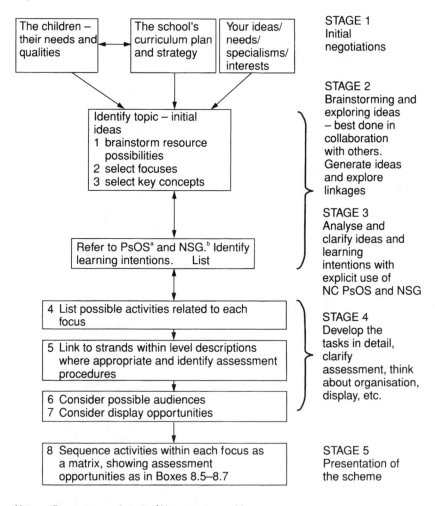

Notes: [a]Programmes of study. [b]Non-statutory guidance.

Figure 8.1 The planning process

OVERVIEW OF RESOURCES

Primary sources

In the whole-school plans, local resources were reviewed: museums, galleries, sites, churches, great homes, municipal buildings, theatres, cinemas. Themes for study units were selected which related to these. Before planning the study unit in detail, it is important to make a preliminary visit to find out (if possible, through discussion with on-site staff) how preparation for a visit and follow-up work can be planned which reflects strands of historical thinking. Some suggestions are given in Boxes 8.1–8.3, which show (in the first column) the historical questions which children may be asked and (in the second column) how these may be related to each kind of historical resource.

The local community

What opportunities for local history can be provided by the local library (maps, street directories, census returns, newspapers, photographs); how can local community centres, workplaces, parents and friends contribute to oral history?

Artefacts

These could be collected, or borrowed from friends, a museum or library.

Extracts from contemporary writings

Use old children's books, advertisements, posters, or even short extracts (for example, from Julius Caesar), diaries (e.g. Pepys, or the diary of a 12-year-old Kentish girl (Kent Archive Office, 1986)) or accounts of Victorian children (Adams 1982).

Videotape

Collect old news items about key events or extracts from old films shown on television which illustrate aspects of daily life in the past: houses, clothes, streets, shops.

Music

Collect sheet music and recorded music related to the period.

Box 8.1 A picture gallery

Are there pictures related to the topic? Will they interest children? Are there pictures of children, of men and women, from different cultural and social backgrounds?

Can they develop awareness that the past is represented in different ways?	Are these pictures about real people and fictional characters?
Are there opportunities to recount episodes from stories?	Is there more than one picture about the same place, event, person? Are there pictures which tell a story?
Are there opportunities to make a distinction between past and present?	Is it possible to compare past and present, in clothes, artefacts, buildings, daily life?
Are there opportunities to find out about the past, and ask questions about the past, from sources?	What questions about the past might the pictures raise? What can children work out from the pictures?

Box 8.2 A museum

How will children be able to recognise similarities and differences between past and present, and between different periods in the past?	Are there collections of clothes or artefacts of the same kind from different periods? Can children compare/identify differences between past and present from the artefacts? Can they explain why they changed?
Will they be able to see how representations of the past are made?	Is there a museum reconstruction?
What questions could children investigate using these exhibits? Can they suggest reasons why people acted as they did?	What could children work out from the exhibits about how they were made and used, and how they affected people's lives?

Simulations and reconstructions

Collect extracts from films or plays on television related to the period. Are there any Living History Reconstructions (see *English Heritage Events Diary*)?

Stories

Collect children's books – stories set in the past, stories about real events (myths and legends if appropriate), old children's books – to use as primary sources and to compare different versions.

Box 8.3 An archaeological site, castle, windmill, church, great house

Will children be able to listen to, find out about, retell and reconstruct events linked to the site?	Is there a story associated with the site? Why was the place constructed?
Can children consider why the building, road, etc. was constructed here and why it may no longer be used, or why its purpose has changed?	What differences could children find between past and present? How has the place changed over time? Why?
What was it like to live and work here? How can children use the site to answer questions about the past? What questions might they investigate?	What questions might children ask about the place? What could they find out about the life and work of the people who lived here?

Secondary sources

Collect children's information books, both recently published books and old history books, to compare different interpretations in text and illustration.

CROSS-CURRICULAR APPROACHES

It is also important to decide what links it is appropriate for individual teachers to plan between history units and other areas of the curriculum. In this chapter there are suggestions about possible links between history-focused topics and other areas of the curriculum (Clothes: Box 8.6, Box 8.4; Castles: Box 8.5, Box 8.2; The Farm: Box 8.7, Box 8.3). These cross-curricular webs are examples of some possible connections. There is guidance (SCAA 1997; DfEE/QCA 1998b) as to how blocks of work in history can be linked to continuing work in English for example, and/or other foundation subjects. Suggestions for links between English, mathematics, and information and communication technology are given in the *National Curriculum for England and Wales* (DfEE/QCA 1999a: 104) and in *History Teachers Guide* (DfEE/QCA 1998a: 16–18). Case studies have explored in more detail appropriate ways of linking history with the Literacy Hour and the Numeracy Hour and ICT (e.g. Cooper 2000b: 94–137). The cross-curricular webs therefore suggest possible links which can be developed in more detail between selected groups of subjects.

At the Foundation Stage, a cross-curricular web can also be a good starting-point for planning. A theme developed over several weeks, for example toys (pp. 177–8), can be organised by identifying possible links between a sequence of history activities and early learning goals in each of the six areas of learning: personal, social and emotional development; communication, language and literacy; mathematical development; knowledge and understanding of the world; physical and creative development. Alternatively, a more general theme, such as changes, may be brainstormed under different strands within Knowledge and Understanding of the World (science, history, geography), each linked to the other five areas of learning, with two weeks planned for the science, two for history and two for geography, in cross-curricular ways.

SELECTION OF FOCUSES

Having decided on resources which are available to their own school, teachers can select focuses within a history topic. Each focus may reflect a particular strand of historical enquiry: sources, time and change or interpretations (Box 7.1). This will ensure that each strand is adequately covered, and make assessment and record-keeping more manageable. Work on castles, for example, may focus on a visit to a castle, castles in stories and the castle today and in the past (Box 8.5). A topic on clothes may focus on clothes in stories about the past, and clothes in photographs (Box 8.6). The history dimension of a topic on a farm (Box 8.7) may focus on inferences about sources, on differences between past and present as illustrated in stories and artefacts, and on different interpretations of life on farms in the past as shown in stories and pictures. Groups of children can work on different focuses then present their work to each other. Alternatively, organising the work in a series of focuses paces it and gives it coherence: work can be drawn together, presentations made and conclusions drawn at intervals.

SELECTION OF CONCEPTS

It is important for teachers to select key vocabulary within a topic so that they can decide, in their planning, when and how to introduce new historical concepts to the class, then how to encourage children to use them independently in writing labels, or captions to pictures, in their own discussions and in play. Teachers will then be clear as to what opportunities they are creating to monitor to what extent children are learning these new concepts. Concepts may be related to the topic (black-out, gas mask, ration book) or to the process of historical enquiry (evidence, maybe, perhaps, because). They may involve the concept of time (now, then, earlier, later) or abstract vocabulary central to all societies (trade, power, defend, attack).

POSSIBLE ACTIVITIES

In order to plan a variety of activities through which children can explore each focus, it may help to review possible opportunities for active learning before deciding which are the most suitable for a particular class and theme. Possible activities include the following.

In pre-school settings

- collecting information by talking to an older person or listening to stories set in the past (pp. 12, 23, 37);
- collecting old artefacts, a local walk, talking about how things were made and used, why they have changed, causes and sequences of events (pp. 30–2, 36);
- exploring the past through free and structured play (pp. 28–32);
- collating information.

Key Stage 1

- collecting information through use of surveys, questionnaires, interviews, databases (recording a gravestone survey, for example, using OUR FACTS database), primary and secondary sources;
- considering the causes and effects of change (e.g. making and explaining sets and time-lines);
- making deductions and inferences;
- writing archaeologists' or historians' reports and explanatory labels for class displays and museums;
- reaching interpretations through free play, role-play, models, drawings;
- presenting results of enquiries in drama, exhibitions, oral and video-tape, and slide presentations.

ASSESSMENT

Assessment opportunities must also be built into the long-term planning. If activities are planned which reflect strands of historical thinking at specified levels, evaluating the resulting work is on-going and formative throughout the unit of study. Work must be planned with clear, expected learning outcomes which can then be recorded. Assessment is an integral part of planning. It could be based on writing a label explaining a time-line, a museum label, an 'archaeologist's' report, a story or poem. It may be made by observing imaginative play, or by listening to children's discussion in a group as they make a model or a painting, discuss a source, or sort into sets of 'old' and 'new'. This could be related to children's self-assessment of their work, either written or oral. It is extremely important that the purpose of activities is made explicit to children (and to parents)

Box 8.4 The history component of an integrated topic, 'Clothes' (the focuses are (1) 'My clothes'; (2) 'Clothes in other places'; (3) 'Clothes in other times')

Science

- Sort according to materials, winter/summer, natural/man-made
- Design and carry out tests for washability, durability, warmth, water resistance

  (Health Education – need to keep warm, clean, dry. Protective clothing matched to occupations)

Art

- Collect fabrics from a variety of countries, decorated using different techniques (e.g. West African print, Batik, woven patterns, embroidery, tie-dye). Discuss how they were made. Collect illustrations in books
- Print own fabric with wax-resist fabric crayons, junk, potatoes; tie-dye, weave, knit

History: Time and change

- Retell true stories or stories set in the 1930s, 1900s, beyond living memory
- Collect photographs, sequence and describe, and try to explain changes in one item of clothing
- Sort newspaper photographs of these periods into 'ordinary people' and 'celebrities'
- Survey: 'Were clothes in — easier to keep clean/smarter than clothes today?

Geography

- Collect pictures of people in hot, cold, temperate climates. Sort into sets. What does each set have in common? Why? Identify on globe/map
- Invite a visitor familiar with locality which has a climate different from Britain to explain/demonstrate traditional clothes and modern modifications
- Do clothes show job or status? How are they suitable for the lives people live in this place? For the climate? What are they made of? How?

Religious Education

Visitors from churches explain special clothes worn by priests in their church, and what they symbolise

Mathematics

- Surveys (e.g. favourite sorts of shoe)
- Time investigations (e.g. which type of fastenings are quickest to do up)
- Measures: shape and space – make outfit for teddy; money (clothes shop)
- Algebra: design a sequence for a bead necklace and record it; make necklace to friend's formula. Is pattern correct?
- Number counting (e.g. for durability test; how many rubs before there is a hole?)

Technology

Design and make an outfit for a very dirty/ragged/cold/hot or wet teddy or doll

Cross-curricular themes

- Citizenship: collect pictures – who are these people? What do they do? Why? Why do they wear special clothes? (e.g. Queen opening Parliament, lords, baronesses, bishops, judges, local mayor, aldermen, members of voluntary organisations, police, firefighters, nurses)
- EIU: house corner play – a clothes shop
- Equal opportunities: (a) traditional dress of various cultures; (b) jobs women do which they did not do in the past, and clothes they wear, e.g. firefighter, police, pilot, bus driver, engineer, scientist

English

- Talking and listening. Interviewing visitor about traditional clothes from another country (geography)
- Reading: labels for fabrics (art), or for photographs (history); stories (e.g. 'The Emperor's New Clothes' and 'The Emperor's Dan-Dan', a West Indian version (see Agard 1992))
- Writing: a (picture) story about a teddy who gets very dirty/ragged/cold/hot or wet

Box 8.5 Example of a history-focused topic showing how activities are planned which reflect history-level descriptions and how they can be assessed: Key Stage 1, 'Castles'

Focus	*Historical strand*	*Resources*
Visit to a castle	**Deductions and inferences from sources** Level 1: find out about the past from sources of information Level 2: answer questions about the past using sources of information Level 3: select information from sources to answer specific questions about the past	Visit to a castle. Record in photographs, drawings. What do we know? What reasonable guesses can we make? What would we like to know? Secondary sources – references books Information about other castles (e.g. Red Fort, Agra, Mughal miniatures, Victoria & Albert Museum, castles in Europe)
Castles in stories	**Interpretations** Level 1: (a) recount episodes from stories in the past; (b) understand that stories may be about real or fictional people Level 2: (a) retell stories about people and events and use terms concerned with the passing of time to order events; suggest reasons why people acted as they did; (b) show awareness that the past is represented in different ways Level 3: (a) demonstrate knowledge of events, people and places they have learned about; discuss causes and consequences of a choice and results; (b) show developing awareness of why past is represented in different ways	Extracts from films (e.g. *Ivanhoe, Robin Hood*) Illustrated fairy stories (e.g. 'Rapunzel', 'Cinderella', 'Puss in Boots') True stories about castle visited
Now and then	**Understanding time and change** Level 1: awareness of differences between past and present Level 2: can make distinctions between their own lives and past times Level 3: can recognise similarities and differences between different periods in the past	Secondary sources; reference books Old recipes (e.g. Renfrew *et al.* 1993), picture cards (postcards, or cards made from brochure) of castle at different periods (e.g. Norman, Medieval, Tudor, 18th Century, today)

Concepts	Activities	Method of assessment
Attack Defend Moat Tower Hall Dungeon Drawbridge Feast Armour Jousting	Make a model; label and explain parts Write booklet or poster for other visitors Draw pictures of parts of castle; label, explain	From model, brochure or picture can: Level 1: describe Level 2: ask questions; refer to other sources to find out more Level 3: make reasonable suggestions based on evidence about how castle was made, used, and why
	Free play (e.g. make flags, 'drawbridge', 'moat', turn house corner into castle tower; hobby-horse tournament). Write proclamations; invitations to feast Teacher observes questions, checks anachronisms, provides resources to find out more, extend Play continues based on new information Story-writing	Level 1: (a) retell story; (b) discuss whether stories are true. How do we know? Level 2: (a) discuss different groups of children's play based on evidence seen in the castle, or in 'true stories' Level 3: (a) can retell 'true stories'; (b) can use vocabulary such as 'I think', 'perhaps', and 'We don't know because . . .'
Now The present Today New	Paint a background for the model of the castle today, and one for when it was new Or make a tape of things you may have heard then and things you hear today, at the castle Or cook food they may have eaten then, and now, or listen to music they may have heard then and music today Put in order/draw pictures of the castle at different periods	Level 1: can contribute background paintings appropriately Level 2: can describe differences between the old and the new and attempt to explain them Level 3: can put pictures of castle at different periods in order; suggest reasons for changes; name periods

Box 8.6 The history dimension of an integrated topic, 'Clothes'

Focus	Understanding changes over time, using sources	Resources
Clothes in other times	Level 1: (a) recount episodes from stories of the past; (b) show awareness of differences between past and present; find out about the past from sources	Illustrated true stories set in the 1930s, 1900s, beyond living memory
	Level 2: make distinctions between own lives and past times. Order objects; suggest reasons why people in the past acted as they did; answer questions about the past using sources	
	Level 3: recognise similarities and differences between different periods in the past. Select information from sources to answer specific questions about the past. Can identify reasons for and results of changes. Awareness that the past is divided into two periods	Photographs over three generations (and beyond living memory)
	Interpretations Level 2: beginning to show awareness that the past is represented in different ways	Collect from newspapers photographs of people at work (ordinary people) and filmstars, politicians, etc., of same date

Concepts	Activities	Method of assessment
Old, new Before, then, next, after, in the end	In a group, take it in turns to tell next stage of story	Level 1: can sequence events correctly Level 2: can refer to factual knowledge of people and events in detail
Edwardian, Victorian, Tudor Fabric: wool, cotton, fur, silk, leather, straw, lace Decoration, jewellery Other special vocabulary as appropriate	Collect photographs of parents (great) grandparents, pictures of people beyond living memory Display them in sequence. Write captions for each photo saying 'I am wearing . . . because . . .' Select one item (e.g. hat or shoes) and copy them from each picture. Present sequence as a fashion commentary to an audience describing changes and suggesting reasons why clothes changed	Level 1: can describe clothes in photographs Level 2: can describe differences, can sequence photographs. Can suggest why people wore these styles of clothes Level 3: can identify differences between particular items of clothing at different periods Can select information from pictures to answer specific questions (e.g. do you think this woman had a job? Why?). Can suggest possible reasons for changes, and effects on people's lives. Can label clothes as, e.g. Victorian/ Tudor/Roman
	Sort photographs of 'ordinary people' and 'celebrities' into sets. In groups, describe what each set tells us about this period	Level 2: Can explain why deductions from 'ordinary people' and 'celebrities' sets give different versions of the period

Box 8.7 The history dimension of a humanities-focused topic, 'The Farm'

Focus	Historical strand	Resources
	Making deductions and inferences from historical sources	
	Level 1: find out about the past from sources of information. Recount episodes from stories of the past	Photographs and drawings made by children on visit (e.g. doors to barn wide enough for cart, iron ring in wall for tying up animals, drinking trough, stile, date over door, name of farm)
	Level 2: answer questions about the past, using sources of information	Collection of old implements
	Level 3: select information from sources to answer specific questions	Old photographs
		Diary extracts, e.g. *Ordinary Times: A Hundred Years Ago* (Adams 1982); *Lark Rise to Candleford* (Thompson 1989: harvest pp.132–7, children's games pp. 87–120). Philip (1993) documents the hardships of rural children
		Old paintings about rural life, both idealised (e.g. *Willie Lot's Cottage*, Constable) and realistic (e.g. *Bird Scaring*, George Clausen)
	Time and change Level 1: show awareness of differences between past and present. Recount episodes from stories about the past	*The Tale of Jemima Puddleduck, The Tale of Sally Henny Penny* and Thompson (1989: pp.132–7, 87–120) retold by the teacher
	Level 2: make distinctions between aspects of their own lives and past times. Order objects. Suggest reasons why people in the past acted as they did	Sequence artefacts, e.g. milk-maid's yoke, milk can, milk bottle, carton
	Interpretations Level 1: understand that stories may be about real people or fictional characters	Folk tales from a variety of cultures about growing and selling crops (e.g. 'The Great Big Enormous Turnip', 'Jack and the Beanstalk', *Shaker Lane* (Provensen and Provensen 1992)
	Level 2: show awareness that different stories can give different versions of the past	
	Level 3: increasing awareness that the past is represented in different ways	Collect images of village life in the past, e.g. photographs of people dressed in old-fashioned clothes (reconstructions), old photographs, nursery rhyme illustrations, pantomime, paintings

Concepts	Activities	Method of assessment
Hay, straw, wheat, barley, sheaves, farm, cultivate, plough, sow, mow, harvest, crops, store, haystack, herd, flock, domesticate, select, breed (*agriculture*) Buy, sell, market, profit (*trade*) Yoke, cart, wagon (*transport*) Patterns, smock Plough, rake, scythe, sickle, pitchfork, butter churn (*tools*) Dairy, barn, stable	Make careful observational drawings. Write explanatory labels Each child writes a question about one of sources collected for quiz. (Display questions next to sources) Leave tape-recorder near quiz display. Children research specific questions posed by teacher or a visitor (e.g. what was it like to be a country child 100 years ago?). Children record any evidence they find on the tape Play back tape to class. Discuss findings	Level 1: can write label (or explain to others) how the artefact/building may have been used. Can recount episode from a diary Level 2: can suggest relevant questions about sources, for quiz. Can suggest or find out possible answers Level 3: can use a range of sources to answer the question
First, then, next; a long time ago, later Old, older, new, newer	Act one of the stories or put separated illustrated pages in order Draw artefacts in chronological sequence	Level 1: can use evidence in illustrations to discuss how the past was different. Can put events in order Level 2: can explain how milk obtained now and in the past; why and how this would have affected people's lives. Can order artefacts
	Discuss whether these stories are about real people. Are diary extracts about real people? How do we know? House corner play stimulated by evidence found on visit about farming in the past (props, e.g. stable door, horse trough, milk-maid's yoke, range) In pairs, sort pictures into sets: 'true', 'maybe' and 'not true'	Level 1: can sort names of characters written on card into sets: 'really lived', and 'not a real person'; explain reasons Level 2: different groups can say how they used the 'props' in their play to tell different stories Level 3: can give reasons for placements, support argument, listen to other views

Figure 8.2 Work in other curriculum areas which links with a history-focused topic, 'Castles'

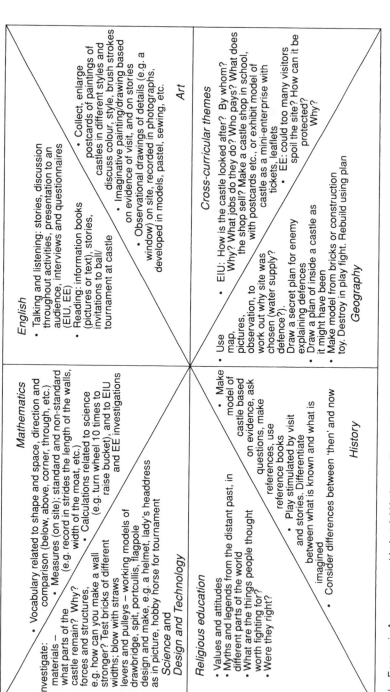

Mathematics

- Vocabulary related to shape and space, direction and comparison (below, above, corner, through, etc.)
- Measures (on site); standard and non-standard (e.g. record in strides the length of the walls, width of the moat, etc.)
- Calculations related to science (e.g. turn wheel 10 times to raise bucket), and to EIU and EE investigations

English

- Talking and listening: stories, discussion throughout activities, presentation to an audience, interviews and questionnaires (EIU, EE)
- Reading: information books (pictures or text), stories, invitations to ball/ tournament at castle

Art

- Collect, enlarge postcards of paintings of castles in different styles and discuss colour, style, brush strokes
- Imaginative painting/drawing based on evidence of visit, and on stories
- Observational drawings of details (e.g. a window) on site, recorded in photographs, developed in models, pastel, sewing, etc.

Cross-curricular themes

- EIU: How is the castle looked after? By whom? Why? What jobs do they do? Who pays? What does the shop sell? Make a castle shop in school, with postcards etc., or exhibit model of castle as a mini-enterprise with tickets, leaflets
- EE: could too many visitors spoil the site? How can it be protected? Why?

Geography

- Use map, pictures, observation, to work out why site was chosen (water supply? defence?).
- Draw a secret plan for enemy explaining defences
- Draw a plan of inside a castle as it might have been
- Make model from bricks or construction toy. Destroy in play fight. Rebuild using plan

History

- Values and attitudes
- Myths and legends from the distant past, in different parts of the world
- What are the things people thought worth fighting for?
- Were they right?

- Make model of castle based on evidence, ask questions, use references
- Play stimulated by visit and stories. Differentiate between what is known and what is imagined
- Consider differences between 'then' and now

Religious education

Science and Design and Technology

Investigate:
- materials – what parts of the castle remain? Why?
- forces and structures, e.g. how can you make a wall stronger? Test bricks of different widths; blow with straws
- levers and pulleys – working models of drawbridge, spit, portcullis, flagpole
- design and make, e.g. a helmet, lady's headdress as in picture, hobby horse for tournament

EIU – Economic Awareness and Industrial Understanding   EE – Environmental Education so that they are involved in deciding to what extent these have been achieved. Many sequences of activities involve all three strands of historical thinking, but it can simplify assessment if one strand in particular is assessed in each focus (Figure 8.2).

POSSIBLE AUDIENCES

It is helpful to decide at the planning stage on possible audiences for each focus of a topic and how the children may present their work to them. This will give a purpose to the work, for children and their teacher, and encourage motivation, quality and quantity. It also makes links between school, home and the wider community, and offers an opportunity for people not necessarily involved in education to learn about and value what is achieved in school. Possible audiences may include another class, the whole school, parents, local libraries and newspapers, teachers' centres, workplaces, and local or national organisations (for example, the Historical Association Young Historian Scheme). Investigations may be presented through structured role-play songs, music and dance in historical contexts, through exhibitions, displays, handmade books, children's presentation of slides, video tape of a visit (with preparation and follow-up work), or audio tape made by children to explain a display.

DISPLAY

It is important to consider at the planning stage how displays can be developed, throughout the project, which are an integral part of the learning process and of the dynamic classroom environment. (Teachers may therefore like to add a column on 'display opportunities' to the planning matrix.) Display can develop and reflect learning as active and interactive. It is important to plan for initial stimuli at the beginning of a unit of study which will interest, involve and raise questions – maybe simply a large artefact related to the topic. Children can then develop increasing ownership of their environment by adding their own contributions, not only of their work, but old toys, things found on 'a dig', or old photographs, as appropriate. These will inevitably stimulate other children's questions and further work. On-going displays might include collaborative model-making or pictures, which evolve as a result of the comments they provoke, the questions they raise and children's resulting research. The learning environment may continue to change as 'props' are made for role-play areas based on the children's own ideas as their play develops, for example, in a castle, a cave or a museum. Children's increasing opportunities for ownership of their environment make it flexible and constantly changing and challenging. They make the learning environment an integral component of a constructivist approach to learning which stems from Piaget, Vygotsky and Bruner.

Figure 8.3 How art, music, maths and science make connections between the history and geography components of a humanities-focused topic, 'The Farm'

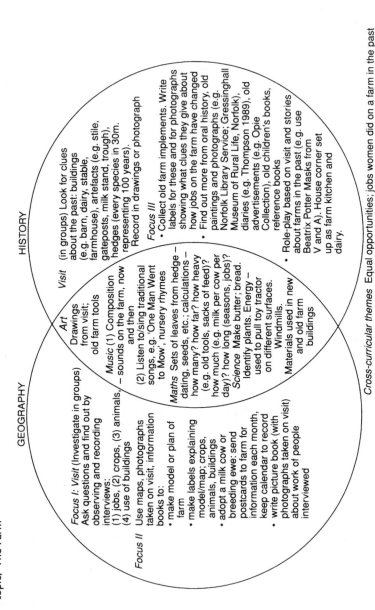

GEOGRAPHY

HISTORY

Focus I: Visit (Investigate in groups) Ask questions and find out by observing and recording interviews:
(1) jobs, (2) crops, (3) animals, (4) use of buildings

Focus II Use maps, photographs taken on visit, information books to:
• make model or plan of farm
• make labels explaining model/map; crops, animals, buildings
• adopt a milk cow or breeding ewe: send postcards to farm for information each month, keep calendar to record
• write picture book (with photographs taken on visit) about work of people interviewed

Art Drawings from visit; old farm tools

Music (1) Composition – sounds on the farm, now and then
(2) Listen to/sing traditional songs, e.g. 'One Man Went to Mow', nursery rhymes

Maths Sets of leaves from hedge – dating, seeds, etc.; calculations – how many? how far? how heavy (e.g. old tools, sacks of feed)? how much (e.g. milk per cow per day)? how long (seasons, jobs)?

Science Make butter; bread. Identify plants. Energy – used to pull toy tractor on different surfaces. Windmills.
Materials used in new and old farm buildings

Visit (in groups) Look for clues about the past: buildings (e.g. barn, dairy, stable, farmhouse), artefacts (e.g. stile, gateposts, milk stand, trough), hedges (every species in 30m. representing 100 years). Record in drawings or photograph

Focus III
• Collect old farm implements. Write labels for these and for photographs showing what clues they give about how jobs on the farm have changed
• Find out more from oral history, old paintings and photographs (e.g. Norfolk Library Service; Gressinghall Museum of Rural Life, Norfolk), diaries (e.g. Thompson 1989), old advertisements (e.g. Opie Collection), old children's books, reference books
• Role-play based on visit and stories about farms in the past (e.g. use Beatrix Potter Masks from V and A). House corner set up as farm kitchen and dairy.

Cross-curricular themes Equal opportunities; jobs women did on a farm in the past (diaries and pictures)

EE Soil experiments: what makes good soil? (mini beasts, humus). Why do farmers use sprays, fertilisers? Hedges: what lives in a hedge?

EIU Pretend play – a farm shop

FROM LONG-TERM PLANS TO WEEKLY AND DAILY PLANNING

First, from the topic web and grid, a weekly planner can be made, showing which part of the study unit can be covered each week, in each curriculum area. This ensures that the amount of work planned is feasible and that there is curriculum balance, although every curriculum area does not have to be included each week. This is also a tried and tested approach which prevents teachers driving themselves crazy trying to do too much! For example, the first two weeks of a unit, or 'Castles', might be planned as in Box 8.8.

Second, activities planned can then be fitted into the class timetable at the beginning of each week. Plans will probably be modified, depending on how much was actually achieved. The weekly timetable can be colour-coded to show concurrent group activities as in Box 8.9.

Third, experienced teachers may not need to write detailed plans for each activity, but they will inevitably remind themselves of learning objectives and assessment opportunities set out in the long-term planning matrix, and they will consider how activities and whole class sessions will be initiated and organised, the sequence of questions they will ask, their own role in extending focused activities, and intervention opportunities.

Fourth, experienced teachers do not usually do a detailed written evaluation of each activity, because this process becomes an innate and integral part of professional reflection. This process is essential in order to inform and modify planning in the light of children's responses. Sometimes this will be part of a formal discussion with colleagues, more often an informal exchange siezed in odd moments. Most often it is, *faute de mieux*, an internal dialogue, in the car or the bath! At whatever level, it is part of a cycle (see Figure 8.4).

However, even the most experienced teachers will need to record what key activities each child has undertaken, and what they have achieved, on some kind of checklist each day or week (see Box 8.10).

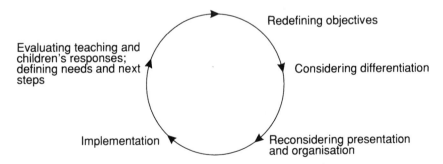

Figure 8.4 Cycle of teachers' self-evaluation

Box 8.8 Planning a unit

Week	History	English	Maths	Science/ Technology	Geography	Art	RE	Music	PE/Dance
5–9 Sept. Numeracy Hour: SHAPE Literacy Hour: Label and captions	Castle visit	Label parts; story about castle	Draw plan	Begin model		Drawing (castles)		Listen to medieval music; make up dance	Based on castle story/visit
12–16 Sept. Numeracy Hour: MEASURES Literacy Hour: Observations of a visit	Use evidence from visit to begin brochure or poster	Role-play	Measure in strides on playground	Continue model			Discuss motives/ values in story about castle		

Box 8.9 Example of a timetable

	8.50–10.30	10.50–12.15	1.20–3.15	Notes
Thursday 8 Sept.	REGISTER	PLAY	LUNCH	4 activities
	Discuss visit (Wednesdays), introduce group work: Literacy Hour	X O # *	Numeracy Hour	X Draw and label parts O Draw plans # Begin model * Free play – castle area
Friday 9 Sept.	X O # *	Literacy Hour	Music	Focused groups for assessment can be highlighted
		PE	Numeracy Hour	
			X O # *	

Box 8.10 Teachers' checklist of each child's achievements

Week	*Record of individual progress*		
Learning intentions	NC reference	Children's initials	Special/urgent action notes

Finally teachers will be able to collect and record more detailed assessments from focused groups they have worked with periodically. This may well allow opportunities for assessment in another curriculum area as well as in history: history and mathematics, history and English, or history and science. Since the introduction of the National Curriculum, assessment has often been seen as the tail wagging the dog. However, when it is an integral part of planning, when curriculum overlap is built into the planning, when formative assessment is recognised as an informal and on-going part of a teacher's inevitable and continuous professional judgement, which is reflected only at intervals in in-depth records, assessment refines teachers' work in an economical way; it gives them confidence because they have evidence that children are progressively achieving a rich variety of objectives in skills, attitudes and knowledge. This was often previously regarded as unquantifiable. Such accountability empowers teachers. It provides a language for valuing, defining, defending and sharing their professional expertise.

HISTORY AND HOLISTIC EDUCATION

The National Curriculum has helped us to identify the central questions and methods of answering them which lie at the heart of each subject and to translate them into activities which even the youngest child can begin to grapple with and also to put Bruner's concept of spiral curriculum into practice:

What we have learned about learning . . . is anything but trivial. Even under the least favourable conditions – psychologically, fiscally, educationally – we still succeed in giving some children a sense of their own possibilities. We do it by getting them (and sometimes their parents) to collaborate in an enabling community.

(Bruner 1996: 76)

Yet the National Curriculum, in spite of its aims of breadth and depth, continuity and progression, tended to fragment the curriculum and lose sight of the development of the whole child. So now there is great emphasis, both at the Foundation Stage and in schools, on identifying ways in which learning experiences created through links between home, school and community can develop children's self-esteem, emotional well-being and sense of identity, and also help them to develop good relationships, spiritual and moral awareness, and an understanding of cultures. There is an expectation that teaching approaches will build on children's own interests and experiences, and provide rich and varied contexts for them to think both creatively and critically (DfEE/QCA 2000: 10–11).

In planning, it is important to identify ways in which history-focused work reflects these dimensions: links with family, locality and community; personal and social education; education for citizenship; spiritual, moral and cultural education; equal opportunities in terms of ability, gender, ethnicity and all kinds of special educational needs. This may be done by colour-coding in a medium-term plan, aspects of personal and social education which can be developed through a history-focused activity. For example, at the Foundation Stage highlight an activity which focuses on children learning to work as part of a group in order to take turns in retelling a story or to discuss an artefact. At Key Stage 1, a story selected to challenge gender stereotypes (p. 169) could be colour-coded under 'equal opportunities'. If we are truly to achieve a principled, integrated and value-laden curriculum, we can take as a starting-point previous tenets of early years education:

A school is not merely a teaching shop. It must transmit values and attitudes. It is a community in which children learn to live, first and foremost as children and not as future adults . . . The school sets out deliberately to devise the right environment for the children to allow them to be themselves and to develop in a way and at a pace appropriate to them. It lays special stress on individual discovery, on first-hand experience and on opportunities for creative work. It insists that knowledge does not fall neatly into separate compartments and that work and play are not opposite but complementary.

(DfE 1967: para 505)

The new emphasis on education which is socially embedded in relationships in the home, school and community, has its roots in the much misunderstood and rarely realised Plowden Report (DfE 1967). Such education provides a stimulating environment and range of experiences which encourage children to learn at first hand, in holistic ways, across boundaries between subjects and between work and play.

Prior to colour-coding links in planning between history and aspects of personal and social education, it may be better to ignore the dead hand of accountability which is driving creativity out of the classroom and, instead, define what identifies creative teachers. For children are changed by creative teaching which leads to creative learning, and it is this that gives them control of their own learning. Woods (1995: Ch. 1) identifies creative teachers as those who:

- are innovative, concerned with the process not the product;
- have ownership of what and how they teach and are able to see alternatives;
- have control, because of a strong commitment to the values they empower;
- make learning relevant, through their holistic perception of children and the curriculum.

Woods describes two schools where teachers were determined to interpret the National Curriculum in ways meaningful to their pupils. In one school of 135 4- to 9-year-olds, of whom 75 per cent were of North Indian ethnic origin and spoke Punjabi as a first language, the teachers, through a 'culture of collaboration', agreed on their basic values and the implications of these for their educational beliefs and teaching approaches. Over two years they articulated those beliefs and illustrated them by practical examples.

They defined their views of learning as 'a process', what is happening inside the child, and they set up a system of home visits and a room for parents and friends. They defined the role of teacher as 'refiner, corrector, editor and consolidator in a collaborative process of learning'. They saw it as the role of the teacher to develop children's confidence and self-esteem by making what is offered in the National Curriculum something the children could make their own, work on and develop, and by encouraging them to take risks. They defined their teaching methods as emphasising real context and purpose within the child's scheme of things, establishing trusting relationships in order to explore with the children their own perceptions and ideas. They even learned some Punjabi in order to reverse roles, so that the children could help them to read stories, recount events, and make labels for artefacts associated with other cultures and beliefs, times and places.

The headteacher in another school described the outside environment as 'a wealthy resource which we can draw upon if we are prepared to plan to do so'. This part of the school's philosophy, in which learning, playing and dreaming have a unity which inspire each other, excite imagination and interest, was defined as:

Involvement
- we learn something by touching, learning, seeing and responding emotionally and spiritually
- we reinforce the experience by talking, reading, writing in the areas of art and music
- our intention is to make learning more abstract and symbolic through concrete starting-points.

Holism
- the interconnectedness of life, rhythm and cycles of creation is recognised
- through celebrating seasons and festivals
- through respect for care and order
- through marking and commemorating births and deaths.

Integrated curriculum
- integration of both the content and the experiences of school life.

The inspectors reported that 'You do a lot more than deliver the National Curriculum. You actually use it as a sort of leap off. . .'

The best way to establish a value-laden curriculum seems to be by agreeing a set of principles, and evolving successful ways of implementing them, relevant to a particular school:

- the children: their interests, backgrounds, needs, learning styles, perceptions of learning;
- the community and its resources: the people, buildings, places, work-places, libraries, galleries, museums;
- the school environment: the layout, areas, furniture, organisation of resources to facilitate choices, selection, independence; the organisation of the curriculum and of time; the outdoor play areas;
- and, not least, the staff: their interests, values and experiences.

History and personal, social, moral, spiritual and cultural education

Certainly it is recognised that history develops more awareness, and social and emotional as well as cognitive growth, not through didactic teaching or exemplary stories but by encouraging children to ask questions, to discuss and speculate about the reasons for people's behaviour, attitudes and values in other times and in other places. Jones (1968), whose work was based on the psychodynamic theories of Erikson (1965), felt that children can and must be encouraged to understand both themselves and the behaviour, ideas and feelings of people in different societies, and that the humanities provide an ideal means of doing this. He saw it as essential that cognitive development should be related to emotional and imaginative growth. 'It is necessary that children feel myth as well as understand it' (Jones 1968: 49). *History in the Primary and Secondary Years* (DES 1985) acknowledged that the great myths of North America, Africa and Asia, as well as those of Europe, are likely to play an important part in the experience of young children. It also said that children between 4 and 7 years are able to relate judgements about people to evidence and to identify with the predicaments and points of view of others. It saw history as part of self-knowledge and the development of moral awareness. It involves asking such questions as, 'What is it like to be someone else?' and 'How do I know that is true?' These questions are assertions of intellectual independence.

There are many opportunities to develop the early learning goals for personal and social education in historical contexts (DfEE/QCA 2000a: 28–43). Discussing how old artefacts may have been made and used and listening to stories of the past from other cultures may involve initiating, listening to and sharing ideas, taking turns, repeating the views and feelings of others. Through role-play in historical contexts children can learn to become independent, form good relationships, consider consequences of words and actions, both in imaginative and actual worlds and, not least, to dress and undress themselves! Through oral history, visits to and visitors from the community and talking about family stories and photographs, children develop increasing awareness of the wider social groups, both past and present, to which they belong.

At Key Stage 1 these understandings can be built upon (DfEE/QCA 1999a: 19–20; 2000b: 7). Children can discuss what might be fair and unfair, right and wrong in the context of all kinds of stories about the past, learn to identify and respect differences and similarities between ways of life in different places and at different times, consider why people may have made the choices they did. In making inferences about artefacts, they learn how they may have been made and used, and how they affected people's lives. They can learn to articulate and defend their opinions.

History and equal opportunities: gender, ethnicity, special educational needs

Principles of inclusion underpin the continuum of early years education. It is important to work with parents to ensure that all children feel secure and valued and that no child is disadvantaged because of ethnicity, culture or religion, home background, family background, special educational needs, disability, gender or ability (DfEE/QCA 1999a: 30–7; 2000a: 11).

These principles underpin planning at all levels. History in particular is a subject which can encourage stereotypical attitudes from an early age. It is also a subject which can challenge traditional attitudes to gender and ethnicity if opportunities are planned and resources and activities are expertly selected to do so.

Gender

It is important to include stories about famous women in the past alongside those of men, and also to interpret stories from female viewpoints (Pounce 1995), to include the lives of ordinary men and women and to discuss how women are portrayed (Ostler 1995). Children's interpretations in role-play may offer opportunities to challenge assumptions. In play about castles, for example, they can be shown medieval sources with illustrations of women defending battlements under siege (Clare 1993) such as the story of Margaret Paston who defended her castle in her husband's absence (Davis 1983) and later, like many widows of the time, ran his business affairs, or the story of Anne Clifford who maintained a vast network of castles across Northern England in the seventeenth century (Clifford 1992). Gender roles of pirates can be contested by stories of the pirate queens (e.g. Martin 1980; Mahy 1987). Stereotypical play about soldiers can be contested by stories of women like Phoebe Hesse, who went to war in the distant past (Moorhouse and Randall 1994), and compared with play about female soldiers and fighter pilots today.

Often teachers need to search out and retell stories from adult texts because such women are under-represented in school books. Miles (1989) warns us not to rely on well-known examples of women who were like men, such as Joan of Arc and Boudicca, which she calls the pop-up, cigarette-card version of women's history. She tells us about a queen who planned the irrigation of Babylon, about Aspasia the 'first Lady of Athens' who taught Socrates and Aristotle, and about a woman called Aristoclea who taught mathematics to Pythagoras.

One year 1/2 class developed some excellent research and role play based on photographs of Amy Johnson, the famous woman aviator, and on information books about early aeroplanes. They compared them with photographs of aeroplanes and newspaper articles about female fighter pilots today, but this required the initiative of the student teacher who planned it.

Old advertising posters in a role-play shop obtained from the History of Advertising Trust compared with modern equivalents provide sound starting-points for talking about the changing roles of women. The National Trust has produced books such as *Scrub-a-dub Nellie* (Woodhouse 1992) through which young children can explore the real lives of ordinary women in the past, possibly linked to a visit to a 'big house' and role-play corner, using a variety of literacy skills, sequencing jobs in Nellie's day as a housemaid, making lists and diary entries. But is it also important to remember that boys and girls may enjoy different aspects of history and choose to respond to them in different ways. Boys may enjoy reading and creating information text (diagrams, plans, instructions, captions, labels) rather than stories. If this encourages their reading and writing skills, which have been shown to lag behind those of girls (Hayes 1998; Sukhnandan *et al.* 2000), then this is another aspect of positive discrimination.

Ethnicity

Claire (1966: 39–79) shows, through practical examples, how stories about the past can promote the ethics of equality and diversity. She provides excellent references and guidance on how to use oral history about families, artefacts and photographs from the past to help young children get to the heart of equality issues about race, class and gender. They learn how to value relationships across generations, make connections, and discover change and continuity. She also gives excellent advice on how to help young children understand through drama, role-play and hot-seating, why interpretations of the lives of famous people may change. She gives references to a range of simple biographies and other resources which avoid bias and sexism.

Special educational needs

The Code of Practice (DfE 1994; DfEE/QCA 2000c) requires teachers and other professionals, when appropriate, to identify children's specific learning difficulties, abilities or disabilities, and to work with the child, parents and other supporting adults to draw up, monitor and review Individual Education Plans, which enable the child to work within the same topics as his or her peers, but at appropriate levels and in suitable ways. It is possible to provide for this wide variety of needs in history because historical sources are varied: they may be written, but can also be visual, tactile, oral (music or talking to a person); sources can be responded to at many levels and in many ways, through signing, touch, play and a variety of information technologies. Here are three examples from classes in different schools.

Elizabeth has Down's Syndrome. She has fluctuating hearing loss. She can be stubborn and bossy. She speaks in sentences, though not always clearly; she likes looking at books and helping. The teacher asks her support assistant Mrs A to observe her playing in the Victorian kitchen area and to intervene occasionally to help her develop her concepts of 'old' and 'new' by finding out how the artefacts were used.

Mrs A watched Elizabeth playing, occasionally saying, for example 'that's a very old kitchen . . . that's how things used to be . . .'. Mrs A then showed Elizabeth a picture of a similar 'old kitchen'. Elizabeth spent a lot of time playing in the kitchen. Mrs A observed her warming the iron by the fire. Elizabeth invited Mrs A in for a cup of tea, and Mrs A showed Elizabeth how to use the toasting fork to (pretend to) toast a piece of bread by the fire for tea. Later in the week, Mrs A and Elizabeth talked about other artefacts in the kitchen, their names, use, shape and materials, and Elizabeth chose to draw the iron and to colour and cut out her drawing for the class display.

Ben has a visual impairment. When his class visited a local church, they found beautiful tactile patterns to explore, many with stories to work out – on the pulpit and the font, memorial stones, statues, brasses, floor tiles. Some children made drawings, some drew a floor plan. Ben's group made rubbings of the floor tiles under the font. Back in school a drawing of the west front was made into a large tactile collage, using bright coloured rope, painted matchsticks and lollipop sticks and other junk materials. Ben's group made their floor tile rubbings into pottery tiles which were glazed and fired. They wrote a book about the church. Ben's entry, in large type, says, 'The church has a font with a wooden lid. The font has patterns on it. There is a patterned floor underneath.'

John is in his first term in a Reception class. He has a Stage 5 full statement of special behavioural needs. Lee is on Stage 2. They both really enjoyed watching with the rest of the class a 'Magic Grandad' video about an old kitchen, and John could identify to his special attachment worker some of the things he had at home which he had seen in the video. John and Lee were both 'on task' in circle time, passing around old and new artefacts and describing them. With considerable individual support during the follow-up group work, they were also able to sort objects into old and new.

Part IV

Three case studies

This section consists of three case studies. They illustrate different approaches to planning and assessment, and different curriculum content and teaching strategies.

Case study 1 (Chapter 9) describes collaboratively planned work in the Nursery and Reception classes in an Early Years Unit which is part of a primary school. The history focus on Toys and Games, Now and Then, based on Early Learning Goals for Knowledge and Understanding of the World (DfEE/QCA 2000a), was developed over four weeks using a High Scope approach. Parents' help was solicited and they became highly involved in the theme, both in and out of school. Their children encouraged them 'not to be shy'. It was a motivating, shared experience for both parents and children. Assessment opportunities identified in the medium-term plans are based on focused observation and discussion.

Case study 2, 'Castles' (Chapter 10) describes work in a year 1 class, which was the history dimension of an integrated topic on 'Buildings' including class, group and individual work. The long-term plan is shown in Box 10.1. A sequence of activities was planned which reflected strands of historical thinking within level descriptors, and assessment was based on the teacher's notes of conversations with the whole class, groups and individuals. Extracts from these notes show how open-ended tasks reflect the complexities of children's thinking and thus the need to return constantly to the same statements of attainment in different contexts.

Case study 3 (Chapter 11) describes how a year 2 class created a class museum. This was a history-focused topic which lasted a term. The teacher had clear ideas of the kinds of historical thinking she was trying to develop, but the work evolved and differentiation was built in through observing children's responses to activities and allowing them to develop their own ideas. As the teacher observed and evaluated, she noted possible alternatives and extensions for a subsequent class. By the end of the term, children themselves were able to suggest a variety of ways in which they might respond to an activity. Assessment was ongoing and formative, based on observations, discussion, writing and drawing.

Chapter 9

Case study 1: A Reception and a Nursery class – 'Toys and Games, Now and Then'

In this case study, a history-focused topic was taught over four weeks to 3- to 5-year-olds in an Early Years Unit attached to a primary school. The Nursery class was taught by Elizabeth Hart and the Reception class by Sarah Spink, both fourth-year BA (QTS) students on their Final Block Placement. Together they developed a shared medium-term plan for each Area of Learning. Box 9.1 shows the plan for history within the area of Knowledge and Understanding of the World.

From these medium-term plans Elizabeth wrote integrated weekly plans for the Nursery class and Sarah wrote individual lesson plans linked by content for the Reception class. There were plenty of teddy bear stories for both classes (for example, Waddell 1990, 1991, 1992, 1994a, 1994b, 1996, 1999a, 1999b).

The unit was organised around Learning Areas on a High Scope basis. At the beginning of a session, each child chose three cards representing the areas in which he or she wanted to work; lists in each area were ticked when a child had finished working there. Elizabeth and Sarah designed a matrix showing available activities each week on one axis and the adults supporting them on the other axis, blocking in the squares to show which activities each was working on. All the adults, those working in the school and parents participating on a voluntary basis, were given notes showing the aim of their activity, possible questions, and intervention and assessment opportunities. The children were pleased to receive me as a visitor to the Teddy Museum at the end of week three. They explained the information they had compiled on how to use the museum, expansively decorated with click-art teddy bears. 'You can look at the teddies, cuddle the teddies, look at their names, show your friends your teddy.' The old teddies on the higher shelves had to be brought down carefully – 'because they're very old'. We read the labels tied with bows around their necks: 'Heather's dad's bear', 'Emma's dad's bear', 'Simon's and Jamie's dad's teddy'. We examined evidence of their antiquity and fragility: 'Lauren's mummy's ted's got a plaster, and it's got stitches in it where it got mended', 'Jodie's mum's ted's got holes in – it's a bit older, and his fur's got ripped.'

Box 9.1 Medium-term plan (weeks 1–4) for Knowledge and Understanding of the World – Nursery and Reception ('Toys and Games, Now and Then')

Week	Learning Objectives	Activities	Links to Early Learning Goals, Knowledge and Understanding of the World	Assessment opportunities
1	To sustain attentive listening, responding to what they have learned with relevant comments, questions or actions	Each day children will describe a favourite toy, explain what it is made of, why they like it, demonstrate how it works. Range of toys may include, e.g. computer game, construction toy, talking doll, puppet, toy car	Show interest in the world in which they live. Investigate objects using all their senses as appropriate. Find out about and identify uses of everyday technology	(Focus children) can speak with confidence, show awareness of listeners, take turns to speak
2	To develop and stimulate interest in an awareness of the past; of changes over time and reasons for changes, and of continuity	Each day a parent or adult working in class shows and describes a favourite toy from their childhood; invites and answers questions. Range may include e.g. teddy, doll, bricks, toy car, fort / doll's house	Talk about similarities and differences between children's favourite toys and parents' favourite toys. Raise questions and suggest reasons for differences	(Focus children) ask questions, identify similarities and differences between their favourite toys and parents' favourite toys

3	To work as part of a class, sharing fairly, understanding need for agreed values and codes for adults and children to work harmoniously together. Extend vocabulary. Use everyday words to decide position; more/less; size; sets	Collect information about parents' teddies. Collect information about parents' favourite toys. Set up a 'teddy bear museum' of 'old' and 'new' teddies using parents' and children's teddies. Agree rules and labels for museum. Make work bank to describe old and new teddies	Find out about past and present events in their own lives and in those of their families	Children and parents work together to complete information sheets on favourite toys and on teddies. Children use teddy museum according to agreed rules. Use appropriate adjectives to describe old and new teddies. Parents visit toy museum with children
4	To move with confidence, control and co-ordination; to use imagination in music, dance (role-play)	Children will learn about and participate in a variety of outdoor games from the past in outdoor play area: hopscotch, hoops, marbles, oranges and lemons, Poor Mary lies a-weeping, The Farmer's in his Den, The Grand Old Duke of York	Find out about past and present; similarities and differences	Children understand that these games were played by children a long time ago. Children participate. Demonstrate understanding of roles in games.

The new teddies provided much evidence not only of their comparative youth, but also of their lives in a contemporary world – football shirts, Coca-Cola advertisements, jewellery. A flag announces that Ryan's teddy had come from Canada and Lauren's bear from the 'Millennium 2000 Collection'. They seemed to live a more colourful and complex life than the previous generation of bears. Indeed, their social group was altogether wider, encompassing La La, a Teletubby, Laura's lamb, Liam's dog, a Koala bear from Canada and Kieran's white polar bear. The new bears also wore labels: 'Ryan O'Sullivan's teddy'. 'That's my name. That's my teddy,' Ryan explained. 'It's a new teddy. That's why I brought it. He's called Eddy.' 'Mine's called Thomas – read the label. He's fluffy because he's young.'

When I remarked on the differences I had inferred between the lives of teddies now and in the past, I was invited to read more about the changes in the lives of teddies.

'Put the teddies back carefully and look at the books,' the notice said. We read about Old Teddies Discovered through History and about collecting bears to make a teddy bear museum (Bryant-Mole 1996), advice which the children told me had been helpful in making their museum. We also found out more about other kinds of toys, new and old (Lemans 1992; Purkis 1991; Blyth 1991).

Then the children showed me the information books they had made for their museum. There was one big folder of letters their parents had scribed for them (completing spaces in a pro forma) giving more details about the teddy each child had brought in. Ian's dad helped him explain that Ian had had his teddy since he was born, and the teddy was therefore four years and ten months old. His name is Mark and Ian likes him 'because he was a present from his grandma and granddad when Ian was born'. In spite of his youth, he has had a not uneventful life: 'his ear tore and mummy mended it'. Teddy Mark enjoys visits to Scarborough to see Ian's grandparents and cousins.

Then the children showed me a second folder of photographed sheets they had compiled with their parents' help, comparing their parents' favourite toys with theirs. Jodie found hers and explained, 'This writing says that I like Harry because he is soft and cuddly and he's 3 years old, and here it says that my mum liked her dolls' pram because you can put things in it and do walks and things.' 'All the mums like to come in to look in the books and talk about them,' Bethany said. 'And the dads,' said Ryan, 'but they all say don't put mine in and they giggle – but we did!'

Then it was time for the Nursery children to round off Friday afternoon with a circle time. Elizabeth's weekly plan for 'language, communication, literacy and PSE' stated that the learning objectives were: to respect others and their possessions; to take turns to share feelings and experiences in the group; and to develop self-esteem. The children passed around one of the new teddies and gave him a big cuddle because, as they said in turn, he feels 'soft', 'really furry', 'cosy'. Then they agreed that Miss Hart should be very gentle with the very old teddy, because 'he's old', 'he's got a wobbly head', 'we have to look after him', 'he looks sad'. Then one child found the page in *Teddy Bears* (Purkis 1991) with a picture of 'the oldest teddy in the world', who, like their Old Ted, looked very sad. Circle time ended with passing the old teddy around, and each child saying why they liked Old Ted, then why they liked someone in the circle.

Chapter 10

Case study 2: year 1 – 'Castles'

This case study illustrates the history dimension of an integrated topic, lasting one term, on 'Buildings', including class, group and individual work. The long-term plan is shown in Box 10.1. The class teacher was Julie Giles.

Box 10.1 Long-term plan for history activities showing assessment opportunities

Activities	Historical thinking	Assessment opportunities
Activity 1: picture reading ↓ Activity 2: class story ↓ Activity 5: collage	*Deductions from sources* Find out about the past from sources of information	Talk about a picture of a castle Listen to children talking as they make their collage, to see how they apply information from picture story and reference books to the collage. Take notes
Activity 3: reinforcing ↓ selected vocabulary Activity 4: draw examples for 'houses now' and 'castles then' (e.g. doors, windows, cooking, lighting)	*Time and change* Identify differences between past and present	Listen to children talking as they identify differences between buildings, and daily life in 'houses now' and 'castles then'
Activity 6: listen to story about Robin Hood	• *Interpretations* Beginning to show awareness that the past is represented in different ways	Ask children in small groups • Do you think Robin Hood is a true story?

• *Time and change* Place in sequence events in a story	• Can you remember what happened in the story?
• *Motive* Suggest reasons why people in the past acted as they did	• Why do you think Robin Hood killed Guy of Guisborne? Why was Little John arrested? Why did Robin Hood rescue Little John?

The activities allow children to demonstrate, by talking to each other and to the teacher, that they have achieved level 1 in each of the attainment targets (and are working towards level 2).

The plans for activities are followed by notes of children's conversations during the activities, recorded for assessment. The selected vocabulary introduced and used included:

drawbridge, gatehouse, moat, stables, stores, guardroom, latrines, well, arrows, slits, lord.

ACTIVITY 1: PICTURE READING (WHOLE-CLASS ACTIVITY)

Aims
- to identify differences between past and present;
- to communicate information acquired from an historical source;
- to make deductions;
- to develop concept of a castle.

Method
- Show children a large tourist poster of people visiting a castle today.
- Ask them what they can work out from the picture.
- Write children's comments around the edge of the picture – each child adds his or her name to his or her comment.
- Have any of the children seen a castle? Where? Was it like this one? Different? How?

ACTIVITY 2: CLASS STORY – A FICTIONAL STORY SET IN THE PAST

Aims
- to help children to imagine what it might have been like to have lived in a castle a long time ago;
- to understand that stories may be about real people or fictional characters;
- to place in sequence events in a story.

Method • Read *The Castle* (Rowe 1991). This is an illustrated story about life in a castle from the point of view of a spit-boy who discovers that 'Grey Fox' is planning to attack.
  • Use information in pictures to discuss differences between a castle and a house, and what it might have been like to have lived in a castle.

ACTIVITY 3: CHILDREN WORK IN PAIRS

Aim • to reinforce selected, specialised vocabulary, introduced in discussing picture, story and information books.

Method • Children are given photocopied plans or picture of a castle and set of cards. Each card has a specialised concept written on it which was previously introduced and used in discussing the picture, story and information books.
  • Children working in pairs take cards in turn and try to link them to parts of the castle plan or picture.
  • Discuss their labels with teacher; modify if necessary.
  • Use cards to label their drawing of a castle.

ACTIVITY 4: INDIVIDUAL

Aims • to help children to identify differences between past and present;
  • to learn and use special vocabulary.

Method • Children choose card(s). On each card is written a feature common to a castle and a house (e.g. door, window, wall, light) or an activity carried out in a castle and a house (e.g. cooking, washing, getting water).
  • Children draw a picture illustrating their card 'now' and 'in a castle'.

ACTIVITY 5: CHILDREN WORK IN SUCCESSIVE GROUPS AS CLASSROOM ORGANISATION ALLOWS

Aims • to use information in picture, story and reference books in order to communicate information from an historical source. This will also involve asking questions about the past, making deductions and developing an awareness that filling in the gaps in the evidence makes different interpretations possible in reconstructing the past.

Method • Using what they have learned from picture, story and reference books, first group discusses the site of a castle with the teacher (need for defensive position – on cliff or hill – and for water for moat and daily use). Sketch in chalk on very large paper with teacher's support. Sponge-print background.

• Second group uses books and previous knowledge to find out, with teacher's help, materials available to build a castle (e.g. wood, stone, thatch), and the requirements of a castle (e.g. defensive walls, keep, drawbridge, portcullis, narrow windows, battlements). Children decide how to represent materials in collage (e.g. balsa for wood, polystyrene for stone, dried grass for thatch). Sketch out the castle on to background with teacher's support. Make collage of courtyard, walls and keep.

• Third group discusses with teacher and finds out from books the people who might live in the castle, their clothes, the jobs they might do; draws people for collage.

ACTIVITY 6: WHOLE-CLASS STORY, FOLLOWED BY DISCUSSION BETWEEN TEACHER AND SMALL GROUPS

Aims • to help children to place in sequence events in a story about the past;
• to suggest reasons why people in the past acted as they did;
• to understand that stories can be about real or fictional characters.

Method • Read a story about Robin Hood to the class.
• Children draw a picture story (or make a zig-zag book) to retell the story.
• As they do this, teacher discusses the story with individuals or small groups and makes notes on their comments.

Notes from children's conversations are recorded for assessment.

Example I: communicate information acquired from an historical source

Activity I: picture reading

K   The castle is made of stone.
M   The windows are narrow.
C   That's to stop arrows hitting them.
M   The windows are rectangles.
K   They don't have glass in.

Deductions:

K   This may be an island. There is water.
M   It's a photograph. A painting would not be so smooth and clear.

Activity 5: children talk as they make a collage of a castle based on information in picture, story and reference books

D   The men go up there to protect the people. (The baddies would climb over.) They have things on their heads to protect them.
E   Yeah – helmets.
D   The door is so people who live there can get in – and visitors.
E   But if an enemy climbed up the ladder you could pull down the ladder.
M   They'd fall in the moat. There's water all around the castle.
J   I've got a fort at home. It's a proper castle. And you can climb up the walls. And I've seen a real castle . . . with a moat . . .
D   Yeah – that's why the bridge comes up. The people come running up and if they're on the bridge they fall in the water.
E   And if they climb up you could put all hot stuff on, and they get burnt.
M   They had a gate that goes up and down. It's a . . . a – yeah – a portcullis. There are windows for the arrows to go out, and people outside can't hit the people because they're too narrow.
D   And there's water in the pots at the bottom of the tower, and flour in the bags.
E   On the next floor there's fire to keep them warm – and to cook.
D   And there's a thing you turn round. It's a . . . a . . . a . . . a spit fire!
E   And there's a spit-boy that turns the wheel.
D   And they eat animals.
E   They kill a cow.
M   And lambs. They have food for all the people in the houses inside the castle.
E   The things in the top room are for when people attack the castle.
D   At home I've got soldiers, and they fight . . . when I don't even *move* them! And the bridge went up, and they fell in the river! . . . (it's not really the river – it's *hard*!) . . . I got squashed on the bridge when I was there! And one of my soldiers got his head squashed! I said, 'Oh – the blood's coming out . . .'

(This is a good example of how evidence and imagination interact for young children.)

Example 2: identify differences between past and present

Activities 3/4: use selected vocabulary to identify differences between 'houses now' and 'castles then'

The children talk as they draw windows, walls and doors, etc.

L   They didn't have glass.
J   They had wooden, protecting things.
L   They had arrow things. . . . They were called arrow slits.
J   No, L. The arrow slits were in the walls.
D   The glass is bigger in our windows.
L   The castle windows are to protect people.
J   Glass can break. We've got a broken window.
L   Yeah – a thief stole my mum's car radio – he just broke the window.
D   There are lots of windows in a castle, but there's no glass and no curtains . . .
J   They had a drawbridge instead of a door.
L   You pulled it up if you didn't want someone to come in to protect themselves. They wanted the castle and they wanted no one to take it away.
E   We haven't got enemies any more. Castles can be dangerous . . . nobody lives in castles any more . . . They're not used any more. People can look at castles now.
L   Even the Queen doesn't live in a castle now.
T   How do you know?
L   I've been past – it's a great big garden . . .
J   There are arrow slits in their walls.
D   Our walls are brick. They've invented bricks now. In a castle they're stone.
J   Stones and cement. They both have cement.
D   Bricks are rectangular – stones are just lumps of rock.
J   In a castle the walls were very big . . .

Activity 1: picture reading

Children's statements are written around the poster, and signed by them:

> The picture is recent.
> We know that because there are cars in it.
> And houses.
> And coaches.
> And caravans.
> And boats.
> The car park is big because all the visitors want to explore the castle . . .

Example 3a: understand that stories may be about real people or fictional characters

Teacher	Do you think the story of Robin Hood is true?
C	I think Robin Hood is true because he does not look like a real person in the books. I've been to Disneyland and I think I saw Robin Hood there. *And* Little John and Maid Marian are true because they're *good* characters and they would fit in with Robin Hood's team . . .

[after listening to E]

	Robin Hood *may* be true, but the picture may not be like Robin Hood was.
A	It *is* true – because there was a man called Robin Hood. Because it said in the story.
K	Yes, because when Robin Hood was alive, when King John was King. He might have been fighting with Prince Richard – Mrs G told us there was a real Prince Richard.
E	I think the story is *not* real because the person who made the book wouldn't be alive when Robin Hood was.
C	I don't know. Robin Hood might still be alive now.
E	*And also* I don't think Robin Hood is real because it's just pictures – and I don't think Robin Hood is so good as they put in the books.

This discussion illustrates the knowledge children need in order to discuss whether a person in a folk tale really lived. They would have found the question easier in the context of a giant's or Cinderella's castle. Nevertheless, the quality of their reasoning and the exchange of ideas is impressive.

The children who said the story was true all tried to support their statement with an argument: *because* . . . I *think* I saw him; *because* . . . they would fit in; *because* it said so in the story; *because* other events in the story were said by Mrs G to be real. It is interesting that within these arguments there are different levels of reasoning: 'it said so in the story' is less carefully reasoned than C's arguments, and K actually cross-referenced with events she knew to be historical. Although E may be correct, and does seem to be trying to express the idea that the story is a legend or folk tale since she implies that Robin Hood is an idealised character, the argument that the author could not be his contemporary and so the story cannot be true, although showing awareness of time, is less valid than K's argument that if Prince Richard is true, so may Robin Hood be true.

It is interesting that the children were engaged in genuine discussion. C was reappraising her arguments after listening to E, although she later decided to stick with them, while E, when challenged, found more arguments to support her own view.

Example 3b: Place in sequence events in a story

Teacher Can you remember what happened in this story? [Robin Hood]
C Robin Hood was in a wood. Little John got captured. He was going to be hung by the neck. Then Robin chopped the rope and he escaped.
A Robin Hood got loads of men – and there's bows and arrows and there's Maid Marian, and she's riding a horse, and there's deer there, and Robin rode in the forest with Little John and Little John was going to get hanged, but Robin saved him.

The story had a complex plot, sub-plots and a number of characters. Robin Hood killed Guy of Guisbourne because he said he had come to kill Robin. Little John was captured. He was going to be killed. Robin, dressed as Guy of Guisbourne, told the sheriff he had come to kill Robin's servant, then rescued him.

It is interesting that both these children selected the characters and sequence of key events (Little John was captured and about to be hanged but Robin saved him). They did not offer any causal explanations. However, they were able to do this when questioned more closely.

Example 3c: Suggest reasons why people in the past may have acted as they did

Activity 6: class story – Robin Hood

Teacher Why do you think Robin Hood killed Guy of Guisbourne?
E I don't think he was *planning* to. He just shot a bow and arrow and got him, right in the shoulder.
C I don't think he meant to. He just wanted to do that so he wouldn't do it any more . . . take poor people's food away . . .
K He was a baddie. Because he was looking for Robin Hood.
Teacher Why was Little John arrested?
E He killed the soldier.
C Because he shot too many of his men. He wouldn't have any crew – any team left.
K He shot one of the King's men.
Teacher Why did Robin Hood rescue Little John?
C He was his friend – one of his team.
E He dressed up as one of his team and said Robin Hood's body was lying on the ground, but it wasn't really him.
K Little John was a goody and if he hangs up he's going to die.

Although these answers are factually correct, they reveal different levels of response. E and C are aware of chance as a cause; A implies that Robin

Hood could not be wicked because of other evidence in the story; E recounts the circumstances which accounted for the rescue. Other answers were simply based on 'goodies' and 'baddies' as sufficient explanation of motive and events.

Chapter 11

Case study 3: year 2 – 'A class museum'

This was a history-focused topic lasting one term taught by Angela Kinsett. It involved sequences of activities investigating artefacts, photographs, and written and oral sources which evolved through enquiries initiated by children and were developed by the teacher.

Throughout the school, work was topic-based. Although this topic had a history focus, other topics had no clear curriculum focus (e.g. air, designing a house, road safety). The ethos of the school centres on collaboration and on co-operative teaching and learning; children are encouraged to plan their own work. Children work in groups or pairs for each task; groups are selected according to children's ability to cope with a specific task. During the course of the day the class meets to share ideas.

This case study was not planned in detail before it was begun as the work developed in response to questions and new evidence. However, the teacher was clear throughout about the aspects of historical thinking she wanted to develop and activities were focused on these.

After discussion about the ways in which people find out about the past, the children unanimously decided to have a museum. Although the teacher had hoped that the museum would be about parents when they were young, the children, who had little experience of working on personal history, were far more interested in their own past and decided to collect information about 'Us as Babies'. They were soon inundated with photographs and artefacts, which gave rise to questions, to looking for differences and making comparisons, using a great deal of time vocabulary.

All the photographs and artefacts were put on display and labelled by the children. They took responsibility for the museum, for keeping it tidy, changing displays, ensuring exhibits were handled carefully and explaining them to visitors.

Children's interest in their own past led them to ask questions about the childhood of their parents and grandparents, and they brought in a variety of older objects and photographs.

Ebony and Sarah wrote explanatory labels for the photographs of their parents as children. They all showed an awareness of change over time and communicated information derived from the photographs. Sarah's photograph raised questions beyond the information in the picture. The children's writing describes parents' different experiences of the past.

> This is my Daddy with my Granny. My daddy is young. Granny is bout 35 in this Picture. My daddy iS about 1 month old in thiS Picture. it iS Summer.
>
> (Emily)

> When my Mummy was young She lived in Jamaica WiTh her grandMa and her two broThers. She had tWo PiCTures Taken in JaMaica tWo OF The PiCTures show a difference about My Mummy. In one of the pictures she is little and in the othew one She is big.
>
> (By Ebony)

> *When my Mummy was young*
> I lived in the country The milk was delivered by horse and cart the large urns were on the back oF the cart. We went to the door with a jug and walter he drove the cart. He measured the milk into the jub. With a ladle. the horse was called dolly. When I was 10 years old I went to secondary school I taravelled by bus through the Country lanes and it took Over an hour. Every year the river Flooded . . .

> *When my daddy was young*
> I Lived on an estate. athe At the bottom ofmy garden was a railWay line and a river. Every day whe I Walked to School I went past a Cotton mill called hardmans Where lots of our neighbours worked. on Saturday mornings I went to the Odean cinema with my brother and our friends.
>
> (Sarah)

The teacher then planned sequences of activities related to other sources: artefacts, photographs and postcards, written and oral sources.

ARTEFACTS

Activity 1: communicating information about an historical source (level 1)

The children were given a selection of objects. They looked at them, handled them, talked about them and shared their ideas. (A tape-recorder was used to record descriptions and for assessment purposes.) Once they were very familiar with the objects, they drew them. The children needed to handle objects to develop observational skills. This activity was repeated a number of times to encourage such development.

Activity 2: using sources to stimulate questions about the past (level 2)

Once children were familiar with handling, observing and talking about objects, they were asked to devise a sheet of questions relating to the investigation of objects. This was an activity for groups. One child in each group had the task of scribing and also of leading the group, thus encouraging active involvement in discussion and relieving the less confident writers of a headache. Sheets were trialled by other groups, followed by discussion and the drawing up of a class sheet for use throughout the project. This was always open to revision.

Activity 3: selecting information from sources to answer specific questions about the past (level 3)

A group of children was given a number of related objects. A box filled with 1950s kitchen utensils led to questions, discussion and guessing (it could have been developed to compare kitchens now and in the 1950s). Once the children were familiar with the objects, they drew them and wrote observations.

Children's questions about sources led them to use information books to help answer their questions. Emily aged 6, brought in an old bottle. She showed the bottle to the class and told them what she knew about it. The children put forward their own ideas and suggestions. Emily then went off to the library to research the bottle and came back with a book showing an identical bottle and some information, which she shared with the rest of the school in an assembly.

Activity 4: putting together information from different sources (level 3/4)

A very successful activity resulted from a suitcase of artefacts being sent in by a parent. All the artefacts related to her childhood. The suitcase contained two swimming certificates, an identity card, a key, two different sized bracelets, a small brown leather purse containing coins and a box camera. The task of investigation was given to a mixed ability group of children. They were given the suitcase to open and to talk about. They were given the task of recording what was inside, as it was not theirs to keep. The children decided between them who would do what. They decided they could find out about Mrs C by asking her questions about the objects in the suitcase and the best way was to write letters. The children set about drafting and redrafting their letters. Questions were not always fruitful, but there was a keen sense of wanting to know.

Within a few days, Mrs C had replied to all the children. She really went to great lengths to answer all the children's questions, to supply the information they wanted, so that they could piece together a small part of her past.

Letters written by Mrs C to the children were a source of information but could also have been used as a basis for distinguishing between facts and points of view, and this could be an area for development.

Activity 5

Children were again able to ask questions about a variety of sources when they visited the Reminiscence Centre run by Age Concern in Blackheath (level 3/4).

The centre is divided into the oil shop, washday and the parlour. Children were able to investigate these three areas, ask questions of the elderly people, listen to their reminiscences, make observational drawings and fill in worksheets if appropriate. They were able to present some of their findings to parents and other children, through drama, as part of their Christmas celebrations.

Natalie became Margaret, one of the ladies who had talked to them. She sat with other children around her and they asked her questions about Christmas when she was young.

Q Did you have Christmas decorations?
A We were too poor to buy decorations, but I remember making paper chains out of newspaper.

A book of Christmas memories at the Reminiscence Centre was also a source of information. It would also be a useful resource in the development of the ability to understand interpretations of history. 'Merry Christmas: greetings in the mother tongue of nine minority groups' (see p. 218) could have added a bilingual dimension.

Activity 6

An adult visiting the school left a Victorian writing slate and a class reading board. This was the beginning of an investigation into 'The Victorian School Room'. A large group of children undertook this task and between them found out how different schools were in the past. They set up their own small class, sat in rows with hands behind backs, and stood up to talk to the teacher. They found out about the clothes they would have worn and the work they would have done, used pen and ink for handwriting (with no blots!), tried out some cross stitch, had a go at learning tables and found out how difficult it is to do the things we do today when confined to a desk.

Activity 7: making deductions from sources, identifying differences between past and present, and placing objects in chronological order

Favourite artefacts turned out to be cameras and teddies.

Cameras

Groups discussed similarities and differences between these and listed lots of questions that needed answering: how do you take a picture with an old camera? Where does the film go? How does it open?

Old photographs or postcards

These formed the basis for observation and questionnaires about what had changed: types of shops, fashion, street furniture, vehicles on the road. Children engaged in activities, generally in pairs. If two children of differing ability worked together, the more able scribed, encouraging the partner to help with initial sounds, and to give ideas. Problems did occur if two more able children worked together. Often they wanted to work independently and not share their ideas. They wanted to produce their own pieces of work. This presented an opportunity to talk about why we collaborate and co-operate in our work; what can be gained by combining ideas and expertise.

When working with postcards, observation and discussion were the first skills to be developed. Each activity took the children a step forward. Children could jump in at the stage most appropriate for them, some progressing further than others. The children were being directed towards an historical approach to questioning. They had the opportunity to share their work with the rest of the class during one of the times they came together.

Activities relating to postcards

Activity 1: communicating information from an historical source orally

In pairs, the children were given a postcard to look at. They talked with their partner about what they could see. They shared their observations with another group or with the class.

Activity 2: communicating information from an historical source in writing

In pairs, the children were given a postcard to look at. They talked about what they could see and wrote down a list of observations. They shared their observations.

Activity 3: recognising that sources can stimulate questions about the past

In pairs, the children looked at a postcard, talked about it and wrote down any questions they wanted to find the answers to. They shared their questions with the class and others began to think about answering the questions.

Activity 4: recognising that sources can help to answer questions about the past

The children were set the task of trying to find the answers to their questions. They could also help find the answers to someone else's questions. This led to discussion on how they could find the answers.

Activity 5: identifying differences between past and present, and describing changes over time

A natural progression would have been to take a theme – buildings, fashion or transport – and to have given the children a selection of pictures relating to a particular period. They could have looked for styles, similarities, differences, particularly in fashion, between rich and poor. If different groups of children had taken different periods, further discussion could have taken place on developments and changes in time. Work could have been displayed on a time-line.

Activity 6: asking questions about a source

Photographs of the local area formed the basis for discussion on what happened in Lee Green during the Second World War. Photographs showed street scenes, people celebrating, an air-raid shelter in the background, the Union Jack at the window, a bomb site. These raised many questions.

Written documents

A letter written by a former resident of the area was investigated by a group of able children. Their first task was to decipher the writing (no mean task!) and to extract relevant information. They were able to sort the information into that about the area and that relating to the Second World War. A development from this was to gather together the relevant artefacts, pictures and information on the Second World War and present these as a section on their own in the museum. It could easily have been investigated further.

Information about the area
The Pond was crowded with skaters.
We Were out in the park every SPare minute.
They had a park next to their house.
They had huge horse chest nuts.
I hope they put back the cherry tree.

Information about the war
Finding out about War.
Bob had just come in from Washing and shaving at the sink, a bomb dropped not far away it landed right upon the sink. Had he been there he would haVe been killed. They had the air raid shelter in the big field. They were underGround. This was they used planes. They tried to bomb woolwich Arsenal. becouse they mod bombs and guns there. The people must have felt scared.

(Both extracts from Mrs C's letter)

ORAL HISTORY

An exciting area of this project was interviewing people about their childhood. Various activities took place before interviews to encourage children to think carefully about questions, to consider the person being interviewed and to get the best out of the occasion.

It was necessary to consider whom to invite to be interviewed – men and women of different ethnic groups and backgrounds. Adults who grew up in different countries are able to offer a new dimension, to develop children's perspective of a wider world, of different cultures and ways of life. This provided an excellent opportunity to discuss similarities and differences. It was necessary to consider what the adult would talk about: childhood, in relation to a specific topic – washday, evacuation, or a particular artefact, 'My favourite toy'. Would the children understand the visitor? Would the visitor hear the children? Had the children planned the questions they wanted to ask? How would the interview be recorded? Was a permanent record of the interview wanted?

Activity 1: a class activity

Once it had been decided to invite a particular person, the children were asked to compose a letter giving some background information about the topic. A few children were given the task of writing out the letter.

Activity 2: a class activity

What questions should be asked? The children were asked for ideas, which were written down. They decided to list their ideas under headings such as home, school, toys, washing, cooking, transport. The children asked questions spontaneously but it was a good idea to have the list available to refer to when necessary.

Mrs C, one of the parents, brought in a washboard, an old iron, a trivet and a carpet beater, all of which fascinated the children. Her interest in anything old resulted in information being at her fingertips and she was able to answer questions prepared by the children. Afterwards, groups of children worked on observational drawings, writing labels for the museum and researching the artefacts further.

Mrs O, a parent from Ghana, brought in a traditional cooking pot and told the children how it was used for cooking, and the types of food cooked in it. The children likened it to cooking on a barbecue. She came in a while later and talked to the children about her childhood in Ghana. The children were delighted to hear that she had lived in a large house, had a swimming pool and servants, and that her mother was a head teacher. After describing life for her family, Mrs O also related how others had lived in entirely different circumstances and still do.

Mrs B was a friend of the school. She was 70 years old and seemed to remember every detail of her childhood. The children had a wonderful time asking her questions. They built up a family tree about her. She remembered the muffin man; beating her carpet on the line each morning; the first time she wore powder; and 'making do' in so many ways!

A variety of activities resulted from these visits:

- Children were eager to word process and desktop publish their accounts and very often worked in pairs on this task.
- Children had a go at developing their own family trees.
- Some children were fascinated by the tale of the muffin man and found out about other nursery rhymes.
- Other children made a display of artefacts Mrs B would have used when she was young, and found information in relevant books.
- Another group re-enacted washday as it would have been for Mrs B as a child.

Before the class museum was dismantled, children had an opportunity to invite a friend to come and visit it. Letters were drafted and written and replies were received. Year 2 children had the delight of sharing their museum, their work, with others.

> i remember when mrss was youny she was not a allowed to wear make up and was allowed to wear powder she had no carpets no electric light she had to scrub the floors and the table. she had no bath room she had a coal fire. the front room was for best only lee on sunday she had an old kettle she never had a fridge when she was 14 years old she went

to wobleworths to buy some clothes and some shoes her father grew some vegetables and they had some stew she had plastic dolls they killed their pet to eat.

ASSESSMENT

Assessment of children's work was on-going. Concepts and ideas understood in discussion were jotted down for inclusion in individual profiles along with special pieces of work which were photocopied.

Children's self-evaluation

The project was rich in opportunities for individual, paired, group and whole-class work, enabling children of all abilities to work together and, in the process of doing so, to discuss, share and evaluate both their own ideas and those of each other. Evaluation of the museum and of activities in progress was continuous. Children's opinions were sought and acted upon; after all, it was their museum.

Teacher's evaluation of the project

The children started to discuss, to compare, to sort and classify, to question, to research, to plan and communicate, to record, in a variety of ways. They became aware of history, of a time before now, that some things are older than others, of chronological sequencing, that changes occur, that things can be similar or different. They realised there is a need to respect 'oldness' and the importance people have in history, that there are many types of evidence which can be used in questioning and developing an understanding of the past.

The class museum generated a sense of curiosity about the past, co-operation between children, perseverance and independence when developing their own work and a keen sense of respect for their own museum and all it entailed. The children were open-minded and eager to find out. They were building on their historical knowledge through their own involvement and growing ability to question.

The development of a class museum was a great success, probably because all the children became so involved regardless of their ability. There were areas which were not developed because time did not allow. Asking for favourite records could have resulted in research into music as far back as the 1920s. Focusing on buildings in photographs could have led to a study of local Victorian houses. Books brought in could have developed work on interpretations of history. The list is endless.

Part V

In-service workshops

Workshops described in this section will draw on information in the previous sections of the book. Children come to school aware of a past and capable of genuine historical thinking. Developmental psychology can inform the development of children's thinking in history. This must be the basis for the planning and assessment of activities in history. History can be an integral part of a broad and rich 'early years' curriculum, based on first-hand, meaningful, experiences. The case studies illustrated how this might be achieved.

The workshops described enable teachers to use this knowledge to develop their own curricula, based on the needs and strengths of their own schools, on the resources of their own localities and on their own interests and those of the children and their families. In this way, teachers can assimilate history within existing good practice, extend their professional expertise and further contribute to our understanding of how young children can learn about the past.

Through participating in the workshops, teachers can work together to write a policy document defining:

1   The nature of history and its importance in the Key Stage 1 curriculum.
2   Activities reflecting aspects of historical thinking.
3   Resources:
    • local organisations, sites, individuals;
    • primary sources; categories collected with criteria for selection and procedures for care and storage;
    • secondary sources; criteria for selection.
4   Planning, assessment and record-keeping:
    • rationale for structuring history topics, with history or humanities focus or as integrated topics;
    • rationale and whole-school plan for topics;
    • long-term teaching and assessment plans for topics selected;
    • procedures for record-keeping;
    • examples of children's work resulting from some activities, at a range of levels.

Useful initial reading for Key Stage 1 history co-ordinators is found in *Primary History 1* (1992: 6–7), *Primary History 5* (1993:12–13) and *Teaching History at Key Stage 1* (NCC 1993: 4–5).

Chapter 12

In-service workshops: some examples

WORKSHOP I

Aim
- to write an introduction to a school policy document which defines the nature of historical thinking.

Resources
- photocopies of articles (for example, appropriately selected extracts from articles in *Teaching History* or from *Remnants, Journal of the English Heritage Education Service*, or the *National Trust Education Supplement* or *Primary History*) on issues related to different aspects of historical enquiry: making deductions from sources; historical imagination; different perspectives (class, race, gender).

Method
- Individually or in small groups read one of the articles (during or before meeting).
- Give a brief synopsis of the article to the whole group.
- Discuss why each of these aspects of historical enquiry is important. (Keep flip-chart notes.)
- Write collaborative introduction to policy document by completing key sentences, for example:
    - We find out about the past by . . .
    - Historical imagination is part of this process because . . .
    - There is no single view of the past because . . .

The following articles were used very successfully in an introductory workshop on a 20-day history course. They enabled teachers to discuss the nature of history as a discipline.

- Making deductions from sources: 'Evidence in the classroom' (Dickinson *et al.* 1978).
- Historical imagination: 'What is historical imagination?' (Little 1983).
- Different perspectives – class, race and gender: 'Whose class is it anyway?' (Jones 1985), 'A way of looking at history: local, national, global' (Collicott 1993), 'Deconstruction to reconstruction: an approach to women's history through local history' (Welbourne 1990).

Through discussing the articles, the teachers reached the conclusion that although facts may be important, facts in themselves are not history, that accounts of the past are made by selecting and interpreting facts, that imagination based on what is known is an important part of this process, and that accounts are written from different perspectives. As a result of the workshop, several participants said, with starry eyes, that they had never thought about history in this way before, and the course got off to a flying start!

WORKSHOP 2

The purpose of this workshop was to experience the processes of historical enquiry in a variety of contexts, relate them to National Curriculum level descriptions and consider how similar activities may be planned for young children.

In small groups, participants select and undertake one of the prepared activities and later report back to the whole group.

Oral sources

Aim • to consider how children can use an oral source to describe, find out about the past, ask questions and make deductions.

Method • Listen to tape-recording of an elderly person talking, for example, about her childhood, or her training and early career as a teacher.
• Consider how you could organise oral history in school.
• Decide on a topic for young children which could include oral history.
• Write a lesson plan for an oral history session, related to this topic.

Buildings

Aim • to consider how to use an old building as an historical source with younger children: communicating information, asking questions, making deductions.

Method • Watch English Heritage video, 'The Key Stage 1 Curriculum', noting teachers' preparations, organisation of visit and follow-up work.
• Outline similar preparations, organisation and follow-up work for a visit to a building familiar to you.
• Write a lesson plan for one activity related to this visit.

Artefacts

Aim   • to consider how children can find out about the past by describing, asking questions and making deductions about artefacts.

Method • Describe one of the artefacts (in words or by drawing all or part of it).
        • Discuss as a group how each artefact was made, how it was used, by whom and how it affected the lives of the people who made and used it.
        • List ideas in three columns: what we know for certain, what we can guess, what we would like to know.
        • Write a work plan for a game or activity which would help children to investigate a question about the past through these artefacts.

Pictures

Aim   • to consider how a painting or photograph can be used as an historical source with young children, to help them to describe, ask questions and make deductions about the past.

Method • Select one of the pictures. These could be enlarged, coloured photocopies of a variety of types of picture, for example, postcards of:
        • toy coach and horses (Bethnal Green Museum of Childhood, London);
        • interior of the Butcher's Shop (Blists Hill Open Air Museum, Shropshire);
        • the kitchen of D. H. Lawrence's home (The Breach House, Eastwood);
        • *A Woman Peeling Apples* (Pieter de Hooch, The Medici Society, London).

   Illustrations in books for older children:
        • reconstruction of life inside a Medieval merchant's house (Clare 1992: 14–15);
        • the birth of Sikri in 1569 (Roberts 1992: 22);
        • women musicians in a fairground in Imperial China (Gleisner 1993: 39).

Sequencing family photographs

Aims   • to experience the process of sequencing family photographs as a context for considering motives, describing differences

between past and present, and explaining reasons for changes over time;
- to list the knowledge and interests which were brought to bear on the process;
- to consider how a similar activity might be planned for young children.

Method • In pairs:
- exchange sets of photographs;
- sequence partner's photographs on a time-line;
- describe to partner what you know, what you can guess and what you would like to know about his or her sequence of photographs;
- partner confirms, corrects, supplements information where possible.
- What did you need to know in order to form the sequence? What were you most interested in?
- How would you plan a similar exercise for young children?

Time and change through stories

Aim • to consider how contemporary fictional stories about everyday life can help young children to examine and understand changes over time.

Method • Select one of the stories.
- Using the format given in Box 12.1, show how it can be used as a basis for introducing historical thinking.

Sequencing events in stories

Aim • to think how fictional stories set in the past may be used to help children to consider the interaction of impersonal and personal factors in shaping people's lives.

Method I • Read *Minnie and Ginger: A Twentieth-century Romance* (Smith 1990).
- Put the pictures (photocopied on separate sheets) in sequence and retell the story from it in your own words.
- How many words/phrases did you use involving time; cause; effect? How many explanations were concerned with public events; with private feelings; with describing places or everyday activities in the past which were different from today?
- How many pictures relate to the same period of time?

Box 12.1 Introducing historical thinking through stories

Category	Title	Author	Publisher	Date	ISBN
Family history	When I was Little	Marie Williams	Walker Books	1991	07445 1765–6

Reading level:	Large print (about 15 words per page, with simple speech bubbles)
Illustration:	Humorous, strip cartoon style, plenty of detail

Historical thinking Granny has rosy recollections of her childhood, when ice-cream tasted of cream and babies never cried

Use primary and secondary sources to consider:	Compare pictures: 'We didn't have these . . . but we did have these' How are they different? Why?
• similarities and differences between past and present	• Make sets of things granny says which are true, and things which may not be true. (This could be done by children each choosing an example to draw, and writing a caption, on separate cards)
• how and why the past is represented in different ways	• Sort the things which might not be true (e.g. weather, facts, feelings, rules, play, warnings, food) • Why do you think your grany said these things? Ask your granny about, for example, the weather when she little, then ask her for photographs of when she was little Do they tell the same story? Make your own 'Granny comes to visit' book Make a page saying 'She didn't have these, but she had these . . .' Compare with other people's 'Granny comes to visit' books Do all grannies tell the same story?

Cross-curricular extensions

Science
- Weather – keep records: 'It never rained in summer'?
- Energy – steam, electricity
- How long do lollipops last? How is ice-cream made?
- Space travel – first man on the moon – the moon . . .
- Materials (we didn't have these but we did have these . . .)

Mathematics
- Journeys to school: 'We walked 4 miles to school'
- Maths – do *we* do it like this?

Geography
- Journey to school
- Foods, now and then
- Grannies who lived in other places

English
- 'Let's pretend' play: when granny was little
- Questionnaires/interviews
- Book making

- Which pictures could be put in a different order without changing the story?
- How could you replace one (or more) of the pictures with your own picture to make a different story?
- Could you reshuffle the pictures to tell a different story?

Method II • How could you develop this activity with young children?

Interpretations through stories

Aims • to consider how different versions of stories may be created, and the similarities and the differences between versions;
- to consider to what extent young children can begin to understand how and why stories differ, and how you can help them to do so.

Method I • Select two versions of a folk tale; a traditional and a modern version of a fairy tale; versions of a folk tale from different cultures, e.g. *The Cinderella Story* by Neil Philip (1989); two accounts of a myth or legend (e.g. a Greek myth, or a story about Robin Hood or King Arthur), or a story told in an old and a modern history book.
- How are the stories the same; different? How do you think the different versions came about? What do you think is probably true; untrue?

Method II • What would children need to be able to do/know in order to discuss whether a story is about real people; in order to compare different versions of stories; in order to understand why there may be different versions of a story?
- How could you help them to do this?
- Is there a sequence in the kinds of stories you would introduce them to in order to do this?

Interpretations through oral history

Aims • to focus on different interpretations of the past, to understand why different stories can give different versions of what happened, and to distinguish between a fact and a point of view.

Method • Decide on an event in the past which many people would remember (e.g. the Coronation of Queen Elizabeth II, or the Gulf War). Interview several people old enough to remember the event. Decide on three questions, e.g. for the Coronation: Describe the event

How did you know about it?

How did it affect you?

for the Gulf War: How did it begin?

What happened?

Why did it end?

- List facts and points of view in interviewees' reports. Consider how the reports are different and why.
- What events might children like to find out about; what topics might such an enquiry be part of?

WORKSHOP 3

Aim   • to initiate school-based collection of primary sources.

Method 1 Decide on categories of artefacts which could be collected:
- related to a particular period (1950s, Second World War, Victorian);
- related to a particular (local) occupation (farming, entertainment, fishing, mining, manufacturing);
- which illustrate change in an aspect of domestic life (cooking, washing, cleaning, clothes, toys, games, children's books).

2 List possible sources:
- parents and friends;
- local organisations;
- car boot sales, junk and second-hand shops.

3 Decide on criteria for selection:
- size;
- value;
- interest;
- relevance to topics, possible deductions;
- safety;
- fragility.

4 Decide on storage, care, cataloguing:
- by children;
- a teacher;
- ancillary worker;
- parent or friend of school.
- Is it possible to enlist help of museum staff?

Write a statement for a school policy document on categories of articles being collected, and storage arrangements. Send a copy to possible contributors.

WORKSHOP 4

Aim
- to agree a policy for evaluating and selecting secondary sources.

Resources
- collection of secondary sources – story books, information books, history schemes.

Method
Each group evaluates one category of secondary sources, using criteria suggested.

1 Stories about past times
- Is there more than one version of the story so that it could illustrate different interpretations?
- Can the illustrations be used as a source to find out about the past?
- Do illustrations show how artists convey different impressions through line, form, scale and colour?
- Does the story allow children to talk about changes over time, why they occurred, why people acted as they did?
- Does it allow children to talk about how and why a time in the past was different from today?

2 Information books
- Is there a clear table of contents and simple index?
- Are there illustrations, photographs or clear drawings from which children can make deductions and inferences?
- Does the text give didactic information without evidence for it?
- Are artists' impressions of events based on what is known?
- Can the book be used at a range of levels (from pictures to text) at different levels of difficulty?

3 Schemes
- Does it provide information and stimulate ideas for activities which teachers can modify to suit their children's needs?
- Are there good starting points for children's own enquiries?
- Are there suggestions for a variety of activities: painting, drawing, model-making, free play, drama?
- Do the enquiries and activities involve genuine historical thinking?
- Are there useful sources which would otherwise be difficult to obtain?
- Is there a variety of sources: paintings, photographs, music, simple written sources?
- Are there good suggestions about how sources could be used, with and without the teacher?

- Do the sources reflect social, gender and ethnic differences; different political, economic, social and cultural perspectives?
- Are there suggestions for links with other curricular areas?
- Are there ideas for presenting findings in different ways?
- Are there manageable suggestions for evaluating and recording children's work, which are intrinsic to the activities, and not simplistic?

Decide whether to amend these criteria, before recording them on a matrix against which each new book can be evaluated and uses suggested. Include in resources section of policy document.

WORKSHOP 5

Aim
- to agree on rationale for whole-school planning of history topics.

Resources
- current curriculum plan for Key Stage 1 history; *The Teaching of History in the Primary Schools* (Cooper 2000b; Chapter 7); History in *The National Curriculum for England and Wales* (DfEE/QCA 1999a); *Teaching History at Key Stage 1* (NCC 1993; DfEE/QCA 1993, 1998a, 2000a).

Method
1 Review existing approach:
   - Is sufficient time spent on history to cover adequate content and develop historical thinking?
   - Are there opportunities for links between history and other areas of the curriculum, which avoid curriculum overload and fragmentation?
   - Are potential resources for history in the local community and environment used to the full?
   - Is there evidence of continuity and progression? How does the plan take into account key skills, inclusion (gender ability, special educational needs, disabilities) and develop personal, spiritual, moral, social, cultural values, health and citizenship education?
   - Would a new approach to curriculum planning be a useful catalyst for stimulating and sharing new ideas?
2 If there is an agreed need for a new approach to topic planning, consider the advantages and disadvantages for teaching history through history-led topics, humanities topics, integrated topics, a mixed approach.
3 Define the rationale for planning history topics within the curriculum for school policy document.

WORKSHOP 6

Aim   • to agree on themes for history topics (or for humanities or integrated topics with a history dimension) for the following year, as a basis for future development.

Method   In brainstorming possible topics, consider:
- local resources;
- cross-curricular themes and dimensions;
- political, economic, social and cultural dimensions;
- children's ethnic backgrounds;
- seasons, if visits outside school are planned;
- rationale for progression;
- Foundation Stage Guidance and Programme of Study for History in the National Curriculum, Key Stage 1. *Note*: Foundation Stage topics must include finding out about past and present events in their own lives and in those of their families and others they know, and beginning to know about their own cultures and beliefs and those of other people.
  Key Stage 1. Topics must involve:
  – changes in the daily lives of children and familiar adults within living memory;
  – life in Britain beyond living memory;
  – key events and the lives of men and women in Britain and other countries;
- Fill in topic grid in Box 12.2 and check that the above aspects are included.

Box 12.2 Topic grid

	Autumn		Spring		Summer	
R						
YR1						
YR2						

WORKSHOP 7

Aim   • to devise detailed plans for teaching and assessing each selected unit of work for inclusion in the Long-Term Plan and school policy.

Method   • Decide whether plans for each year group should reflect statements of attainment for one level (expecting differentiation within the level), or for several levels.
           • There may be opportunities within one activity for assessment at a range of levels.
           • There may be opportunities within an activity for assessment in more than one aspect of historical thinking.
           • Models and matrices for planning schemes are given in DfEE/QCA 2000a.
           • Teachers work together on long-term plans for their own topics.

WORKSHOP 8

Aim   • to maintain progression from the Foundation Stage to year 2. Ideally, practitioners working in early years settings and year 1 and year 2 teachers will have met previously to plan for progression in thinking across agreed topics (pp. 140–2). Examples of a case study investigating progression from 3- to 7-year-olds, in a primary school and a feeder play group, are given in Cooper and Sixsmith (2002).

Resources • Topic grid identifying strands of historical thinking from Foundation Stage to year 2 (Box 7.4).
           • Examples of records showing progression based on *Early Learning Goals Stepping Stones* (DfEE/QCA 2000a) and National Curriculum Level Descriptors.
           • Examples of children's work for each topic, which is average and significantly below or above average. It is expected that three broad levels identified in schemes of work or medium-term plans (e.g. Box 8.5, 8.6, 8.7) describe the levels of achievement which will help teachers to decide whether a pupil has made markedly more or less progress than the rest of the class and to note possible reasons, but detailed individual records for history are inappropriate (DfEE/QCA 1998a: 16).

Method   • Select one of the strands of historical thinking which run through the Foundation Stage to year 2 identified in Box 7.4

(e.g. sequence events, extend vocabulary, or ask-and-answer questions about the past).
- Discuss, supported by evidence where possible, how children responded to this strand across the age-phase.
- Collate examples which illustrate progression.

WORKSHOP 9

Aim
- to consider opportunities for making links between the National Literacy Strategy (DfEE/QCA 1998b) and history, from Reception to year 2.

Resources
- Photocopy the summary of the Range of Work for Each Term (DfEE/QCA 1998b). Cut out the Range of Work for Each Year, R-Y2, and stick each in the middle of a separate sheet of A3 paper.
- Photocopy the text related to Early Learning Goals for Communication, Language and Literacy (DfEE/QCA 2000a: 62), and stick it in the middle of a sheet of A3 paper.

Method
- Teachers for each age group (Foundation Stage to year 2) brainstorm a range of history-related texts for each genre they have used or could use. Record as a spider diagram on the A3 sheet for each year group.
- Draft literacy hours for some of the texts, and show how they could be used at text, sentence and word level and also linked to a history topic.
- List possible extended history activities linked to the topic which could support the Literacy Hour.
- Collate as a resource which can be added to.

WORKSHOP 10

Aim
- to develop partnership with parents and guardians.

Method   Review possible approaches, in order to record philosophy and method in policy document.

Long-term:
- At the beginning of the year (term or topic), explain to interested parents, either at brief meeting or in a letter, what is planned, why and how it will be taught.
- Display long-term plans in classroom.
- Explain how possible visits (e.g. to a Roman fort or a windmill while on holiday may relate to school history topics).
- Explain, in meeting or letter, requests for photographs, oral

history, artefacts – what is needed, their purpose, how they will be used, how they will be cared for (e.g. will they be displayed, can they be touched?).

Short-term:

- Preparatory information (workshop?) for adults accompanying a visit.
- Organisational information: timetable for day, toilet, eating and safety arrangements; groups, rules, expected products, e.g. photographs, interviews, drawings.
- Historical information: educational notes, maps, plans, historical information.
- Questions to ask to extend children's thinking:
  - general open question for each group;
  - possible ways to investigate it (clues available);
  - two categories of question to ask about clues:
    (a) How was it made? How was it used? How did it affect the lives of people who made/used it?
    (b) What do you know for certain? What can you guess? What would you like to know?
- Reasons for detailed observational drawing.
- Parents could try, in a workshop session, asking their own questions and making drawings of artefacts.
- Parents could assist in follow-up work in school: pottery models, embroidery, bookmaking, cooking, weaving, etc.
- Parents and friends could function as informed and questioning audience for presenting results of enquiry orally, or in play and display.

Finally, the curriculum leader needs to devise a rolling programme for:

- review, modification, alteration of topics selected and methods of record-keeping;
- evaluation of resources, storage, extending and updating as appropriate;
- sharing ideas with colleagues in other schools;
- inviting guest speakers to stimulate further ideas;
- less frequent but finely focused staff meetings, for example, to investigate the kinds of inferences children across the three-year age span make about the same source; how play becomes increasingly based on evidence as children grow older; how children of different ages respond to the same story. Such case studies would be valuable in, for example, *Teaching History*;
- monitoring children's development over the Key Stage, by discussing collected samples of work by the same child;

- extending an awareness among parents, and in the wider community, of the quality and value of young children's work in history through displays, presentations, children's tape-recorded discussions and adult participation in projects.

Lomas (1994) gives an excellent checklist of questions for monitoring good practice in the teaching and learning of history in the primary school. He also outlines the role of the headteacher and the co-ordinator in developing the contribution that history can make to children's spiritual, moral, social and cultural development and to the broad curriculum, and includes sections on meeting special educational needs through history.

Many teachers began early years history because it became a statutory requirement, then discovered how enjoyable and appropriate it can be. It is to be hoped that this book has sparked off further ideas, possibilities, insights and questions, which, in turn, will stimulate further books. Enjoy it; it's fun!

IN CONCLUSION

I should like to return to my initial acknowledgement of the students and teachers with whom I have worked. In the first edition I wrote how, after hearing teachers, schools and state education denigrated by an 'academic' colleague from a prestigious university, I had received Margaret Taylor's lesson plans describing work she had undertaken on a 'Victorian Kitchen' in a school for children with severe learning difficulties. I wept in anger for all the teachers I have known who have given their all, their spirit, time and professional expertise, in often difficult circumstances, because of a strong moral commitment to what they consider to be good and right for all children, whatever their backgrounds or difficulties. Margaret Taylor's case study is not included in this second edition because it was felt an appropriate response to the revised curriculum was to weave into the book references to children with special educational needs in mainstream classrooms. The 'academic' colleague has not changed his position, but Margaret is now deputy headteacher of a large primary school.

Historians take a long view of the past. I wrote in the Introduction about my grandmother who, aged 5 in 1869, was awarded a history of the world as a school prize. Later, she became a headteacher of one of the Board Schools which, for the first time in any society, offered an education for all. Her son, my father, became a headteacher of one of the first secondary modern schools, which extended these opportunities beyond elementary education.

Recently, I listened to a tape recording my mother had made for an oral history in-service session, describing her years as a young teacher in the 1930s. It included a vivid and deeply moving account of how the young and newly qualified infants teacher with whom she shared digs in a poor inner-city area had, by half-term, become exhausted by her Reception class of 56 children. She had little money for food or clothes, caught pneumonia at the school jumble sale and died in her room. The teacher's father was out of work and too poor to travel from South Wales to the funeral. The response of the infants school headteacher on hearing the news was, 'I'm not surprised. She didn't wear woollen combinations.' After a proper interval, the teachers in the in-service session asked, 'What are combinations?' (Answer: woollen vest and knickers buttoned at the waist!)

Society and education have changed for the better and not just because none of us now wears woollen combinations. We may grumble about tests and targets and core skills, but we also have new endorsement for both play and history in the early years curriculum, and many innovative and creative teachers to implement it.

So I shall end this edition on the same lyrical note as the last one by quoting Tennyson's *Ulysses*:

> Come, my friends,
> 'Tis not too late to seek a newer world.

Resources referred to in the text

Articles of Antiquity, The Bury Business Centre, Kay Street, Bury.

Bethnal Green Museum of Childhood, Cambridge Heath Road, London, E.2.

Butser Iron Age Village Farm, Queen Elizabeth National Park, Hampshire.

Dolls' House Emporium, Victoria Road, Ripley, Derbyshire.

English Heritage Education, http://www.HeritageEducation.net

English Heritage Education Service, Keysign House, 429 Oxford Street, London, W.1.

Folklore Society, School of Scottish Studies, Edinburgh University, St George's Square, Edinburgh.

Haringey (London Borough of), Multicultural Resource Centre for under fives.

Historical Association, The, 59-A Kennington Park Road, London SE11 4JH.

History Box; new and traditional stories from Wales, audio cassettes and teachers' and pupils' books, National Language Unit of Wales, Brook Street, Treforest, Pontypridd.

History in Evidence, TTS, Monk Road, Alfreton, Derbyshire DE55 7RL, sales@tts-group.co.uk

History of Advertising Trust, HAT House, 12 Raveningham Centre, Raveningham, Norwich NR14 6NU, hat@uea.ac.uk

Honeychurch Toys Ltd, Woodlands, Lodge Hill, Market Lavington, Wiltshire.

Ironbridge Gorge Museum Trust (*Under Fives and Museums: Guidelines for Teachers*), The Ironbridge Gorge Museum, Ironbridge, Telford, Shropshire.

Maritime Museum, The, http://www.history.org.uk

Mary Rose Trust, The, No. 5 Boathouse, HM Naval Base, Portsmouth PO1 3PX.

MEGSS, 'Merry Christmas: greetings in the mother tongue of nine minority groups', Minority Ethnic Group Support Service, Lancashire Education Authority.

Morwellham Quay Copper Mine, Tavistock, Devon.

Mrs Tanner's Tangible History, Gill Tanner, 9 Selvy Road, West Bridgford, Nottingham, NG2 7BP.

National Trust, 36 Queen Anne's Gate, London, S.W.1.

Our Facts database, R.M. Nimbus version, 1988, NCET.

Past Times Historical Gifts, Whitney, Oxford OX29 7BR.

Sara Liptai, Philosophy for Children, SAPERE, 7 Cloister Way, Leamington Spa CV32 6QE, http://www.SAPERE.net

Victoria and Albert Museum, South Kensington, London, S.W.7.

Yorvik Viking Centre, Coppergate, York.

West Stowe Anglo-Saxon Village Trust, Bury St Edmunds, Suffolk.
Women's History Network, Key Stage 1 Biography Project, Department of History, University of York.

Some useful information and communication technology resources

Clicker grids, www.cricksoft.com/cgfl/index.htm
Clip-art is available from: Anglia TV, Norwich NR1 3JE.
Concept Keyboard, REM, Great Western House, Langport, Somerset TA10 9YU.
'Find It', Actis Ltd, Rutland Mills, Market Street, Ilkeston, Derbyshire DE7 5RY, tel: +44(0) 115 944 8300, fax: +44(0) 115 944 8311, email: welcome@actis.co.uk, http://www.actis.co.uk/.
'Front Page Extra' is available from: Newman Publishing.
'My World', 'My World 2' and 'Optima' are available from: SEMERC, 1 Broadbent Road, Watershedding, Oldham L14LB.
'Our Facts' is available from: The Babbage Centre, Devon.
'Primart' is available from: Minerva, Exeter.
'Textease', Softease Ltd, Market Place, Ashbourne, Derbyshire DE6 1ES, tel: +44 (0)1335 343421 fax: +44 (0)1335 343422, email: sales@softease.co.uk, http:// www.textease.com.
'Talking Write Away', BlackCat Software, Granada Learning, Granada Television, Quay Street, Manchester M60 9EA, tel: +44 (0)161 827 2927, fax: +44 (0)161 827 2966, email: info@blackcatsoftware.com, http://www.blackcatsoftware.com.

Curriculum support

http://www.mape.org.uk

http://www..mape.org.uk/curriculum/history/ict.htm
(Young Children Using ICT)

http://www.mape.org.uk/curriculum/history/keystage1.htm
(Key Stage 1 Understanding History)

http://www.devon.gov.uk/babbage/content.htm

http://www.r-e-m.co.uk/catalogues/yearbook.htm

Useful history sites on the Internet

http://www.liv.ac.uk/~evansjon/humanities/history/history.html
(UK Schools History Resources)

http://www.open.gov.uk/heritage/eduindex.htm

http://www.english-heritage.org.uk
(English Heritage)

http://www.nmm.ac.uk/index.html
(National Maritime Museum)

http://www.nt-education.org
(The National Trust)

http://www.history.org.uk
(Historical Association)

http://www.local-history.co.uk
(Local History Magazine)

http://www.learnfree.co.uk
(Starting point for finding history sites)

http://www.nationalgallery.org.uk/collection/content.htm
(The National Gallery)

http://www.npg.org.uk/search

http://www.npg.org.uk/roomsg.htm
(The National Portrait Gallery)

http://www.british-museum.ac.uk/
(The British Museum)

http://www.genealogy.bookpub.net
(Trace your ancestors)

http://www.britannia.com/history

http://www.24hourmuseum.org.uk
(General information sites about English Heritage, museum websites, etc. can be accessed from here.)

Bibliography

Adams, C. (1982) *Ordinary Times: A Hundred Years Ago*, London: Virago.

Adams, J. (1998) 'Read all about it: Using newspapers as an historical source in an infant classroom', in P. Hoodless (ed.) *History and English in the Primary School*, London: Routledge.

Agard, J. (1992) *The Emperor's Dan-Dan*, London: Hodder & Stoughton.

Ahlberg, J. and Ahlberg, A. (1983) *Peepo*, London: Puffin.

—— (1984) *The Baby's Catalogue*, UK: Puffin.

Aldred, D. (1993) *Castles and Cathedrals*, Cambridge: Cambridge University Press.

Anderson, D. (1989) 'Learning history in museums', *The International Journal of Museum Management and Curatorship* 8: 357–68.

—— (1993) 'Myth and story telling', Key Stage 1 workshop at the Primary Conference of the Historical Association, Victoria and Albert Museum, London.

Arnheim, R. (1974) *Art and Visual Perception: A Psychology of the Creative Eye*, Berkeley: University of California Press.

Ausubel, D. P. (1968) *Educational Psychology. A Cognitive View*, New York: Holt, Rinehart & Winston.

Bage, G. (1999) *Narrative Pattern: Teaching and Learning History through Story*, Lewes: Falmer Press.

Baker, J. (1991) *Where the Forest Meets the Sea*, London: Walker Books.

Ball, B. (1989) *Stone Age Magic*, London: Hamish Hamilton.

Barnard, P. (1989) *Escape from the Workhouse*, Saffron Walden: Anglia.

Barnes, J. (1993) 'The saints: close observation and drawing', Historical Association Primary History Conference, Victoria and Albert Museum, London.

Batho, G. R. (ed.) (1994) *Schools, Museums and Primary History*, London: The Historical Association.

Bearne, E. (1992) 'Myth and legend: the oldest language?', in M. Styles, E. Bearne and V. Watson (eds) *After Alice: Exploring Children's Literature*, London: Cassell.

Bateson, G. (1985) 'A theory of play and fantasy', in J. S. Bruner, A. Jolly and K. Sylva (eds) *Play, its Role, Development and Evolution*, London: Penguin.

Bennet, N., Woods, E. A. and Rogers, S. (1996) *Teaching through Play: Teachers' Theories and Classroom Practice*, Milton Keynes: Open University Press.

Bernot, L. and Blancard, R. (1953) *Nouville, un village français*, Paris: Institut d'Ethnologie.

Bhatia, M. (1988) *Happy Birthday Bhini* (English/Gujarati), London: Magi.

Bicknell, G. (1998) 'Peel appeal: talking about the past with Nursery and Reception children', in P. Hoodless (ed.) *History and English in the Primary School*, London: Routledge.

Blake, William (1981) *Selected Poetry of William Blake*, New York: New American Library.

Blume, J. (1988) *The Pain and the Great One*, London: Pan/Macmillan.

Blyth, A. (1990) *Making the Grade for Primary Humanities*, Milton Keynes: Open University Press.

Blyth, J. (1991) *Old Toys* (A Sense of History Series), Harlow: Longman.

Blyth, J., Cigman, J., Harnett, P. and Sampson, J. (1991a) *Ginn History, Key Stage 1 Teacher's Resource Book*, Aylesbury: Ginn & Co.

—— (1991b) *Ginn History Stories*, Aylesbury: Ginn & Co.

—— (1991c) *Ginn History Topic Books*, Aylesbury: Ginn & Co.

Board of Education (1905) *Suggestions for the Consideration of Teachers and Others Concerned in the Work of Public Elementary Schools*, London: HMSO.

—— (1927) *Handbook of Suggestions for Teachers*, London: HMSO.

Booth, W. (1985) 'Narrative as a mould of character', paper given at Language in Inner City Schools Conference, London.

Borke, H. (1978) 'Piaget's view of social interaction and the theoretical construct of empathy', in L. E. Siegal and C. J. Brainerd (eds) *Alternatives to Piaget*, London: Academic Press.

Bowyer, E. (1992) 'Time boxes: an investigation of time using artefacts for Key Stages 1 and 2', *Young Historian Scheme 4*, London: Historical Association.

Bradley H. (1974) *Miss Carter Came With Us*, London: Jonathan Cape.

Bradley N. C. (1947) 'The growth of the knowledge of time in children of school age', *British Journal of Psychology* 38: 67–8.

Brown, R. (1982) *If at First You Do Not See*, London: Beaver, Arrow Books.

Bruce, T. (1991) *Time to Play in Early Childhood Education*, Sevenoaks: Hodder & Stoughton.

Bruner, J. S. (1963) *The Process of Education*, New York: Vintage Books.

—— (1966) *Towards a Theory of Instruction*, Harvard: Belknap Press.

—— (1983) *Child's Talk: Learning to Use Language*, Oxford: Oxford University Press.

—— (1986) *Actual Minds; Possible Worlds*, Cambridge, MA: Harvard University Press.

—— (1989) 'Culture and human development: a new look', paper given at the annual meeting of the Society for Research in Child Development, Kansas City Missouri.

—— (1996) *The Culture of Education*, Cambridge, MA: Harvard University Press.

Bryant-Mole, K. (1996) *Old Teddies Discovered*, London: A & C Black.

Burningham, J. (1984) *Granpa*, London: Picture Puffin.

—— (1985) *Time to Get Out of the Bath, Shirley*, Oxford: Picture Lions.

—— (1992) *Come Away from the Water, Shirley*, London: Jonathan Cape.

Burton, V. L. (1978) *The Little House*, New York: Houghton Mifflin.

Butler, D. (1988) *Babies Need Books*, London: Penguin.

Christenson, K. (1995) *Rachel's Roses*, Bath: Barefoot.

Chukovsky K. (1968) *From Two to Five*, Berkeley: University of California Press.

Claire, H. (1966) *Reclaiming Our Past: Equality and Diversity in the Primary Curriculum*, Harlow: Trentham Books, Longman.

Clare, J. D. (1992) *Medieval Towns* (I was There Series), London: Bodley Head.
—— (1993) *Knights in Armour* (I Was There Series Investigation Pack), London: Bodley Head.
Clark, K. (1969) *Civilization: A Personal View*, London: BBC/John Murray.
Clements, G. (1987) *The Normans are Coming*, London: Macmillan Children's Books.
—— (1988) *The Truth about Castles*, London: Pan/Macmillan.
Clifford, D. J. H. (ed.) (1992) *The Diaries of Lady Anne Clifford*, Stroud: Alan Sutton.
Coate, L. (1991) *Grandma's Attic*, Brighton: Tressell.
Cole, B. (1987) *Prince Cinders*, London: Hamish Hamilton.
Collicott, S. L. (1993) 'A way of looking at history: local – national – world links', *Teaching History* 72: 18–23.
Collingwood, R. G. (1939) *An Autobiography*, Oxford: Oxford University Press.
—— (1946) *The Idea of History*, Oxford: Clarendon.
Cook, E. (1969) *The Ordinary and the Fabulous*, Cambridge: Cambridge University Press.
Cooper, H. (1991) 'Young children's thinking in history', unpublished PhD thesis, University of London.
—— (1992) *The Teaching of History*, London: David Fulton.
—— (1995) *The Teaching of History in the Primary Schools*, London: David Fulton.
—— (1997) 'History in its Own Write', *Primary English Magazine* 3.2: 14–17.
—— (1998a) 'History in its Own Write', *Primary English Magazine* 3.3: 16–18.
—— (1998b) 'Writing about History in the Early Years', in P. Hoodless (ed.) *History and English in the Primary School*, London: Routledge.
—— (2000a) 'Primary school history in Europe: a staple diet or a hot potato?' in J. Arthur and R. Phillips (eds), *Issues in History Teaching*, London: Routledge.
—— (2000b) *The Teaching of History in the Primary Schools* (2nd edn), London: David Fulton.
Cooper, H. and Etches, P. (1996) 'Church-going Kendal', *Teaching History*, 83: 30–4.
Cooper, H. and Sixsmith, C. (2002) *Teaching Across the Early Years 3–8*, London: RoutledgeFalmer.
Cooper, H. and Twiselton, S. (1998) 'Victorian alphabets: a sampler for the literacy hour?' (1), *Primary English Magazine* 4.2: 7–11.
—— (1999) 'Victorian alphabets: a sampler for the literacy hour?' (2), *Primary English Magazine* 4.3: 18–21.
—— (2000) *Art and Artists: Impressionism (7–9)*, Reading for Information Series, Leamington Spa: Scholastic.
Costello, P. (2000) *Thinking Skills in Early Childhood Education*, London: David Fulton.
Cox, K. and Hughes, P. (1990) 'Early years history', unpublished paper, Liverpool Institute of Higher Education.
—— (1998) 'History and children's fiction', in P. Hoodless (ed.) *History and English in the Primary School*, London: Routledge.
Cox, M. V. (1986) *The Child's Point of View: The Development of Cognition and Language*, Brighton: Harvester Press.
Cramer, I. (1993) 'Oral history: working with children', *Teaching History* 71: 17–20.
Crowther, E. W. (1982) 'Understanding the concept of change among children and young adolescents', *Educational Review* 34(3): 279–84.
Curtis, S. (1993) 'Constructing tasks for mixed ability groups', *Teaching History* 73: 16–22.

Davis, N. (ed.) (1983) *The Paston Letters: A Selection in Modern Spelling*, Oxford: Oxford University Press.

Dahl, R. (1986) *Boy*, London: Penguin.

de Paolo, T. (1988) *Bill and Pete Go Down the Nile*, Oxford, Oxford University Press.

Department of Education and Science (DES) (1967) *Children and their Primary Schools: A Report of the Central Advisory Council for Education*, (The Plowden Report) London: HMSO.

—— (1985) *History in the Primary and Secondary Years: An HMI View*, London: HMSO.

—— (1989a) *Curriculum Matters 14: Personal and Social Education from 5–16*, London: HMSO.

—— (1989d) *Aspects of Primary Education. The Education of Children Under Five*, London: HMSO.

—— (1990) *History for Ages 5–16: Proposals of the Secretary of State for Education and Science* (The Rumbold Report), London: HMSO.

—— (1991a) *History in the National Curriculum*, London: HMSO.

—— (1991b) *Starting with Quality. Report of the Committee of Enquiry into the Quality of Educational Experiences Offered to 3 and 4 Year Olds*, London: HMSO.

Department for Education (DfE) (1992a) *A Survey of the Use of Artefacts and Museum Resources in Teaching National Curriculum History*, London: DfE Publications Centre.

—— (1992b) *A Survey of the Use of Artefacts and Specimens in Schools*, HMI, London: DfE Publications Centre.

DfE (1994) *Code of Practice on the Identification and Assessment of Pupils with Special Educational Needs*, London: HMSO.

—— (1995) *History in the National Curriculum*, London: DfE Publications Centre.

Department of Education and Employment/Qualifications and Curriculum Authority (DfEE/QCA) (1998a) *History Teachers' Guide: A Scheme of Work for Key Stages 1 and 2*, London: QCA. www.open.gov.uk/qca

—— (1998b) *The National Literacy Strategy*, London: DfEE/QCA.

—— (1999a) *The National Curriculum for England and Wales: Handbook for Primary Teachers in England*, London: HMSO. www.nc.uk.net

—— (1999b) *All Our Futures: Creativity, Culture and Education*, London: HMSO.

—— (1999) *The National Numeracy Framework: Framework for Teaching Mathematics from Reception to Year 6*, Sudbury: DfEE Publications.

—— (2000) *Art and Artists: Impressionism (7–9)*, Reading for Information Series, Leamington Spa: Scholastic.

—— (2000a) *Curriculum Guidance for the Foundation Stage*, London: QCA. www.qca.org.uk

—— (2000b) *History Teacher's Guide Update*, London: QCA.

—— (2000c) *Special Education Needs: Special Edition*, London: HMSO.

Dickinson, A. K. and Lee, P. J. (eds) (1978) *History Teaching and Historical Understanding*, London: Heinemann.

Dickinson, A., Gard, A. and Lee, P. J. (1978) 'Evidence in the classroom', in A. K. Dickinson and P. J. Lee (eds) *History Teaching and Historical Understanding*, London: Heinemann.

Dickinson, M. (1989) *Smudge*, Sevenoaks: Picture Knight, Hodder & Stoughton.

Doise, W., Mugny, C. and Perret Clermont, A. N. (1975) 'Social interaction and the development of cognitive operations', *European Journal of Social Psychology* 5: 367–83.

—— (1978) *Groups and Individuals: Explanations in Social Psychology*, Cambridge: Cambridge University Press.

Donaldson, M. (1978) *Children's Minds*, London: Fontana.

Douloubakas, G. (1985) *Hare and the Tortoise*, London: Luzac.

Doonan, J. (1993) *Looking at Picture Books*, Stroud: Thimble Press.

Dupasquier, P. (1987) *Jack at Sea*, London: Picture Puffin.

Eliot, T. S. (1986) *Collected Poems*, London: Faber & Faber.

Elton, G. R. (1970) 'What sort of history should we teach?', in M. Ballard (ed.) *New Movements in the Study and Teaching of History*, London: Temple Smith.

English Heritage (2001) *Seaside Holiday Photopack: Toys, Games in the Past*, London: English Heritage. www.HeritageEducation.net

Eno, P. (1993) 'In touch with the past', *Times Educational Supplement*, Resources III, 10 September.

Erikson, E. H. (1965) *Childhood and Society*, London: Penguin.

Fairclough, J. and Redsell, P. (1987) *Living History: Reconstructing the Past with Children*, London: English Heritage.

Flavell, J. H. (1985) *Cognitive Development*, Englewood Cliffs, NJ: Prentice-Hall.

Fox, M. (1987) *Wilfred Gordon McDonald Partridge*, London: Picture Puffin. (Also available as a Big Book, La Jolla, California: Kane Miller.)

Franklin, I. L. (1992) *The Old, Old Man and the Very Little Boy*, New York: Athaneum, Simon and Schuster.

Friedman, W. (1978) 'Development of time concepts and children', in H. W. Reese and L. P. Lipsett (eds) *Advances in Child Development and Behaviour* vol. 12.

Fryer, P. (1989) *Black People in the British Empire: An Introduction*, London: Pluto.

Furth, H. G. (1980) *The World of Grown-ups*, New York: Elsevier Press.

Gagné, R. M. (1977) *The Conditions of Learning*, London and New York: Holt, Rinehart & Winston.

Gallagher, C. (1998) 'The future of history: a plea for relevance'. Paper given at the School History Project Conference, Leeds, 3–8 April.

Garland, S. (1996) *Seeing Red*, London: Andersen Press.

Garvey, C. (1977) *Play*, The Developing Child Series, edited by J. Bruner, M. Cole and B. Lloyd, London: Collins/Fontana.

Gaunt, J. (1990) *Little Nora Goes South*, London: Hodder and Stoughton.

Gleisner, C. (1992) *Imperial China*, Oxford: Oxford University Press.

Goalen, P. (1992) *India: From Mughal Empire to British Raj*, Cambridge: Cambridge University Press.

Gombrich, E. H. (1977) *Art and Illusions*, New York and London: Phaidon Press.

Goodall, J. S. (1986) *The Story of a Castle*, London: André Deutsch.

Gould, D. (1990) *Granpa's Slide Show*, London: Penguin.

Grafoni, A. (1989) *The Village of Round and Square Houses*, London: Pan/Macmillan.

Greenaway K. (1991) *Nursery Rhymes Classic*, London: Cresset Press.

Grifiths, V. (1987) *My Class Visits a Museum*, London: Franklin Watts.

Guest, G. 'Developing design and technology through history', *Primary History* 17: 4–6.

Hampshire Inspection and Advisory Service (1999) *A Nursery Rhymes Resource Pack*,

Hampshire History Centre, Southampton: Hampshire Education Authority (tel: 023–92377546).

Hague, M. (1984) *Mother Goose Treasury: A Collection of Classic Nursery Rhymes*, London: Methuen.

Hammond, N. (1993) 'New discoveries challenge views on hieroglyphics', *The Times*, 24 August: 14.

Harner, L. (1982) 'Talking about the past and the future', in W. Friedman (ed.) *The Developmental Psychology of Time*, New York: Academic Press.

Harnett, P. (1993) 'Identifying progression in children's understanding: the use of visual materials to assess primary school children's learning in history', *Cambridge Journal of Education* 23.2: 137–54.

—— (1996) 'Questions about the past: responses to historical pictures from primary school children', *Welsh Historian* 25: 19–26.

—— (1998) 'Children working with pictures', in P. Hoodless (ed.) *History and English in the Primary School*, London: Routledge.

Harpin, W. (1976) *The Second 'R': Writing Development in the Junior School*, London: Allen & Unwin.

Harrison, G. (1993) 'Into battle; an infant archaeology project', *Remnants Journal of the English Heritage Education Service* 21: 1–3.

Harrison, J. (1992) *Timothy's Teddy*, London: Picture Lions, Harper Collins.

Harrison, S. (2000) 'Students in primary history: onward and upward? a view from Ofsted', *Primary History* 26: 7–9.

Haskell, F. (1993) *History and its Images: Art and the Interpretation of the Past*, New Haven: Yale University Press.

Hastings, S. (1992) *Sir Gawain and the Loathly Lady*, London: Walker Books.

Hayes, D. (1998) *Can Do Better: Raising Boys' Achievement in English*, London: QCA.

Holdaway D. (1979) *The Foundations of Literacy*, London and Sydney: Ashton Scholastic.

Holmann, M., Banet, B. and Weikart, D. P. (1979) *Young Children in Action*, Ypsilanti, MI: High/Scope Press.

Hoodless, P. (1998) 'Children's awareness of time in story and historical fiction', in P. Hoodless (ed.) *History and English in the Primary School*, London: Routledge.

Hughes, P., Cox, K. and Goddard, G. (2000) *Primary History Curriculum Guide*, London: David Fulton.

Hulton, M. (1989) 'African traditional stories in the classroom', in D. Atkinson (ed.) *The Children's Bookroom: Reading and the Use of Books*, Stoke-on-Trent: Trentham.

Hutchins, P. (1973) *Rosie's Walk*, London: Picture Puffins.

Isaacs, S. (1930) *Intellectual Growth in Young Children*, London: Routledge & Kegan Paul.

Isherwood, S. (1987) *Tim's Knight*, London: Hamish Hamilton.

Jahoda, G. (1963) 'Children's concept of time and history', *Educational Review* 15: 2.

Jenkins, K. (1991) *Re-thinking History*, London: Routledge.

Jones, I. (1985) 'Whose class is it anyway?', *Teaching History* 43: 8–10.

Jones, R. M. (1968) *Fantasy and Feeling in Education*, London: London University Press.

Ker Wilson, B. (1990) *The Turtle and the Island*, London: Francis Lincoln.

King-Smith, D. (1990) *The Toby Man*, London: Puffin.
—— (1993) *Lady Daisy*, London: Puffin.
Kingsbury, B. (1998) 'Picture books for teaching history', *Primary History* 20: 17–18.
Klausmeier, H. J. and Allen, P. S. (1978) *Cognitive Development of Children and Youth: A Longitudinal Study*, London: Academic Press.
Klausmeier, H. J. and associates (1979) *Cognitive Learning and Development*, Cambridge, MA: Ballinger.
Klein, G. (1989) '"Is going two days now the pot turn down": stories for all', in D. Atkinson (ed.) *The Children's Bookroom: Reading and the Use of Books*, Stoke-on-Trent: Trentham Books.
Lee, L. (1989) *The Illustrated Cider with Rosie*, London: Cresset Press.
Lee, P. J. (1984) 'Historical imagination', in A. K. Dickinson, P. J. Lee and P. J. Rodgers (eds) *Learning History*, London: Heinemann.
Lee, P. J., Dickinson, A. and Ashby, R. (1998) 'History is an information culture'. Paper given at the Symposium on Teaching and Learning as Epistemic Acts, American Educational Research Association Conference, San Diego, California.
Lello, J. (1980) 'The concept of time, the teaching of history and school organisation', *History Teacher* 13: 3.
Lemans, M. (1992) *Just Bears*, London: Pelham Books
Light, P. (1983) 'Social interaction and cognitive development: a review of post-Piagetian research', in S. Meadows (ed.) *Developing Thinking Approaches to Children's Cognitive Development*, London: Methuen.
Line, K. (1989) *Lavender's Blue*, Oxford: Oxford University Press.
Little, V. (1983) 'What is historical imagination?', *Teaching History* 36: 27–32.
Lively P. (1991) *City of the Mind*, London: Penguin.
Loader, P. (1993) 'Historically speaking', *Teaching History* 71: 20–2.
Lomas, T. (1994) *A Guide to Preparing the History Curriculum in Primary Schools for an Ofsted Inspection*, London: Historical Association.
Lynn, S. (1993) 'Children's reading pictures: history visuals at Key Stage 1 and 2', *Education 3–13* 21.3: 23–9.
MacIntosh, D. (1999) *Travels in Galloway: Memories from Southwest Scotland*, Glasgow: Neil Wilson Publishing.
McKee, D. (1980) *Not Now Bernard*, London: Andersen Press.
Maclure, M. and French, P. F. (1986) 'Comparison of talk at home and at school', in G. Wells (ed.) *Learning Through Interaction: The Study of Language Development*, Cambridge: Cambridge University Press.
McNaughton, C. (1991) *King None the Wiser*, London: Mammoth.
Marbeau, L. (1988) 'History and geography in school', *Primary Education* 88: 20–2.
Martin, S. (1980) *Pirates*, London: Macmillan.
Mahy, M. (1987) *The Man Whose Mother Was a Pirate*, London: Puffin.
Meek, M. (1988) *How Texts Teach What Readers Learn*, Lewes: Falmer.
Miles, R. (1989) *The Women's History of the World*, London: HarperCollins.
Milne, A.A. (1979a) *When We Were Very Young*, London: Magnet.
—— (1979b) *Now We Are Six*, London: Magnet.
Ministry of Education (1952) *Teaching of History*, London: HMSO.
Mitchelhill, B. (1991) *Princess Victoria*, History Key Stage One Stories, Set A, Aylesbury: Ginn.

Moorhouse, R. and Randall, C. (1994) *Herstory: The Life of Phoebe Hessel*, Brighton: Queens Park Books.

Moyles, J. R. (1989) *Just Playing? The Role and Status of Play in Early Childhood Education*, Milton Keynes: Open University Press.

Munsch, R. (1988) *The Paper Bag Princess*, UK: Hippo Scholastic.

Nicholl, H. (1975) *Meg's Castle*, London: Heinemann.

Nulty, P. (1998) 'Talking about artefacts at Key Stage 1', in P. Hoodless (ed.) *History and English in the Primary School*, London: Routledge.

Office for Standards in Education (Ofsted) (1999) *Primary Education 1994–98: A Review of Primary Schools in England*, London: HMSO.

—— (2000) *Inspecting Subjects 3–11: Guidance for Inspectors and Schools*, London: HMSO.

Opie, I. and Opie, P. (eds) (1973) *The Oxford Book of Children's Verse*, Oxford: Clarendon.

Osoba, F. (1993) *Benin Folklore*, London: Hadada Books.

Ostler, A. (1995) 'Does the National Curriculum bring us closer to a gender-balanced history?', *Teaching History* 79: 21–4.

O'Toole, J. (1992) *The Process of Drama*, London: Routledge.

Parsons, M. L. (1996) 'Let's take a granny off the street: the problems of oral history and how they can be minimalised', *Teaching History* 84, 30–3.

Philip, N. (1989) *The Cinderella Story*, London: Penguin.

—— (1993) *Victorian Village Life*, Spring Hildbury Oxfordshire: Albion Press.

Phillips, R. (1998) *History Teaching, Nationhood and the State: A Study in Educational Politics*, London: Cassell.

Piaget, J. (1926) *The Language and Thought of the Child*, London: Routledge.

—— (1928) *Judgement and Reasoning in the Child*, London: Kegan Paul.

—— (1951) *The Origin of the Idea of Chance in the Child*, London: Routledge.

—— (1952) *The Child's Conception of Number*, London: Routledge.

—— (1956) *The Child's Conception of Time*, London: Routledge.

Poster, J. (1973) 'The birth of the past', *The History Teacher*, August.

Pounce, E. (1995) 'Ensuring continuity and understanding through teaching of gender issues in history 5–16', in R. Watts and I. Grosvenor (eds.) *Crossing the Key Stages of History*, London: David Fulton.

Prisk, T. (1987) 'Letting them get on with it, a study of an unsupervised group task in the infant school', in A. Pollard (ed.) *Children in their Primary Schools*, Lewes: Falmer Press.

Provensen, A. and Provensen, M. (1991) *Shaker Lane*, London: Walker Books.

Purkis, S. (1991) *Teddy Bears* (A Sense of History Series), Harlow: Longman.

Qualifications and Curriculum Authority (QCA) (1998) *Maintaining Balance and Breadth at Key Stages 1 and 2*, London: QCA.

Redfern, A. (1998) 'Voices of the past: oral history and English in the primary school', in P. Hoodless (ed.) *History and English in the Primary School*, London: Routledge.

—— (1999) 'Oral history in primary schools', *Primary History* 23: 14–15.

Renfrew, J. (1985) *Food and Cooking in Prehistoric Britain*, London: English Heritage.

—— (1993) *Food and Cooking in Medieval Britain*, London: English Heritage.

Roberts, F. (1992) *India 1526–1800*, London: Hodder & Stoughton.

Rodgers, E. and Rodgers, P. (1991) *Our House*, London: Walker Books.

Rodgers, P. (1989) *Me and Alice go to the Museum*, London: Bodley Head.

Rogers, P. (1995) 'Silver lining: using the elderly as a resource', *Primary History* 10: 14–15.

Rosen, C. and Rosen, H. (1973) *The Language of Primary School Children*, Harmondsworth: Penguin.

Rotheroe, D. (1990) *London Inn Signs*, Princes Risborough: Shire Publications.

Routh, C. and Rowe, A. (1992) *Stories for Time: Resourcing the History Curriculum KS1*, University of Reading: Reading and Language Information Centre.

Rowe, A. (1991) *The Castle*, History Key Stage One Stories, Set B, Aylesbury: Ginn.

Rowse, A. L. (1946) *The Use of History*, London: Hodder & Stoughton.

Ross, R. (1991) *Little Red Riding Hood*, London: Puffin.

Salter, K. (1996) 'Grace Darling and Reception children', *Primary History* 14: 18–19.

Samuel, R. (1993) 'Photography The "eye of history"', *New Statesman and Society*, 18 Dec.

Schools Curriculum and Assessment Authority (SCAA) (1997) *Planning the Curriculum at Key Stages 1 and 2*, London: SCAA.

Sciescka, J. (1991) *The Three Little Pigs*, London: Puffin.

Scott, B. (1994) 'History in the National Curriculum', *Primary History* 6: 11–12.

Scott, D. (1986) *Caribbean Poetry Now*, S. Brown (ed.), London: Hodder & Stoughton.

SEAC (1993) National Foundation for Educational Research publication, Windsor: Nelson.

Sendek, M. (1970) *Where the Wild Things Are*, Harmondsworth: Penguin.

Shamroth, N. (1992) 'A rolling drama gathers much talk', *TALK, The Journal of the National Oracy Project* 5: 37–42.

Silvera, P. and Cawood, I. (2000) 'History and the literacy hour: a case study', *Primary History* 24: 9–10.

Simmonds, P. (1988) *Lulu and the Flying Babies*, London: Picture Puffin.

Singer, D. G. and Singer, J. L. (1990) *The House of Make Believe*, Cambridge, MA, London: Harvard University Press.

Shemilt, D. (1984) 'Beauty and the philosopher; empathy in history and the classroom', in A. K. Dickinson, P. J. Lee and P. J. Rogers (eds) *Learning History*, London: Heinemann.

Shuter, J. and Reynoldson, F. (1991) *Sunshine History Planning and Assessment Guide*, London: Heinemann Educational.

—— (1991) *Sunshine History Starter Pack 1: People in History*, London: Heinemann Educational.

Smart, L. (1999) 'Any place for a database in the teaching and learning of history at Key Stage 1?', *Primary History* 23: 8–10.

Smith, B. (1990) *Minnie and Ginger*, London: Pavilion Books.

Smith, E. and Holden, C. (1994) 'I thought it was for picking bones out of soup', *Teaching History* 76: 6–9.

Smith, F. (1989) *Writing and the Writer*, London: Heinemann Educational.

Smith, R. N. and Tomlinson, P. (1977) 'The development of children's construction of historical duration: a new approach and some findings', *Educational Research* 19(3): 163–70.

Steptoe, J. (1992) *Mufaro's Beautiful Daughters: An African Tale*, London: Hodder & Stoughton.

Stobart, M. (1996) 'Tensions between political ideology and history teaching: to what extent may history serve a cause however well-meant?', *The Standing Conference of European History Teachers Association Bulletin* 6.

Stones, R. and Mann, A. (1987) *Mother Goose Comes to Cable Street*, London: Picture Puffin.

Stow, W. (1998) 'An investigation into aspects of children's understanding of historical time', unpublished M.A. thesis, Canterbury: Christ Church University College.

Suknandan, L., Lee, B. and Kelleher, S. (2000) *An Investigation into Gender Differences in Achievement*, Slough: NFER.

Sylva, K., Roy C. and Painter, M. (1980) *Childwatching in Playgroup and Nursery School*, London: Grant McIntyre.

Tanner, G. and Wood, T. (1993) *Bathtime; Shopping; At School; Cooking; Toys; Travelling; Washing*, History Mystery Series, London: A. & C. Black.

Taylor, A. (1988) *Lights On, Lights Off*, Oxford: Oxford University Press.

Temple, A., Nathan, R. and Burns N. (1982) *Beginning of Writing*, Boston, London, Sydney and Toronto: Allyn & Bacon Inc.

Testa, F. (1982) *Never Satisfied*, London: Abelard/North-South.

Thomas, E. (1993) 'Irony age infants', *Times Educational Supplement*, 23 April: 5.

Thompson, F. (1989) *The Illustrated Lark Rise to Candleford*, London: Cresset Press.

Thornton, S. J. and Vukelich, R. (1988) 'Effects of children's understanding of time concepts on historical understanding', *Theory and Research in Social Education* 16(1): 69–82.

Tilbury, L. and Fordham, J. (2001) 'Don't forget key skills', *Primary History* 27: 13–15.

Tizard, B., Blatchford, P., Burke, J., Farquar, C. and Plewis, L. (1988) *Young Children at School in the Inner City*, London: Lawrence Erlbaum Associates.

Tough, J. (1976) *Listening to Children Talking*, London: Ward Lock.

Toye, N. and Prendiville, F. (2000) *Drama and Traditional Story in the Early Years*, London: Routledge.

Trevelyan, G. M. (1919) *The Recreations of an Historian*, London: Nelson.

Tucker, N. (1981) *The Child and the Book*, Cambridge: Cambridge University Press.

Unwin, R. (1981) *The Visual Dimension in the Study and Teaching of History*, Teaching History Series 49, London: Historical Association.

Vass, P. (1993) 'Have I got a witness? A consideration of the use of historical witnesses in the primary classroom', *Teaching History* 73: 19–24.

—— (1999) 'History, story and the teaching of history at Key Stage 1', *Primary History* 22: 14–15.

Vygotsky L. S. (1962) *Thought and Language*, Chichester, New York: Wiley.

Waddell, M. (1990) *Sailor Bear*, London: Walker Books.

—— (1991) *My Great Grandpa*, London: Walker Books.

—— (1992) *The Hidden House*, London: Walker Books.

—— (1994a) *Let's Go Home, Little Bear*, London: Walker Books.

—— (1994b) *When the Teddy Bears Came*, London: Walker Books.

—— (1999a) *Well Done, Little Bear*, London: Walker Books.

—— (1999b) *Can't You Sleep, Little Bear?* London: Walker Books.

Waddell, M. and Dale, P. (1989) *Once There Were Giants*, London: Walker Books.

Waddell, M. and Mansell, D. (1991) *My Great Grandpa*, London: Walker Books.

Warlow, A. (1977) 'Kinds of fiction: a hierarchy of veracity', in M. Meek, A. Warlow and G. Barton (eds) *The Cool Web: The Patterns of Children's Reading*, London: Bodley Head.

Warner, M. (1994) *From the Beast to the Blonde*, London: Chatto & Windus.

Warton, C. (1993) 'Chalkface assessment and green paint', *Primary History* 4: 13–14.

Wasu, K. (1986) *Bilingual Nursery Rhymes*, Barking: Cheetah Books.

Waterland, L. (1985) *Read with Me: An Apprenticeship Approach to Reading*, Stroud: Signal.

Welbourne, P. (1990) 'Deconstruction to reconstruction: an approach to women's history through local history', *Teaching History* 59: 16–21.

Wells, G. (1981) *Learning through Interaction: The Study of Language Development*, Cambridge: Cambridge University Press.

West, J. (1981) 'Primary school children's perceptions of authenticity and time in historical narrative pictures', *Teaching History*, February.

Wild, M. (1995) *Remember Me*, Morton Grove, IL: Albert Whitman & Co.

Wildsmith, B. (1987) *Mother Goose*, Oxford: Oxford University Press.

Williams, M. (1991) *When I Was Little*, London: Walker Books.

—— (1992) *Joseph and His Magnificent Coat of Colours*, London: Walker Books.

Wilson, H. (ed.) (1988) *There's a Wolf in my Pudding*, London: Pan Macmillan.

Winnicott, D. W. (1974) *Playing and Reality*, Harmondsworth: Penguin.

Woodhouse, M. (1992) *Scrub-a-dub Nellie*, London: The National Trust.

Wood, E. and Holden, P. (1997) 'I can't remember doing the Romans': the development of children's understanding in history', *Teaching History* 89: 9–12.

—— (1995) *Teaching Early Years History*, Cambridge: Chris Kingston Publishers.

Woods, P. (1995) *Creative Teachers and Their Primary Skills*, Buckingham: Open University Press.

Wright, D. (1984) 'A small local investigation', *Teaching History* 39: 3–4.

Zolotow, C. (1992) *This Quiet Lady*, London: Greenwill, HarperCollins.

Index

Note: Most references are to teaching history in the early years unless otherwise stated.

RA
644
A25
SOC

CENTRE FOR HEALTH ECONOMICS
INSTITUTE FOR HEALTH STUDIES

Social Care &

HIV-AIDS

The Hull-York Research Team

London : HMSO

© Crown copyright 1993

Applications for reproduction should be made to HMSO
First published 1993

ISBN 011 701718 3